Knowledge, Identity and School Life Series: 3

After Postmodernism:
Education, Politics and Identity

Edited by

Richard Smith and Philip Wexler

 The Falmer Press

(A member of the Taylor & Francis Group)
London • Washington, D.C.

UK   The Falmer Press, 4 John Street, London WC1N 2ET
USA   The Falmer Press, Taylor & Francis Inc., 1900 Frost Road, Suite 101,
       Bristol, PA 19007

First published in 1995

**A catalogue record for this book is available from the British
Library**

Library of Congress Cataloging-in-Publication Data are
available on request

ISBN 0 7507 0441 1 cased
ISBN 0 7507 0442 X paper

Jacket design by Caroline Archer

Typeset in 10/12 pt Bembo by
Graphicraft Typesetters Ltd., Hong Kong.

*Printed in Great Britain by Burgess Science Press, Basingstoke on paper
which has a specified pH value on final paper manufacture of not less than
7.5 and is therefore 'acid free'.*

After Postmodernism

Knowledge, Identity and School Life Series

Editors: Professor Philip Wexler, Graduate School of Education and
Human Development, University of Rochester, New York,
NY 14627, USA and
Professor Ivor Goodson, Faculty of Education, University of
Western Ontario, Canada.

Contents

Contents

Acknowledgments

Planning, organizational and social skills for the seminar at Griffith University Gold Coast were provided by Ms Fiona Howroyd, who also ensured that participants' scripts were distributed in advance. Fiona's assistance in linking Phil Wexler and Richard Smith by the usual technologies and her work as Assistant Editor is also acknowledged.

Prologue

Richard Smith

In the introduction to his 1988 edited collection *Universal Abandon?*, Andrew Ross pointed out that postmodern criticism arises from particular social and political conditions. Postmodern politics are framed as a politics of difference in which voices from the margins have challenged the hitherto accepted dominance of heroic white western male actors and universal theorizing. At the same time, welfare capitalism has been 'revealed as a social vision with only limited, and not universal, applications.' In cultural and social analysis, these two currents have been realized, not only in a retreat from neo-marxist and 'critical' theorizing, but also as an exploration of ways to apprehend and discuss contemporary conditions. The 'new times' clearly need new ways to understand, and act on, new social forms and manifestations of older politics.

Nowhere is this complex of contradictory conditions more evident than in education. Whereas Bernstein (1990, p. 88) refers to the shift of state regulation from the economy to symbolic control in a wider process of transition to a 'communications' age, 'which appears to be taking place', our view is that the shift has long since occurred. Everywhere education systems have been organizationally restructured and turned to the purposes of international capitalism. In the Australian context for example, corporatist politics have had major effects on the relations between capital and labour so that the union movement is irrevocably implicated in micro-economic reform, especially industrial matters. The former boundaries between the business and the public-education sector have long since disappeared as resource restrictions encourage education systems, teachers, academics and institutions to seek substantial funding beyond the public sector.

The communications revolution spanning technologies such as the internet, multimedia, satellite video, cable TV, flexible delivery modes and so on has already had an impact on education management discourse and, as this language is altered, so too are traditional patterns of school and university life. In every part of the education sector, plans have been formulated for the transformation of education-delivery management and governance. Client-centred education policy is more the rule than the exception. It is, then, no longer appropriate to talk about the *imminent* transformation of education or to rediscover and defend liberal welfarism *per se*. The new order has already

1

brought arrangements of power and patterns of inequality that require expla-nation and action. What is at stake is a redefinition of 'education' itself in a post-postmodern age and the possibilities for the future (Wexler, 1987).

Without wishing to compartmentalize history into discrete periods, the idea of 'post'-postmodernism is a useful fiction that takes on the political effects of the 'postmodern condition'. For our purposes, it includes a descrip-tion of material circumstances marked by communications technology, changes in the global economy and the commodification of culture which together dismantle traditional patterns of social life and are accompanied by the loss of moral cohesion (Alexander and Sztompka, 1990). The major reverberations of postmodern emergence, Gergen (1991) argues, are brought about by 'social saturation' in technologies and immersion in multiple perspectives which herald a new consciousness. In this sense, postmodernism is a state of things which challenges and transforms existing hierarchies in all spheres of contemporary life.

While the scope and range of postmodern social theory is contentious, it is characterized by the social construction of reality which relativizes claims to knowledge and authority; multiple realities, multiple goals and diverse evalu-ation criteria so that the concept of rational decision-making is threatened; self-reflection and irony (Gergen, 1991; Laclau, 1988; Featherstone, 1988; Bohman, 1993). Such theory blurs formerly delineated genres so that the quintessential theoretical homology is the replacement of literal models of truth and knowledge by figural representations (Denzin, 1991, p. 26). There is freedom to theoretically combine and synthesize so that as Ross (1988, p. xv) observes, '(e)verything is contestable; nothing is off limits; and no out-comes are guaranteed'. The notion of 'post'-postmodernism seeks to optimize the nascent possibilities of an already existing set of historical conditions that are characterized as 'postmodern', to play on the versatility in social life that nascency provides (Olalquiaga, 1992, pp. xii, xiv).

The speed of change and the realization of its immensity in educational affairs often leads its critics and participants to label education as a 'crisis' area. Historically, this is not surprising if the idea of crisis is normalized as the most symptomatic root metaphor of the late twentieth century (Holton, 1991, p. 4). There is a logic then to those critical accounts of postmodern education that are premised on the assumption that the education system should be dedicated to human self-realization and expressions of democratic will (e.g., McLaren, in press). In contrast, there are those postmodern accounts of edu-cation which argue that the State is neither informed by fundamental demo-cratic and emancipatory principles nor possesses the means to realize them (Hunter, 1994; Meredyth, 1994). In the Australian setting, the debate that rages about what it is possible to do in the present and foreseeable future in both academic and practitioner circles, has tended to polarize around these positions and to be either unduly pessimistic (everything is lost) or excessively unconcerned about institutionalized power and its effects (power resides everywhere).

In response to this impasse between the 'critical' and postmodernist theorists, we discern a new sense of urgency to intervene in education practice both theoretically and materially as a *post*-postmodernist concern (e.g., Bourdieu, 1989). There is an emergent impatience with the apocalyptic impulse in postmodernist theory and practice which tends to dominate educational criticism of postmodernism and its effects by litanies of crisis and of the imminent doom of individuals or institutions. There is a growing awareness of the self-defeating nature of the 'apocalyptic fallacy' or B-Effect (Zurbrugg, 1993, pp. 7–12), in which the end of truth is identified with discrediting theories of truth. The B-Effect is, Zurbrugg argues, a 'needlessly catastrophic sense of critical and creative crisis' in which there is no future. He contrasts this with the C-Effect or the possibilities of restarting by rejecting the limitations of the past and worrying about the limitations of the present and the future.

Akiba Lerner (1994) captures what we mean:

> Instead of developing a framework by which all the various forms of struggle could be integrated into a sustainable vision for the good and for the future, the generation of the Sixties fell prey to valorizing each and every form of localized resistance without providing a universal understanding of how specific forms oppression and resistance could be integrated into constructive forms of growth and unity. The generation of the Sixties fell prey to thinkers such as Foucault and others whose main message was, 'Forget about changing the fundamental structures of society, it can never really happen'. Instead, most focussed in on a specific group with which they could identify. . . . As a result, . . . my generation is faced with the 'masadization' of politics. (Lerner, 1994)

The chapters in this book originated in an invited seminar at the Griffith University Gold Coast campus on the occasion of a visit by Philip Wexler in December 1993. The intent of the seminar was to explore ways and means of transcending a 'postmodernist' analysis of education. All are concerned with overcoming the mere reiteration of crisis that emerges from much 'critical' theory and the further fragmentation of politics and theory that accompanies postmodern concepts. The participants have longstanding track records in grappling with what Bauman (1992, p. 94) refers to as the 'growing sense of failure, inadequacy or irrealism of the traditional functions and ambitions [of intellectuals]' under postmodern conditions in universities. In particular, as teachers and/or managers, each of the authors is concerned with the practicalities of working within publicly funded institutions and engaging in activities like teacher education and government consultancies, while criticizing them. There is also concern about the intellectual role as such in an age when it is increasingly perceived as irrelevant by the very people whose interests academics value. All of the authors *intend* that things should be different and despite theoretical constraints, all seek breaks with orthodox theorizing about postmodern circumstances.

The papers explore an educational politics that is grounded in a sociology of postmodernity, rather than a postmodern sociology (Bauman, 1992, p. 111). While the examples are predominantly Australian, the issues are profoundly international. The major themes include the theoretical implications of a refusal to abandon universals and the justification for intervening in educational policy; the efficacy of different kinds of interventions and what a theoretically driven action agenda might be; and dealing with the new range of inequalities which are consequences of postmodern transformations at both the institutional and existential levels. These broad themes provide the organization of the book into five sections, namely: Social Theory of Education, Pedagogy, Identity and Politics. Philip Wexler's Epilogue concludes the book by proposing a new direction in educational theory.

Social Theory of Education

Robert Young poses the paradox of learning: learners cannot understand reasons until they have already acquired a view. The purpose of critique then is a problem of access to some opportunity to intervene in creating reality by undermining networks of power/knowledge in modern societies. Critique then goes beyond reactions to the colonizer and the uncritical celebration of the myths of the colonized.

Young identifies the postmodernist problem as a confusion about the relative weight of power and difference and their interdependence. He chides Foucault for confusing power with difference and Derrida for emphasizing difference rather than power. He defines the post-postmodern project as the elaboration of power defined as the 'political organisation of ontogenetic voice'.

John Knight's continuing theme is that of humanism, the denial of human agency and the rejection of modernity. His view is that in postmodernity, something is lost: 'This is indeed the post-human.' He makes a distinction between anti-humanism or a rejection of previous humanisms and post-humanism which 'follows' but is discontinuous with older humanisms. Anti-humanism assumes a knowledge of humanism whereas posthumanism exists on a terrain 'constituted by and of simulacra'. He links Lyotard's (1984) conception of 'performativity', in which notions of truth are replaced by notions of use and the emergence of control over information as a major element of global capitalism. In this scenario humanisms are not rejected; 'they cannot exist'.

Knight argues that the full elaboration of the postmodern is yet to come. He shows that 'postmodern' theoretical positions do not preclude action and critique. The postmodern education question for Knight is not whether schools will change but the directions in which they will move and the values that will underlie the changes.

Jane Kenway parodies postmodern feminism, and in turn, postmodern theory, in order to make the point that contemporary emancipatory movements need an active and informed politics. Kenway makes the important point for this book that some university teachers and researchers, faced with the paradoxes of postmodern theory, either leave the university or seek post-postmodern ways of thinking. Renewal of work in this way does not entail the abandonment of postmodern theory but the appropriation of the modern emancipatory traditions and postmodern discourses.

Kenway's paper underlines a recurrent theme in the book: how to write about and take political action in the postmodern world that makes a difference when dominant postmodern theoretical modes undermine and dissipate the very mechanisms that are needed to do the job. Kenway's review and analysis of material feminism indicates that postmodern imperatives depoliticize social and cultural life unless patterned asymmetric power relations are understood. Such power can be used on behalf of the non-dominant and in this respect, the case is made for feminists academics to practise their authority as intellectuals in the postmodern age.

Philip Wexler's chapter attempts to offer a new foundation for critical social theory in education by reinterpreting Durkheim and Weber in a non-positivist, religious reading and by reviving selected romantically influenced social theorists — largely from left Freudianism and religious, utopian existentialism. He reviews social and cultural changes of a so-called 'new age' and tries to draw the implications of cultural and social theoretic shifts for understanding and practising education.

Pedagogy

Allan Luke begins with reference to Michael Apple's critiques of postmodernists who ignore questions of political and economic control over official knowledge. He uses this as a starting point to argue that academics can intervene in state education policies. His position is that postmodern work (poststructuralism, feminism, postcolonialism) enables rather than forgets. He shows that public-sector curriculum-development work is 'profoundly polysemic and heteroglossic' and that the 'local sociologies' of educational interventions can have intended political effects. By way of example, he undermines the notion that there is a necessary connection between the conditions of institutional production of the text (political economy); the codes and semiosis (of the text); the institutional conditions of interpretation of the text (audience/readership).

In this way, Luke makes the strong claim that the language of hybridity is more than a theoretical and empirical aberration. He proposes the notion of a 'provisional politics' — making it up as we go along, or picking the spot to deploy a particular identity in relation to material power — to characterize what he calls 'strategic hybridity'. In his view, '(h)ybrid targets are harder to hit' for 'fast capitalism'.

5

Jennifer Gore believes that power matters. She is interested in the micro-level functioning of power relations and explains how Foucault's analysis of these can be translated into empirical educational research. She identifies a 'structured circulation of power relations' which point to a more macro-political analysis than is usual with a Foucauldian analysis.

Gore understands pedagogical practices and research techniques to be neither postmodern, modern or poststructural. Instead, she proposes that pedagogical practices and research techniques should be judged by the questions they pose; by the analyses conducted; and the reports written.

Wendy Morgan and Erica McWilliam are particularly critical of the 'lecture' as a means of teaching. They argue that postmodern teachers are caught in assumptions about theory that is all about heterogeneity, hybridity, uncertainty, regionalism and the multiplicity of subject positions and the personalist faith that one's own position is sufficient. They extend their criticism to flexible delivery modes as well because many such packages are 'bolted to their foundations' in modernist theories of knowledge. They explore the dilemmas of the educational intellectual who wishes to take a political stand when the attempt to summarize theory may 'lead to a classroom discourse which is apparently imitative'. In these circumstances, even a resistant reading of a given text becomes a new orthodoxy. They find a partial answer to their dilemma in a deictic pedagogical practice.

Identity

Lindsay Fitzclarence, Bill Green and Chris Bigum make a case for an 'adequate form of educational theory for these new times'. They indicate that the school and education reforms of the 1980s and early 1990s have been instituted juggernaut-like and that there is a need for a critical analysis of their effects on young people. A 'new critical sociology of education', they write, 'will need to show who wins and who loses because of the restructuring of the education system'.

They argue that media culture has a new significance for identity formation and for educational practice because in the post-postmodern period it points to the renewal of class as a significant category of social analysis. The relationships between class and schooling and class and identity formation become crucial in this period as the means of production are discursive. As Wexler (1987, p. 174) suggests, the mass communication–individual relation now better exemplifies the education relation than the school does, which is surpassed as new forms of education emerge.

Robert Funnell, a former public-sector employee who was involved in the restructure of a state-training sector, explores the theoretical dimensions of such a process. His analysis shows how contemporary debates about the effects of organizational changes in the private and public sectors fail to explain why people suffer a loss of self and how people can deal with necessary changes in work patterns. He proposes that both the critiques of corporatist management and its effects and their opponents are locked into different forms of libertarian social democratic critique. His contention is that this model is incapable of dealing with problems of stress and alienation in emergent institutions. He argues for a social psychology that deals with both changes in the patterns of governance and the mechanisms through which subjectivities are transformed from one set of codes and values to another. In this way, organizational changes that fit contemporary and future conditions will be matched with a better understanding of how and why people might creatively adopt them.

Parlo Singh's paper crystallizes many of the worries that emerged during the postmodern period of educational theorizing. While educational theorists attempted to move beyond the constrictions of received theories derived from post-Marxism and textual criticism, new orthodoxies were put in place that paralleled the very objects that were displaced. Singh locates some of these difficulties in the neglected spaces in modernist theory and the discourses of the Enlightenment.

Singh argues that educational theory needs some realignment to account for the political and economic dimensions of global educational restructuring. Her view is that while considerable advances have been made in feminist theory to acknowledge a range of hitherto silenced voices, theorizing the relationships between class, race, gender and social division is rather less adequate. Consequently, 'white middle class' feminists have been reluctant to deal with 'others' in the category of 'other'. Moreover, Singh is critical of the political orientation that speaks for the 'sexed' individual humanist self-defined from the perspective of the academy without forming alliances with other struggles, including those of men. In this respect, Singh voices a growing concern that the generations of the 1960s and 1970s supported and became involved in struggles for black liberation, women's liberation and sexual liberation but failed to develop a framework for integrating various forms of struggle.

Politics

James Ladwig is concerned with the contribution of academics at an international level. He is especially critical of academic criticisms of corporatist educational politics that ignore the cultural context in which the theoretical materials were developed and their fit with Australian (or any other) conditions. Like Hunter (1994) and Meredyth (1994), he challenges the assumption that the 'universal' education system is founded on the need for human self-realization and for expressions of democratic will. Instead of pursuing criticisms of corporatism, Ladwig argues for an alternative form of sociological analysis grounded in the 'thought experiment' of the 'nomadic educational intellectual'. Such a person exploits the already constrained position of employment

by the State, the availability of a plethora of information technology for networking and distribution purposes and the potential for involvement in educational research and policy (see Luke in this volume). Moreover, Ladwig
adopts the view that the historical role of educational corporatism 'remains an
open book' and nomadic educational intellectuals might establish an international, universalizing force in educational research and other pursuits.

Richard Smith and Judyth Sachs review the impact of national political
agendas which restrict university resources while placing new teaching, research and administrative demands on both institutions and academics. They
criticize calls for the re-establishment of a more 'collegial' workplace as a
response to 'economic rationalism' and 'managerialism' as a self-seeking and
ahistorical response by academics. The argument is made that attempts to
reconstruct organizationally the tenets of a previous academic age and culture
are inappropriate (and futile) in a period when universities are being
deinstitutionalized. Philip Wexler's Epilogue indicates why new intellectual
resources are required to deal with the fall out from postmodern social relations and suggests some directions for doing it.

References

ALEXANDER, J.C. and SZTOMPKA, P. (Eds) (1990) *Rethinking Progress: movements, forces
and ideas at the end of the 20th century*, London, Unwin Hyman.
BAUMAN, Z. (1992) *Intimations of Postmodernity*, London, Routledge.
BERNSTEIN, B. (1990) 'Social class and pedagogic practice', in *The Structuring of Peda-
gogic Discourse, Volume IV: Class, Codes and Control*, London, Routledge, pp. 63–
93.
BOURDIEU, P. (1989) 'The corporatism of the universal: the role of intellectuals in the
modern world', *Telos*, 81, pp. 99–110.
BOWMAN, J. (1991/1993) *New Philosophy of Social Science*, Cambridge, Mass., MIT
Press.
DENZIN, N. (1991) *Images of Postmodern Society: social theory and contemporary cinema*,
London, Sage.
FEATHERSTONE, M. (1988) 'In pursuit of the postmodern: an introduction', *Theory
Culture and Society*, 5, 2–3, pp. 195–216.
GERGEN, K. (1987) *Dilemmas of Identity in Contemporary Life*, New York, Basic Books.
HOLTON, R. (1990) 'Problems of crisis and normalcy in the contemporary world', in
ALEXANDER, J.C. and SZTOMPKA, P. (Eds) (1990) *Rethinking Progress: movements,
forces and ideas at the end of the 20th century*, London, Unwin Hyman, pp. 39–52.
HUNTER, I. (1994) *Rethinking The School: subjectivity, bureaucracy, criticism*, Sydney,
Allen and Unwin.
LACLAU, E. (1988) 'Politics and the limits of modernity', in Ross, A. (Ed) *Universal
Abandon? The politics of postmodernism*, Minneapolis, University of Minnesota Press,
pp. 63–82.
LERNER, A. (1994) 'My generation', *Tikkun*, 9, 2, pp. 56–8.
LYOTARD, J.-F. (1984) *The Postmodern Condition: A Report on Knowledge*, Tr, BENNING-
TON, G. and MASSUMI, B., Minneapolis, University of Minnesota Press.

McLaren, P. (1995) *Australian Journal of Education*, 39, (1), p. 1.

Meredyth, D. (1994) Education And Its Critics: Principles and Programmes in Australian Education Policy, Brisbane, Griffith University, Unpublished PhD Thesis.

Olalquiaga, C. (1992) *Megalopolis: contemporary cultural sensibilities*, Minneapolis, University of Minnesota Press.

Ross, A. (1988) (Ed) *Universal Abandon? The politics of postmodernism*, Minneapolis, University of Minnesota Press.

Wexler, P. (1987) *Social Analysis of Education: after the New Sociology*, New York, Routledge Kegan Paul.

Zurbrugg, N. (1993) *The Parameters of Postmodernism*, London, Routledge.

Part 1

Theory of Education

1 Liberalism, Postmodernism, Critical Theory and Politics[1]

Robert Young

The Failure of Liberal Models of Critical Learning

Liberal theories of criticism, including educational criticism, celebrate the idea of critique, but both poststructuralist and Habermasian views of education find common ground in rejecting liberal models of critique, albeit for partly different reasons. Both approaches may be subjected to a reading which pragmatically seeks to find complementary moments between them. There may be advantages to a reading of this kind, advantages that more oppositionary readings lack.

The central concern of liberal models of education has been the avoidance of 'indoctrination'. The term itself was coined by one of Dewey's students (Garrison, 1986). Avoiding indoctrination has generally been defined as so ordering the educational experience that learners come to accept views only on the basis of reasons which seem valid to them as individuals (see Young, 1984). The crucial issue for this account is that of the possibility of the kind of rational autonomy that the theory calls for.

The liberal view of indoctrination leads to a kind of paradox. Reasons cannot be assessed atomistically. As Quine/Duhem and other holistic analyses make clear, reasons take on meaning systemically, because of their imbeddedness in a theoretical context.[2] Derrida's view is rather similar. His account of significance leads us to a seamless web of semiotic relations, an archi-*écriture* rather than to an architectonic. Foucault makes similar points about the systemic character of regimes of power/knowledge, which include complex sets of institutional and discursive relations. Constructivist learning theory rests on a similar schema-related understanding of meaning. Habermas' view of the ontological implications of discursive redemption of claims has a similar implication. The upshot of all this is: learners cannot understand reasons until they have already acquired a view. Another way of stating the same point is that criticism always presupposes a schema, background, worldview, *vorhabe*, or tradition. It always works from within a historical/biographical horizon, to borrow Gadamer's terminology (Gadamer, 1975). Put crudely, in order to be critical you must first be indoctrinated.

This paradox has also been called the paradox of learning (see Bereiter, 1985). In this form, it is expressed as the problem of the conflict between schematically based interpretation of incoming 'information' and schema change. The problem is that since interpretation can only occur within a schema, schema transcending experience should be uninterpretable.

Suspicion of the liberal model centres on the adequacy of the notion of the autonomous judgment with which learners already possessed of a worldview, however limited, are supposed to evaluate incoming claims and reasons for their validity. That is no doubt why Foucault makes the otherwise surprising statement that in the issue of pedagogy and power he was '. . . not certain that self-management is what produces the best results. Nothing proves,' he went on to say, '. . . on the contrary, that that approach isn't a hindrance.' (Foucault, 1984). The reason for Foucault's doubts here must be excavated archaeologically from his works, since he does not comment further, but the gist of it follows Bernauer's interpretation of Foucault as a 'mystic', and Foucault's own assertion that his thinking about subjectivity rested on a refusal to accept the explicability of either freedom or obedience to a tradition (see Bernauer, 1988; Bernstein, 1991).

The Political Task of Critique

While the psychology and micro-sociology of rational autonomy remain problematic, the macroscopic political task of critique is clearer, at least for perspectives other than liberal ones. There is convergence among various kinds of critical theory on the questions with which a theory of critique and the possibility of *critical* agency must grapple. Questions of colonialism, power and patriarchy, have joined questions of economic class in the re-examination of the rather transparent notions of rational agency that tended to characterize what Toulmin has called 'high modern' understandings of constructive agency (and associated liberal theories of citizenship and politics). Despite differences in the source and kind of power implied by distinctions among patriarchy, political power, power/knowledge, colonialism, and class it might be useful to gloss all of these as problems of *ontogenetic* power — the power to create 'reality'.

Accordingly, critique becomes a problem of freedom or access to some opportunity to intervene in creating or inscribing reality. For instance, it is implicit in Derrida's claims for deconstruction that it offers a means of 'taking a position'. Derrida states that 'Deconstruction is not [politically] neutral. It *intervenes*'. (Derrida, 1991). Similarly, Foucault has more than once endorsed what he calls the 'critical principle' of symmetrical dialogue as the means whereby intellectuals can have a role in undermining the networks of power/ knowledge in modern societies (Foucault, 1984). And in recent discussions of colonialism by poststructurally influenced thinkers such as Spivak (1987), Niranjana (1992), the possibility of a form of critical dialogue, although earlier condemned, has again been canvassed, as it is recognized that colonized peoples must go beyond 'nativist' responses which simply react by rejecting the colonizer and by uncritical celebration of myths of the colonized.

Habermas, as is well known, has always endorsed the possibility of more or less critical dialogues. In his own linguistic turn, post-1978 (Habermas, 1978), he has theorized the possibility of interpretation in terms of critical validity judgments of speakers and hearers. For Habermas, to understand what someone is saying it is necessary to understand the claims of an ontic, ethical and personal kind being made. These claims go beyond the semantic content of what is being said to the implied claims of a background of commitments — a world — in which the speech concerned finds its frame of reference. Interlocutors, as a normal part of understanding speech or writing, understand not only in what worlds the specific claims of the present talk are being made, but also to what extent these claims are in agreement or disagreement with their own understandings of those worlds. As I pointed out recently, this means that interlocutors ordinarily are aware of the *weight* of any particular claims, if by weight we stipulate: the logical ramifications of a claim within a world.[3] In turn, the weight of a claim is a part of its meaning. Claims mean partly by virtue of their weight. Of course, Habermas goes on to elucidate the assumptions of interlocutors about communication when they are oriented to understanding each other, pointing out that these are counterfactual or *as if* assumptions. Initially, he tried to elaborate this dimension of his theory using quasi-Kantian categories, such as the notion of communicative universals or the 'ideal speech situation', but since 1986 he has abandoned these, retreating to a more modest analysis of the presence of counterfactual thinking in communication, the details of which need not delay us here, except to say it would be reasonable to gloss this thought as the assertion that would-be communicators hope for an as yet unachieved state of understanding and proceed in the present in the light of that hope.

There is also something of a convergence on the issues which must be dealt with in any account of the conditions that a theory must satisfy if it is to be critical — in the political dimension this means that the theory has to account for the possibility of a communicatively achieved undermining of communicatively constructed domination, since the problems of politics are essentially problems of the tension between power and freedom. The convergence concerned can be constructed as a recognition of the significance of the attitude toward 'the other of dialogue'. Some theorists go little beyond acknowledgment of respect for the otherness of the other (see Bernstein, 1991). Other theorists explore the many ways in which apparent dialogic openness can mask various forms of surreptitious denial of the other's right to make claims in discourse from their own genuine starting point (see Derrida, 1992). In Foucault's final works, the possibility of knowing this starting point and the ethical disciplines for discovering it when it is hidden from us were the focus of theoretical attention (Foucault, 1986).

What we can learn from many sources, from Nietszche, through Adorno and Heidegger, to Habermas, Foucault and Derrida is that the conditions necessary for fully open dialogue cannot exist in real, historically and biographically situated dialogue. Openness is at best, a matter of degree. The problem of the other in dialogue is central in any critical conception of dialogue. If situations where the parties to talk around a problem do not have equal rights to communicate, or do not have equal freedom from internal constraints are unavoidable, how can we speak of some process of critique through openness to the other of dialogue? In such situations, learning cannot be critical, it would seem, because both problem-definition and schema-change for at least one class of participants will not reflect the success criteria of that class of participants. What results is domination in class, patriarchal or colonial terms. As we will see below, where different critical theories differ, is in the account they give of the possibility of overcoming distortion in this dialogic process. However, I would like to signal a crucial distinction here. It is the distinction between an absolute criterion, even if it is a hidden absolute, and an historical, developmental one. Some readings of postmodern thought display a tendency toward a kind of absolutism of relativism, where a cautious, evolutionary perspective might be more appropriate, as Derrida's discussions of emergent teleology would indicate.

Scepticism and Hope

Poststructuralist statements about the immersion of knowledge in power, or about the ineffability of meaning, may be felicitously read as methodological devices of a sceptical trajectory, rather than as absolute claims. If so, there is room for the hidden humanism of these approaches to be read between the performatory detail of their writing.

In the light of this form of reading, we need to go beyond characterizing poststructuralism as simple scepticism, as Bernstein did (Bernstein, op. cit.). A closer examination of the sceptical traditions reveals Foucault's position as a subspecies of scepticism called 'fideism'. The (academic) sceptical position, following Arcesilas c.315–241 BC, holds that no true belief is possible through reason. The fideist variety of it nonetheless holds that it is possible still to simply adopt a position on faith, and that would appear to be just what Foucault does. He rejects the model of the self as capable of potentially autonomous reason and replaces it with a fideistic model of the care and creation of the self through aesthetic, ethical and ascetic means. Derrida's fideism is more open.

Derrida addresses the possibility of rational autonomy more indirectly. He speaks of 'letting be' whereby we allow the other sufficient respect to be other and of the relationship of this letting be to freedom. He writes of 'choosing' to accept an inscription directed toward our identity or of rejecting it. But he undercuts the liberal idea of a responsive, reasoning dialogue by deconstructing the idea of claim and response, as well as by deconstructing the idea of intended meaning:

The overweening presumption from which no response will ever be free not only has to do with the fact that the response claims to measure up to the discourse of the other, to situate it, understand it, indeed, circumscribe it by responding thus *to* the other and *before* the other. The respondent presumes, with as much frivolity as arrogance, that he can respond to the other and before the other because, first of all he is able to answer for himself . . . (Derrida, op. cit., p. 17)

Nevertheless, he also affirms the possibility of authorship. He does not fly straight to the opposite position to that adopted by liberal thought but rather moves toward a displacement of its oppositions.

Habermas deals with these issues more clumsily, but not necessarily less powerfully. First, the idea of transparent giving and evaluating of reasons in Habermas' theory is an idea of *counterfactual* conditions of dialogue (Habermas, 1990). In a number of places he describes the empirical conditions that prevent genuine dialogue from occurring, including aspects of the development of subjectivity (Habermas, 1982). The purpose of struggles around these empirical conditions, both personal and social, is not to achieve the counterfactual state, nor are they to be measured by comparisons with an ideal of perfectly reciprocal and open dialogue. The purpose of struggles around issues of voice and who gets the speaking parts in the drama of the social construction of reality is strategic. And strategy is a fallible, pragmatic art — a social art as well as an individual art of the care of the self.[4] Strategy can be guided by models for thinking, and the counterfactual idea of unconstrained communication is a model for thinking with — in an apophatic way (and therefore in a way functionally quite similar to the tropes of poststructuralist sceptical fideism) (see Bernstein, op. cit.).

While Habermas now allows that his model of the ideal speech situation was too static and detached to be useful, he nonetheless continues to argue for the necessity of the counterfactual imagination in critique (Habermas, 1990). With this imagination we are able to engage in an ethic of care for the other through communicative respect — one which tackles both obstacles to autonomy *and* to solidarity (without domination). To hyperinflate the 'otherness' of the other without a corresponding recognition of desire or passion — a unitative emotion — is to give in to a universalization of the sense of alienation characteristic of French intellectuals. Derrida honours the other, Foucault honours the self, both effectively stumble when they reach toward the possibility of bridging the gap between persons. They reject the liberal account of the autonomous reasoning agent because they take the classical sceptical position that all knowledge claims must be asserted in bad faith, but in rejecting liberal claims on *these* grounds they also reject the very possibility of communicatively achieved ethical progress. They nonetheless reaffirm this possibility fideistically, each in his own way.

Certainly, Habermas does not theorize dialogue convincingly or fully. Foucault's agonized attempts to come to some *rapprochement* with his own sado-masochistic and self-destructive sexuality, led to his final reflections, which offer us more insight into our inwardness and our inner dialogue; Derrida's 'affirmative interpretations' offer us more insight about the many forms of imposition of our self upon the other of communication. But Habermas is right to insist that we desire more. Perhaps Richard Bernstein's injunction for us to hold the thought of Derrida and Habermas in productive tension — not as a synthesis, but as a constellation — might be appropriate, if minimalist, advice for us to follow, at least as far as the account of dialogue and its role in pedagogy is concerned (Bernstein, op. cit.). If so, we must be concerned in pedagogical dialogue with the desire for oneness *and* the problem of otherness, and keep open the possibility of 'letting difference be' as a pedagogical outcome. In other words, we must keep liberal hope alive, while deconstructing successive approximations of it.

The Political Dimensions of Critique

So far, we have been examining critique through the lens of dialogue (and deconstruction) but the notion that either deconstructive writings or argumentative dialogue can have real political effect has been heavily parasitic on the linguistic turn in social theory and on the idea that social reality is dialogically constructed. It has also been parasitic on an inflated estimation of the significance for social change of intellectual discourse and of what might be called the 'theoretic' layer in social structure. As realist and neo-Marxist critics of postmodernism have pointed out, this is scarcely adequate to the sheer mass and inertia of sociocultural reality, hardly cognisant of the instruments of force which back up institutional structures, barely reflective of the degree to which everyday practices are habitual adaptations to circumstances and virtually silent about the reasons for the effectiveness (rather than the form) of technology (see Callinicos, 1989).

While every macropolitics must have a micropolitics, a kind of methodological individualism runs through the debate about discourse which is fatal for any coherent account of political strategy.

Fraser and Nicholson, writing about the adequacy of Lyotard's postmodernist account of politics for the needs of the women's movement, present a more general argument that more than a local, specific, micropolitics is required:

> . . . effective criticism . . . requires at a minimum large narratives about changes in social oganisations and ideology, empirical and social-theoretical accounts of macrostructures and institutions. (Fraser and Nicholson, 1990)

While both Derrida and Foucault claim political relevance for their work they both retreat theoretically from the macropolitical. As Richard Bernstein says,

'. . . there is a strong undercurrent in these writings that gravitates towards ethical-political issues' (Bernstein, op. cit., p. 6), but an absence of an intellectual resource for a macropolitics.

For Derrida, ethical-political questions call for responsibility and commitment but are in essence 'undecideable' (Derrida, 1988). Derrida has himself been politically engaged at the level of public-opinion formation, institutional critique, policy critique and the like, but all the while explicitly recognizing this as '. . . incommensurate with my intellectual project . . .' (Derrida, 1984).

Foucault, too, was politically active during one period of his life, but again, as Michel Foucault not as a poststructuralist theorist. Foucault was brought back again and again to this issue by interviewers and critics. At times, he acknowledged the problem of a gap between his recommendation for a local and specific role for intellectuals and the need for intellectuals to play a role in wider political strategy. Foucault wavered between acknowledging critical principles of a distinctly Habermasian kind and denying the possibility of an intellectually guided political strategy. With Derrida, Foucault declared such questions undecideable and described his approach as 'anti-strategic' in the political sense (Foucault, 1981).

In this attitude, both Foucault and Derrida share common ground with Weber, who saw political questions as lying in a realm of warring gods, beyond the reach of expeditions of reason. However, in his critique of Weber, Habermas argued that this view is a product of a limited conception of reason — the reduction of reason to what Weber called *zweckrationalität* or means–ends reason. In the case of poststructuralist thought, despite notorious and extensive differences among different thinkers, the source of scepticism about political reason is the same, or at least it is ground to Weber's figure. Like Weber, the poststructuralists sometimes seem to have erected an impossible conception of reason (albeit one which high modernity took to be its true self-image), and in denying its possibility took themselves to be denying all reasonableness.

At times, and in some readings, Derrida and Foucault contend against conceptual windmills — a conception of communication as perfect sharing of meaning (Derrida), and of knowledge as warranted true belief (Foucault). Space precludes a full treatment of issues here, but it is possible to retrace the tropic structure of Derrida's and Foucault's arguments and show that by aggrandizing that against which they fight they also elevate the status of their own assertions. Foucault's dystopias are models of societies that are simpler and more functionally closed than real societies. The texts Derrida chooses to deconstruct are only some among the proof texts of modernity. A more modest, less absolutist conception of communication and knowledge might be more valuable, despite problems. Certainly, Foucault was a stranger to moderation, and his discovery of its role in Greek thought, late in his life, greatly troubled him spiritually and intellectually (see Bernauer, op. cit. and Colapietro, 1990). The later work of Derrida, too, displays a greater willingness to forestall more absolutist readings. Perhaps it would be interesting for

Derrida to focus on the texts of nuanced, critical modernism. There is reason to wonder whether an attempt to deconstruct, say, Adorno might not result in a simultaneous deconstruction of Derrida.

For the purposes of a macroscopic, institutional politics of education in culturally and socioeconomically pluralistic settings, a more modest conception of marginal and relational gains in truth or understanding is of greater value than the political agnosticism and fideism more absolute criteria drive us toward. Pragmatist philosophy of knowledge provides a more reasonable, fallibilist account of the possibility of effective cognitive adaptation. In his turn, Habermas provides some of the basic elements of a theory of institutional politics of inquiry and education in his critique of Parsons, Luhmann and Mead, and in his most recent political essays (Habermas, 1993). Admittedly, it is a lousy theory but that is not what is at issue. What is at issue is whether it is the best lousy theory we have. No doubt, it is also a theory vulnerable to specific forms of cooption. Poststructuralist thought may provide necessary, if dystopian and sometimes jaundiced correctives to Habermasian critical theory, playing Socrates to his Plato. For the foreseeable future, the micropolitical suspicions of Derrida and the micropolitical strategies of Foucault may provide one kind of measure of the adequacy of specific, critical, macropolitical strategies.

Conclusion

What we discover when we address the question of the social process whereby each of us meets the other person and brings our candidate standards for critique into some process of dialogue with theirs, and we struggle with the problem of the inadequacy of liberal accounts of this, is that we are dealing with a cluster of questions that are crucial for our particular historical circumstances — how to make our quasi-democratic societies reflect our plurality while at the same time celebrating our diversity — how to deal, in a genuine democracy, with the cultural and personal plurality of valuing without giving up the dialogue about the best ways of valuing. This problem is lent urgency, and any solution to it thereby given crucial status, by the obvious cultural uncertainty and moral turmoil that societies like ours display.

Just as there is a macropolitics and a micropolitics there is a macroeducation and a microeducation. Habermas speaks of macroeducational questions when he talks of the 'learning level' of societies like ours. In the Deweyian language of problem-solving learning, or inquiry, which Habermas also employs at times, the macroproblem characteristic of our time is the problem of difference. It is easy enough to see the roots of this in the world-historical process of the globalization of communication and cultural interaction. It shows up in our school systems in problems of minorities, value and lifestyle differences.

But the microproblem is the problem of critique. This problem manifests itself as a problem of interpretation, dialogue and the, in some sense 'relatively autonomous', praxis of intellectuals and professionals, including teachers and learners. Of course, as Toulmin's analysis of 'high modernity' shows, the problems of difference and critique are intertwined (Toulmin, 1990). High modernity was specifically a technology for providing a form of critique which overcame specificity, localism and cultural and religious difference in the newly forming nation states of Europe.

Foucault's failure is that he has construed the macroproblem as a problem of power, not difference, and Derrida's failure is that he has construed the microproblem (of texts, authorship and meaning) as a problem of difference not power. Habermas' virtue is that he has not made either mistake, thus sharing Foucault's critique of Derrida and Derrida's critique of Foucault.[5] But Habermas' failure, which can only be corrected by a synthesis with pragmatism, a failure which both Foucault and Derrida share, is that he has construed the problem of power as a struggle about meaning, that is, as a problem of ideology, when it is just as much, but not more so, an ontological problem, or a problem of political organization of ontogenetic voice, and of the contingent formation of courage and other attributes of character necessary to this voice — the formation of virtue, hope and love. Perhaps in an account of the specific, concrete character of the form of virtue in our time and condition, we can find the basis for an account which transcends the obstacles to authentic self-representation that cause liberal theory to stumble.

Notes

1 Paper delivered to the Conference on poststructuralism and education at Griffith University, Gold Coast, Australia, 8–9 December 1993.
2 The Quine/Duhem thesis is also referred to as the thesis of the 'theory-ladenness of observation'.
3 The issues here are complex. Some are discussed in my 1990 paper 'Habermas' Ontology of Learning: Reconstructing Dewey', *Educational Theory*, 40, 4, pp. 471–82 and in (1992) *Critical Theory and Classroom Talk*, Clevedon, Philadelphia and Adelaide, Multilingual Matters.

   In general, the reader would not go far wrong if they joined the ontogenetic emphasis of my 1990 work with Charles Hamblin's logical analysis of dialogue with a contribution from Dewey's (1966) *Logic: The Theory of Inquiry*, New York, Pantheon.
4 Foucault tends to limit the notion of strategy to individual action.
5 The debate between Foucault and Derrida about Derrida's reading of Descartes is instructive: J. Derrida, (1978), 'Cogito and the History of Madness', in *Writing and Difference*, London, Routledge and Kegan Paul, and Foucault's 1972 response in the appendix to *Folie et Déraison*, Paris, Gallimard. See also Frow, J. 'Foucault and Derrida', (1985) *Raritan*, V, 1, pp. 31–42.

Robert Young

References

BEREITER, C. (1985) 'Toward a Solution of the Learning Paradox', *Review of Educational Research*, 55, 2, pp. 201–26.

BERNAUER, J. (1988) 'Michel Foucault's ecstatic thinking', in BERNAUER, J. and RASMUSSEN, D. (Eds) *The Final Foucault*, Cambridge, MIT Press, pp. 45–82.

BERNSTEIN, R. (1991) *The New Constellation*, Cambridge, Polity Press.

CALLINICOS, A. (1989) *Against Postmodernism*, Cambridge, Polity Press.

COLAPIETRO, V. (1990) 'The Vanishing Subject of Contemporary Discourse: A Pragmatic Response', *Journal of Philosophy*, pp. 644–55.

DERRIDA, J. (1984) 'Dialogue with Jacques Derrida', in KEARNEY, R. (Ed) *Dialogues with Contemporary Continental Thinkers*, Manchester, Manchester University Press, p. 120.

DERRIDA, J. (1988) 'Afterword', *Limited Inc*, Evanston, Northwestern University Press, p. 116.

DERRIDA, J. (1991) in KAMUF, P. (Ed) *A Derrida Reader: Between the Blinds*, London, Harvester Wheatsheaf.

DERRIDA, J. (1992) 'Passions: An Oblique Offering', WOODS, D. (1992) (Ed) *Derrida: A Critical Reader*, Oxford, Blackwell, pp. 5–35.

FOUCAULT, M. (1981) 'Is it useless to revolt?', *Philosophy and Social Criticism*, VIII, 1, pp. 1–9.

FOUCAULT, M. (1984) in RABINOW, P. (Ed) *The Foucault Reader*, London, Penguin. p. 379.

FOUCAULT, M. (1984) 'Politics and ethics: An interview', pp. 373–380 in RABINOW, P. (Ed) *The Foucault Reader*, London, Penguin, pp. 373–80.

FOUCAULT, M. (1986) *The History of Sexuality*, 3, *The Care of the Self*, New York, Pantheon.

FRASER, N. and NICHOLSON, L. (1990) 'Social Criticism without Philosophy: An Encounter between Feminism and Postmodernism,' in NICHOLSON, L. (Ed) *Feminism/Postmodernism*, New York, Routledge and Kegan Paul, pp. 19–38.

GADAMER, H-G. (1975) *Truth and Method*, New York, Seabury Press.

GARRISON, J. (1986) 'The paradox of indoctrination: A solution', *Synthese*, 68, pp. 261–73.

HABERMAS, J. (1978) *Communication and the Evolution of Society*, London, Heinemann Educational Books.

HABERMAS, J. (1982) *The Theory of Communicative Action*, 1, London, Heinemann Educational Books, pp. 328–38.

HABERMAS, J. (1990) 'Discourse ethics: Some notes on a program of philosophical justification', in BENHABIB, S. and DALLMAYR, F. (Eds) *The Communicative Ethics Controversy*, Cambridge, MIT Press.

HABERMAS, J. (1993) *Postmetaphysical Thinking*, Cambridge, MIT Press.

NIRANJANA, T. (1992) *Siting Translation*, Berkeley, University of California Press.

SPIVAK, G. (1987) *In Other Worlds: Essays in Cultural Politics*, London, Methuen.

TOULMIN, S. (1990) *Cosmopolis: The Hidden Agenda of Modernity*, New York, The Free Press.

YOUNG, R. (1984) 'Teaching equals indoctrination: The epistemic practices of our schools', *British Journal of Educational Studies*, 32, 3, pp. 231–42.

2 Fading Poststructuralisms: Post-Ford, Posthuman, Posteducation?

John Knight

Abstract

Mass schooling is characterised by a split referentiality in which humanistic education stands for the infinite re/production of schooled workers. The introduction of post-Fordist forms of schooling, allied with current presses for efficiency and effectiveness, is seen as allowing for a more thorough-going commodification of knowledge and workers. Arguably, it is also consonant with the growing influence of corporatism on public education. Here is not an anti-humanism which is aware of its binary formulation with humanism, but a post-humanism.[1]

Modifications of poststructuralist thought, including much recent feminist work, along with some of the more thoughtful critiques of poststructuralism, are seen as raising the possibility of new humanisms. However, forthcoming developments in biology, psychology and sociology may offer new and effective technologies of behaviour for the post-human and a corporatised post-Fordist posteducation.

In the title of this book I find a certain liberty (as much given as taken) to be impertinent. What I attempt, therefore, in this chapter is to assert, to irritate, to provoke, to transgress, to dissimulate, to be serious, to speculate, to inquire. In short, to write. There are aporia: questions, puzzles, gaps, for which I cannot find satisfactory conclusions. There are fictions where I would find truth. Humanness, progress, truth, the individual, society, education are under erasure. But what will be written over the fading poststructuralisms of the present?

I begin with the recognition that despite the rhetorics of classical humanism, liberal humanism, child-centred education, personal growth and progressivism which have been deployed variously in education's justification, mass schooling has been characterized by practices which are substantially otherwise. There is, in Ricoeur's (1981) terms, a process of 'split referentiality', in which in a metaphoric framing, one thing (here, humanistic assertions of the worth of the individual, the value of 'our' cultural heritage, and the development of the human through education) stands for something other (here, the attempt to produce personalities and subjected and docile bodies suited to the needs of work and the practices of power; the infinite reproduction of schooled workers). In short, to equate mass schooling with a humanistic education is almost certainly to commit an oxymoron. Nevertheless, the use (which would once have been termed 'ideological') of such formulations, representing schooling as that which it is not, is significant. For, *inter alia*, this schizophrenic (metaphoric) representation opens a space for critical reflection and action on the nature and processes of schooling, and (on paper at least) for deconstructing and reconstructing its purposes and practices. Can you imagine what the schooling of the nation (and the schooling of teachers) might have become without such deception?

The essay speculates on an end to the present settlement of education/schooling. What it anticipates is the 'restructuring' of schooling in an amalgam of corporate forms of management, contemporary technologies of behaviour, and post-Fordist processes of production. 'Education' is replaced by the (re)production of flexible human units of production/consumption. What follows is the excision of even the representations of humanism from schooling. Baudrillard's depiction of a situation in which distinctions of 'signifier' and 'signified', 'medium' and 'message', 'simulacrum' and 'reality' collapse, implode is pertinent. With the disappearance of the (human-educational) referent, in this (post)-'political economy of the sign' there are only simulacra, and

> It is no longer a question of a false representation of reality (ideology), but of concealing the fact that the real is no longer real . . . (Baudrillard, 1988, p. 172)

With such a degree of (post)consonance, there is no further need for the split referentiality of education/schooling. Hypocrisy requires the existence of virtue; here there will be neither. This is indeed the posthuman.

In this setting, posteducation is the new educational settlement in the shift from industrial to what has been variously described as 'postindustrial society' (Bell, 1973), 'late' or 'disorganized capitalism' (Lash and Urry, 1987), or 'flexible postmodernity' (Harvey, 1989). As suggested above, there will be a shift from the massified reproduction of Fordist forms of schooling to the flexible simulations of post-Fordist production and a restructuring of the inflexible strictures and archaic fixtures of state bureaucracies to more devolved and 'self-managing' systems of social formation. Which means (in a sort of Orwellian double-speak) continuing transformations of 'reality' and the assemblages of 'citizens' in 'our' 'free' and 'democratic' 'society'. This is to say, they will be continual consumers in a universal market. In this situation, distinctions of 'public' and 'private' have no substance. Boundaries are fluid, forms have no abiding substance: they collapse, coalesce and recoalesce.

And so as public schooling becomes more adaptive, responsible and 'private' (in short, more 'autonomous'), it is the more thoroughly monitored and directed. Hence the range of accountability mechanisms is far more searching and thorough than any earlier processes of inspection: national goals, national reporting, performance indicators, generic competencies, outputs, subject and student profiles . . . Such discursive constructions are indexical: they point up the expedient coming conjunction of corporation and market in posteducation and the all-embracing message/medium of the postmodern. But what forms and conceptions of the posthuman will be inscribed within and upon this new settlement?

The uses and abuses of poststructuralist theorizing in analysing and reforming schooling are celebrated widely. Working variously in and out of poststructuralist, deconstructive, feminist, postmodernist, postpositivist and postcolonial frames, such noted (notorious) figures of the radical academic educational establishment as Philip Wexler, Stephen Ball, Bronwyn Davies, Henry Giroux, Jane Kenway, Patti Lather and Peter McLaren have been most effective in the production of critiques of current practice and the predication of various alternatives to the old humanisms. Nevertheless, thus far the structures and processes of schooling have proved remarkably resistant to change. And indeed schooling (whether francophone or anglophone) continues as if the strictures of poststructuralism (and neo-marxism) had never been uttered. (The populace at large remains unregenerately modernist. Bannet (1989) makes a similar point with respect to the inertia of the French academy despite Lacan, Barthes, Foucault and Derrida.)

Certainly, poststructuralist critiques (demolitions) of 'humanism' are well-known in the academy (though whether that humanism was somewhat of a straw person will be addressed shortly). At any rate, as Dews (1987, p. xi) points out, the result has been 'the dismantling of stable conceptions of meaning, subjectivity and identity'. In such anti-humanist framings, the individual subject is decentred, fragmented, inconsistent, pluriform, a product of their changing and contradictory discursive and extra-discursive positionings. Rationalism is subverted by anti-rationalism (though not irrationalism). Notions of 'truth', 'progress' and human 'emancipation' are rejected for 'the unmasterable historicity, heterogeneity and cultural relativity of all values' (Connor, 1992, p. 1). Issues of aesthetics, values and ethics are thereby problematized. The implications for any political and educational project beyond the local and the immediate are substantial. 'Revolution' has been replaced by 'resistance', 'progress' by 'change', 'emancipation' by 'empowerment' and 'struggle', 'truth' by 'commodified knowledge', and the 'global' by the 'local'.[2]

Despite such apparently extreme relativism, leading poststructuralist writers have been politically active in support of minority groups and 'democratic' issues. They would reject charges of nihilism or passivity. Nevertheless, some of the more thoughtful critics of poststructuralism have expressed serious concerns over its apparent anti-humanism, denial of human agency, and rejection of the project of modernity, and these will be addressed shortly.

There is also a growing sense in the academy that poststructuralism has been something of an interregnum. (I do not say cul-de-sac, for I believe its uses, its insights and its spirit of play have been and continue to be needed and invaluable.) But, increasingly there are discomforts over its elevation from 'theory' to 'Theory' and from *bricolage* to totalizing framework in some Anglo-American (and Australian) poststructuralist work. As Bannet (1989) observes, the texts of the poststructuralist theorizings of Barthes, Lacan, Foucault and Derrida are often treated (and *mea culpa* — I too have sinned) as universals rather than as coming from (and in the first instance addressing) specific cultural and historical contexts, in particular the literary and classical humanist curriculum of the French academy, the standardized, centralized and hierarchical authority structures of the French State. That given, the 'humanism' which is condemned may not be in all particulars the humanism of our reconstructions. This recognition may perhaps be a part of an emergent new humanism.

Thus, certain feminist theorists working across and against poststructuralisms (e.g., Fraser, 1989; Lather, 1991) may be seen as reworking the various poststructuralist anti-humanisms into a range of what might be termed 'new humanist' approaches. This is the case with a number of members of the Australian academy. Thus, with respect to education, Davies (1989, 1993) sees the opportunity for moving beyond the 'male–female dualism' and its 'associated binary metaphors' and shifting from discourse to discourse as appropriate to circumstance and need. Kenway (1992) draws on poststructuralist thought and practice to address 'gender reform in schools through a post-structuralist lens'. Gilbert and Taylor (1991) examine ways of using popular culture to challenge and change adolescent female identity. Morgan (1992, 1993) shows how 'a post-structuralist English classroom' was run and what a postcolonial pedagogy might be. McWilliam (1992) presents a postpositivist approach to research 'with and for' rather than on her pre-service teacher-education students. (There is, of course, no necessary connection between feminism and the new humanisms, and neither is virtue gendered. There are also simulacra, posthumanisms.)

That said, let's return to the question of the sort of intellectual and cultural settlement (if any) most likely in the immediate future and the implications for education/schooling. The reading of the prefix 'post' is critical. Does it mean 'after' (as in 'postwar'), a temporal sequence which may well be disjunctive or does it mean 'post' as in 'dialogue with or response to'? etc. (The debate over the place of the 'postmodern' is analogous. Is the postmodern the successor to the modern, is it a *fin-de-siècle* modernism, or is it as Lyotard (1992) concludes, the constantly reworked interface between past and future?)

In this chapter my usage of the term 'post' is at best ambiguous. I accept the usual constructions of 'poststructuralism' as extending, modifying and denying an antecedent 'structuralism'. Thus poststructuralism may presage a full-blown postmodernism, but it is by and large a manifestation of, and from, late modernity and a critique and deconstruction of the modern. Yet the 'postmodern' also has temporal and epistemological continuities and discontinuities with the 'modern'. I agree with Giddens (1990) that the post-modern as 'a new and different order' is yet to come, but my construction of that 'after' differs markedly from his. For the present, elements of modernity still coexist with postmodernity; we have yet to see the full elaboration of the postmodern.

To compound this 'post'-ambiguity, and to make the points I want to make in this essay, a somewhat arbitrary distinction is drawn between 'anti-humanism', a reaction to, or rejection of, some form or other (or all forms) of 'humanism', and 'posthumanism', which follows but is discontinuous with the old humanisms. That is, anti-humanism presumes a knowledge of humanism, and humanism–anti-humanism form a binary, they exist in the same epistemic field. Posthumanism, however, is situated on a different terrain, a terrain constituted by, and of, simulacra. From chimera to simulacrum.

I want to reference certain matters from some of the more thoughtful critiques of poststructuralist theorizings. They present matters of some substance on the place of values, ethics, aesthetics and the human agent in the project of human emancipation. In various ways they ask what is to be inscribed in place of, over or beyond, the old signifying humanisms of modernism, liberalism and socialism. Perhaps they will help us discern some of the broad features of certain pluralized and pluralizing new humanisms which may yet withstand (however impossibly) the simulacra of the posthuman.

Thus, addressing the binary of critical theory and poststructuralism, Dews (1987) concludes,

> the rejection of the claims of an integrated critical standpoint in poststructuralism, in the mistaken belief that such a standpoint implies repressive totalization, is far from providing a more decisive liberation from the illusions of philosophy, and a more powerful illumination of the contemporary word . . . [C]ritique is not a question of the arbitrary and coercive espousal of premises and precepts, but rather of commitments to that coherence of thought which alone ensures its emancipatory power. (Dews, 1987, p. 242)

Thus, arguing that '[t]he ideology of post-modernism permanently seals off any attempt to find an escape hatch for inquiry beyond the textual surface of discourse' (p. 4), Dorothy Smith (1990) calls for a materialist mode of inquiry into 'the relations of ruling' which seeks

> access to the extended or macro-relations organizing the society through an analysis of the micro-social . . . Without a totalizing theory or externalizing master frame . . . [it] begins where people are and explores the actual practices engaging us in the relations organizing our lives. (Smith, 1990, p. 10)

Thus Freadman and Miller (1992) ask, 'how can "the strategic goal of human emancipation" be served or secured in the absence of a theoretical account of the emancipated individual subject?' (p. 194). Against a *melange* of poststructuralisms which they characterize as 'constructivist anti-humanism', they argue for a revivified humanism, in which

> [one:] substantive conceptions of the individual subject are indispensable, both in respect of literature and of politics; . . . [two:] language . . . can give us access to significant features of a reality that is not itself a linguistic construct; . . . [and three:] discourses of value, both aesthetic and moral, are indispensable . . . (Freadman and Miller, 1992, p. 4)

Thus Frank (1989), working in a hermeneutic frame, inquires,

> how can one, on the one hand, do justice to the fundamental fact that meaning, significance and intention — the semantic foundations of every consciousness — can form themselves only in a language, in a social, cultural and economic order (in a structure)? How can one, on the other hand, redeem the fundamental idea of modern humanism that links the dignity of human beings with their use of freedom and which cannot tolerate that one can morally applaud the factual threatening of subjectivity by the totalitarianism of systems of rules and social codes? (Frank, 1989, p. 6)

It is in this frame that he concludes, 'Above all, we need *an archaeology of individuality*' (p. 447) and in consonance with (rather than repeating) Habermas, he calls for satisfying the 'claims for universality' 'in postmetaphysical times' 'by means of a will to universal nonrestrictive communication', for

> [t]he work of conceptualisation demands more from those who claim to engage in it than that they execute *their own* thoughts well; it also demands that they confront the thoughts of others in transindividual and, what is more, transcultural and transnational communication. (ibid., p. 449)

Thus Connor (1992), faced with the ongoing conflict between those who espouse absolute or relative value, concludes paradoxically that these positions are not only mutually exclusive but also necessary correlates, each of which 'requires, confirms and regenerates the other'. Hence, rather than being resolved into a choice between or synthesis of each other, they should be 'thought together'. That is,

> one should refuse to surrender either the orientation towards universal, absolute and transcendent value, or the commitment to plurality, relativity and contingency. (Connor, 1992, p. 1)

Value, here, is 'the irreducible orientation towards the better, and revulsion from the worse' (p. 2) Hence, also,

> The values that we prize come into being because of acts of energetic, painful appraisal; values are the sedimental deposits of the imperative to value. But all values must remain continually vulnerable to appraisal. The imperative to value therefore turns out to involve an extreme reflexivity . . . (ibid., p. 3)

It follows also that ethical and aesthetic values are necessarily and inescapably interactive. And this continuous questioning of value is indeed 'a discourse of emancipation', first because emancipation from 'hunger, poverty, exploitation, autonomization, degradation and exclusion' is a necessary precondition for such questioning, and second because individuals need 'rational interchange with the greatest plurality of emancipated subjects' in order to have 'maximally free transaction of value' (p. 5).

Thus, finally, Habermas' (1983) concern to reinstate 'the incomplete project of modernity' and Giddens' (1990, p. 150) assertion of the need for a 'radicalized modernity'. For Giddens, radicalized modernity

1　Identifies the institutional developments which create a sense of fragmentation and dispersal.
2　Sees high modernity as a set of circumstances in which dispersal is dialectically connected to profound tendencies towards global integration.
3　Sees the self as more than just a site of intersecting forces; active processes of reflexive self-identity are made possible by modernity.
4　Argues that the universal features of truth claims force themselves upon us in an irresistible way given the primacy of problems of a global kind. Systematic knowledge about these developments is not precluded by the reflexivity of modernity.
5　Analyses a dialectic of powerlessness and empowerment, in terms of both experience and action.
6　Sees day-to-day life as an active complex of reactions to abstract systems, involving appropriation as well as loss.
7　Regards coordinated political engagement as both possible and necessary, on a global level as well as locally . . .

Let me turn (back) to education. John Dewey's critique of conventional forms of schooling is well known. Dewey recognized that their pedagogy and practices were antithetical to preparation for life in a democratic society. He saw that the distinction of liberal from vocational forms of education perpetuated the divisions between dominant social groupings and the working classes. Given a rapidly changing society, he argued that any form of training for specific future conditions was futile; the best preparation schools could give for a future life was to give children command of themselves. They should be able to draw on the resources of the past and their own powers to reconstruct their contexts for socially democratic ends. Dewey's words, written just prior to his death in 1952, remain pertinent to any 'progressive' programme for a new humanism in education:

> For the creation of a democratic society we need an educational system where the process of moral-intellectual development is in practice as well as in theory a cooperative transaction of inquiry engaged in by free, independent human beings who treat ideas and the heritage of the past as means and methods for the further enrichment of life, quantitatively and qualitatively, who use the good attained for the discovery and establishment of something better. (Dewey and Dewey, 1962, p. xix)

More recently, the noted liberal humanist, Robert Hutchins (1970), laid out the possibility of achieving 'the learning society', a society in which technology would liberate all people from the demands of work so that a lifelong education might enable them to become more fully human. In this utopic situation, the transformation of social values would make 'learning, fulfilment, becoming human', the goal of all social institutions and the central purpose of education (p. 133). Nowadays, such totalizing narratives are out of favour. But what then can we say to a situation in which the totalizing economic narrative of the capitalist market represents massive and chronic unemployment as the necessary consequence of increased productivity through new labour-saving technologies?

Notions of the redistribution of wealth are currently unfashionable. The principles of progressive education or notions of a learning society are too unrealistic for 'practical' political agendas. Indeed, they have become almost inconceivable. What we see, instead, is the corporatist programme for the 'reform' of schooling and the new 'training' agendas for human capital in a postindustrial society.

Thus a major recent development in Australian schooling (and similar developments are taking place elsewhere) has been the attempt by various agencies of government, industry and the unions to articulate 'education' and 'training' more closely, and to specify and develop 'generic' and 'industry-specific' competencies in all students. The system of schooling is also being 'restructured' and corporatized on managerialist and economic rationalist lines for greater efficiencies of process and effectiveness of outputs. This is part of the process of reforming education 'in the national interest'. That is, schools, TAFE colleges and universities function in corporate fashion to produce flexible and multiskilled workers with the 'human capital' necessary for a successful post-Fordist economy. In this shift to corporatist forms and processes, whatever elements of the humanist tradition may have remained in public education are under erasure or at best subverted for instrumental ends. The project of human emancipation has been (once more) overwritten. A new project, establishing a first world, post-Fordist and postindustrial (these assumptions are at best doubtful, at worst specious) Australia, is under way. Regardless, outside of an increasingly prolonged period of schooling (now reaching to postsecondary and tertiary levels for the great majority) and an artificially extended adolescence, the outlook for Australia's youth continues to be bleak.

Underlying this transformation of 'knowledge' into 'competencies' for corporate ends there is something very like Lyotard's (1984) notion of postmodern 'performativity', in which,

> The question . . . now asked . . . is no longer 'Is it true?' but 'What use is it?' In the context of the mercantilization of knowledge, more often than not this question is equivalent to: 'Is it saleable?' And in the context of power-growth: 'Is it efficient?' Having competence in a performance oriented skill does indeed seem saleable . . . and it is efficient by definition. What no longer makes the grade is competence as defined by other criteria true–false, just–unjust etc. — and, of course, low performativity in general. (Lyotard, 1984, p. 51)

In such a framing, as Lyotard notes, the nature of knowledge is transformed. No longer (if it ever was) an end in itself, it has become a commodity which is produced, sold and consumed. (The same fate applies to the (once) 'human'.) More, it has now not only become 'the principle force of production', it is 'a major — perhaps *the* major — stake in the worldwide competition for power'. Where once territory and raw materials were occasions of national conflict, the coming scenario envisages disputes over 'control of information' (1984, pp. 4, 5). And this is the way of things in 'late', 'global' or 'consumer capitalism' (Jameson, 1991).

I have already suggested that there is no purchase for any antecedent humanisms in such scenarios. It is not that they are rejected, they cannot exist. In this (post)ethos of the universal market and its (de)valuing of the individual to the status of commodity, there is no place for the project of human emancipation, indeed there is little place for the human. Here then is not an antihumanism which is aware of its binary opposite, but a posthumanism. And not the hopeful new humanisms on which we speculated earlier either.

I spoke earlier of a coming shift from bureaucratic and Fordist to post-Fordist and corporatized forms of schooling. The inadequacies, inefficiencies, and limitations of the current grade/classroom system are well-known, yet little has changed since the devising of mass schooling in the latter part of the nineteenth century. Mass schooling was to be cheap, but it was seldom efficient. Typically, one teacher still stands in front of twenty or thirty students. Yet modern technologies (IT, 'programmed learning', hypertext, 'distance' and 'open' education . . .) now make traditional forms of schooling (and teachers) obsolete.

While such 'innovations' as 'team-teaching', 'machine learning' and the like have been around for decades, teachers and their unions have generally resisted them. More recently, the 'advanced-skills teacher' concept, which promised much, has delivered little, again because of the distortion of a 'professional' development for 'industrial' ends. However, investigations are currently proceeding on new forms of work and organization in the National Project for Quality in Teaching and Learning and the newly formed Australian Teaching Council may also address these matters. Ashenden (1992) proffers an (economical) educational post-Fordist solution: fewer (but fully professional) teachers, deployed in specialist fashion, and a plethora of paraprofessionals, aides and support services.

The availability of technologies (the metaphor itself is significant) for transforming schooling intersects with the need for flexible and multiskilled workers for a (presumed — this is an item of faith) post-Fordist situation in industry and with presses for economies in the public services. Offe's (1984) paradox, in which at the very time when there is the greatest demand for resources for unemployment, health, education, etc., there is the greatest scarcity of available resources, is well-known. In such a situation, 'economic rationalism' and new more efficient forms of 'management' (as in the recent corporate restructurings of state systems of education) provide a metatechnology for reforming schooling. Meanwhile, we have all learned that more can be done for less, either by 'working cleverer' (which is the new slogan of micro-economic reform) or (more likely) by working harder.

This is the situation in which award restructuring and the drive for micro-economic reform and corporatization of schooling leads to an emphasis on the 'productivity' of 'education', with 'performance indicators' for (measurable) 'outputs'. What is demanded is the efficient deployment of teachers, where teachers are themselves competent producers, and the efficient reproduction of pupils as flexible workers (the notion is an oxymoron, surely?) for an indecipherable future. Here is indeed the end of commodification: the production and reproduction of knowledgeable (or more properly skilled) posthumans in the education industry (Knight, 1992) for the needs of an all-pervasive market.

The question is, not whether schooling will change, but what forms that change will take, what ethical considerations underwrite it, what constructions of humanness are disabled and enabled, what values are affirmed or denied. For example, will the new settlement inscribe a new humanism which resituates and restates notions of human improvement, progress, and enlightenment within the materiality and struggles of the present, not as inevitable consequences of modernity, but as a continuing testing and contesting, writing and rewriting, of the practices and assumptions of everyday life (Lusted, 1986). Or will it be a vertiginous and multiple series of displacements, dissections, transmutations, dehumanizations, marketizations of the subjected (dis-)organism. In short, the posthuman. (By writing, 'for example', I mean that these are not binary formulations.)

Meanwhile, the world goes on. And despite (indeed, ignoring) post-structuralisms, postmodernities, literary theories, nihilisms, existentialisms, sociologies, phenomenologies, hermeneutics, science continues to search for the grail of a unifying field theory, biology continues to advance towards 'a fully developmental theory of the phenotype from gene to organism' and 'the dissolution of the nature–nurture dichotomy' (Gottlieb, 1992), and psychology extends our knowledge of the brain–mind interface.

What, then, of a new settlement? Is the age of totalizing frameworks and metanarrative truly past? It may yet return. And if it does, it may be quite other than such new humanisms as we may have conjectured. Let us suppose, *as I fear*, that there is a new synthesis of biology, psychology, sociology. We may indeed then have a thorough understanding of 'human nature', a new and effective technology of behaviour, a posthuman constructing indeed. It might also indeed be consonant in its theory and practice with emergent corporatist forms of posteducation. But it would hardly support either the various humanisms of the past or the anti-humanisms of poststructuralism. Or the new humanist critiques of both.

Edmund Wilson (1975) inscribes a preface for this less than brave new posthuman world and (I fear) the forms of schooling/training appropriate for it:

> The transition from purely phenomenological to fundamental theory in sociology must await a full, neuronal explanation of the human brain. Only when the machinery can be torn down on paper at the level of the cell and put together again will the properties of emotion and ethical judgement come clear . . . Having cannibalised psychology, the new neurobiology will yield an enduring set of first principles for sociology. (Wilson, 1975, p. 575)

Meanwhile, we continue to debate the number of subject positions on the point of a pin.

Notes

1   I have found few references to 'posthumanism'. It is not in the recent revisions of the Oxford English Dictionary. Yet it is not a neologism. Spanos (1993) equates posthumanism with poststructuralism. Lather (1989, p. 2) describes a 'turning point . . . called variously postmodernism, poststructuralism, post-humanism, post-marxism, and, my least favourite, post-feminism.' Philipson (1989), in a nice double entendre, presents a letter 'to the post-man'.

2   It will be evident that in speaking of a particular set of anti-humanist framings, I do not deny the existence of others. For example, the Skinnerian 'technology of behaviour' or the Nazi construction of the *herrenvolk*, though this last is surely an example of irrationalism. Nor, though Margaret Thatcher and poststructuralism concur that 'there is no such thing as society', do I value all anti-humanisms equally.

John Knight

References

ASHENDEN, D. (1992) 'Award restructuring and productivity in the future of schooling', in RILEY, D. (Ed) *Industrial Relations in Australian Education*, Sydney, Social Science Press, pp. 55–74.

BANNET, E. (1989) *Structuralism and the Logic of Dissent*, London, Macmillan.

BAUDRILLARD, J. (1988) *Selected Writings*, POSTER, M. (Ed) Cambridge, Polity Press.

BELL, D. (1973) *The Coming of Post-Industrial Society: A Venture in Social Forecasting*, New York, Basic Books.

CONNOR, S. (1992) *Theory and Cultural Value*, Oxford, Blackwell.

DAVIES, B (1989) *Frogs and Snails and Feminist Tales*, Sydney, Allen and Unwin.

DAVIES, B. (1993) *Shards of Glass,* Sydney, Allen and Unwin.

DEWEY, J. and DEWEY, E. (1962) *Schools of Tomorrow*, New York, Dutton.

DEWS, P. (1987) *Logics of Disintegration*, London, Verso.

FRANK, M. (1989) *What Is Neostructuralism?*, Minneapolis, University of Minnesota Press.

FRASER, N. (1989) *Unruly Practices: Power, Discourse and Gender in Contemporary Social Theory*, Cambridge, Polity Press.

FREADMAN, R. and MILLER, S. (1992) *Re-Thinking Theory*, Cambridge, Cambridge University Press.

GIDDENS, A. (1990) *The Consequences of Modernity*, Stanford, Stanford University Press.

GILBERT, P. and TAYLOR, S. (1991) *Fashioning the Feminine: Girls, Popular Culture and Schooling*, Sydney, Allen and Unwin.

GOTTLIEB, G. (1992) *Individual Development and Evolution: The Genesis of Novel Behaviour*, New York, Oxford University Press.

HABERMAS, J. (1983) 'Modernity — An incomplete project', in FOSTER, H. (Ed) *Postmodern Culture*, London, Pluto Press, pp. 3–15.

HARVEY, D. (1989) *The Condition of Postmodernity*, Oxford, Basil Blackwell.

HUTCHINS, R. (1970) *The Learning Society*, Harmondsworth, Penguin.

JAMESON, F. (1991) *Postmodernism, or, the Cultural Logic of Late Capitalism,* London, Verso.

KENWAY, J. (1992) 'Making "Hope Practical" rather than "Despair Convincing": Some Thoughts on the Value of Poststructuralism as a Theory of and for Feminist change in Schools,' Paper delivered at AARE Conference, Deakin, November.

KNIGHT, J. (1992) 'The political economy of the education industry in the Dawkins Era', *Unicorn*, 18, 4, pp. 27–38.

LASH, S. and URRY, J. (1987) *The End of Organised Capitalism*, Cambridge, Polity Press.

LATHER, P. (1989) 'Deconstructing/Deconstructive Inquiry: Issues in Feminist Research Methodologies', Paper presented at NZ Women's Studies Association Conference, Christchurch, August 25–7.

LATHER, P. (1991) *Feminist Research in Education: Within/Against,* Geelong, Deakin University Press.

LUSTED, D. (1986) 'Why pedagogy?,' *Screen*, 27, 8, pp. 2–14.

LYOTARD, J.-F. (1984) *The Postmodern Condition: A Report on Knowledge*, Tr, BENNINGTON, G. and MASSUMI, B. Minneapolis, University of Minnesota Press.

LYOTARD, J.-F. (1992) *The Postmodern Explained to Children*, PEFANIS, J. and THOMAS, M. (Eds).

McWILLIAM, E. (1992) 'Towards Advocacy: Post-positivist Directions for Progressive Teacher Educators', *British Journal of Sociology of Education*, 13, 1, pp. 3–17.

MORGAN, W. (1992) *A Post-Structuralist English Classroom: The Example of Ned Kelly*, Carlton, VATE.

MORGAN, W. (1993) 'Whose English Down Under? The Example of a Post-colonial Australian Classroom', Address to the Fifth International Convention on Language in Education, the University of East Anglia, April.

OFFE, C. (1984) *Contradictions of the Welfare State*, London, Hutchinson.

PHILIPSON, M. (1989) *In Modernity's Wake: The Ameurunculus Letters*, London, Routledge.

RICOEUR, P. (1981) *Hermeneutics and the Human Sciences: Essays on Language, Action and Interpretation*, THOMPSON, J.B. (Ed) Cambridge, Cambridge University Press.

SMART, B. (1993) *Postmodernity*, London, Routledge.

SMITH, D. (1990) *Texts, Facts and Femininity: Exploring the Relations of Ruling*, London, Routledge.

SPANOS, W. (1993) *The End of Education: Towards Posthumanism*, Minneapolis, University of Minnesota Press.

WILSON, E. (1975) *Sociobiology: The New Synthesis*, Cambridge, Mass, Harvard University Press.

3 Having a Postmodernist Turn or Postmodernist *Angst*: A Disorder Experienced by an Author Who is Not Yet Dead or Even Close to It

Jane Kenway

There is a defiant spirit in my title to this chapter. However, I don't feel defiant and I do feel more close to death than I'd like to. I'm not dying — at least not 'by chocolate' unfortunately — but I do feel a certain political unease, wariness and weariness; if not a sense of hopelessness then at least a reduced optimism with regard to feminism in and maybe beyond education.[1] I am disturbed but not surprised at the recent backlash against feminism in Australian education and health systems (this is most evident in the rise of the boys' and the men's rights movements[2]), but I am also unsettled, agitated and anxious about some of the current directions in feminism in education and I want to publish my anxieties and see if others share them.[3] I say I am anxious, others say I am paranoid. I say there is a range of reasons to be both and others say some of these reasons are more my problem than feminism's. I say maybe that is true, but let me at least express my anxieties and see if they strike a chord — publish and be damned. Others say if you do publish, you will be damned; you will experience a feminist backlash. Yet others say that, in these current backlash times, I should defend feminism, not criticize it. They say that feminists, 'progressive educators' (whatever that means) and 'Left academics' (whatever that means) should promote feminist (and other) worthy causes, and that criticism should be directed particularly at those who detract from, and undermine, such causes and who benefit most from current inequitable social and educational arrangements.

I agree to some considerable extent with this last imperative. How could I do otherwise when I live in the Australian state of Victoria, a state governed by radical conservatives who, since coming to power less then two years ago, have vandalized the school system, removed 8,200 teaching positions, closed or amalgamated over 230 schools, wound back the provision of educational support services, pushed schools into a market mode, instituted a model of management which has turned educational leadership into a form of institutional management devoid of educational concerns, undermined the morale of teachers, almost totally destroyed the teachers' unions, officially removed the concept of social justice from the educational agenda, shaved $300 million off the state education budget and increased aid to private schools by 15 per cent in real terms (see further Marginson, forthcoming). I agree that there is an urgent and pressing need for educators to speak out strongly and courageously against those types of educational manoeuvres, to deconstruct the truth claims which have been mobilized to justify and legitimate such moves and to name them for what they are. I also think it is equally important that the broader national and global political, cultural and economic shifts which have helped to provide the conditions for this great leap backwards are identified and critically named. And here comes the rub, or at least one of them, with regard to much work by feminist academics in education. I have to be critical of such work in order to encourage more feminists to become critical education activists not just with regard to the obvious gender politics of education but with regard to these and other current directions which often have more subtle implications for girls and women. In the third part of this chapter I will suggest some directions that feminism in education may take if it is to accept my implicit challenge.

I believe that in recent times feminism in and for education has become so preoccupied with its own 'internal' theoretical and political difficulties and differences that it has not paid due and proper attention to what is going on in the rest of the 'restructured' educational world. I also believe that it has become so infatuated with various versions of poststructuralism and/or postmodernism, so influenced by the concerns and interests and intrigued by the debates and challenges of these fields that it has, in many senses, let the educational policy world go by.[4] Certainly exploring the implications of these theories for education policy has not been high on the agenda. This is not to say that any of its postmodernist concerns are unimportant, rather it is to say that a great deal of other really important educational ground is being lost and that feminism seems to be sacrificing much of its critical edge in those Political (the big P is intentional) circles where education policy is made. It seems to be off in a space by itself somewhere, meanwhile something is burning, and it's not Rome.

If I am correct, a matter always open to dispute as my friends eagerly and constantly tell me, then the obvious question to be asked is 'why?'. I attribute part of the reason to the 'nature' (for want of a better word) of popular or dominant versions of postmodernism, to the selective appropriations from the fields that some feminists in education have made and to the ways in which they have translated these ideas into the worlds of education. I also believe that feminist educators have not deployed certain insights from postmodernism as wisely and strategically as they might have in current times and that their engagement with postmodernism has not been as critical as it should have been. I know these are harsh words and in saying them I do not wish to imply that I am innocent or that I am on higher moral or political ground than others. Far from it. I have been just as infatuated and uncritical as the next person, as some of my recent feminist research and writing indicates (see for example, Kenway, Willis, Blackmore and Rennie, 1994). Indeed, it hasn't been my feminist work that has led me to be as concerned as I am. It has been my work examining the rise of market forms in education in association with other major policy shifts and in the context of the commodification and technologization of western culture.[5] This complex world of practice, commentary and analysis in and beyond but connected to education is barely touched by the ideas of feminists in education and yet it is this world which is largely shaping education's future. Feminists from outside of education have not been quite so tardy with regard to matters associated with the commodity and technology, although the volume of their work is not great.

One way to proceed from here would be to go back through the literature and carefully document and substantiate my claims. This would fit comfortably within the cleverer and 'holier than thou' traditions of academic scholarship. I could add to this a 'humbler than thou' dimension and identify the deep flaws in my own recent research and writing. Certainly, I could develop a catalogue of sinners and write myself into it, and this would be one route towards making the case that feminism needs to consider either moving past the post or into a more politically astute relationship with it. However, I am not inclined to take this route (call me irresponsible or cowardly if you will). Rather, what I will do is offer a short satirical piece which fondly but irreverently names what I see as some of the problems and issues. This involves what Rosemary Hennessy calls a 'double move between solidarity and critique' (1993, p. xviii). When I feel the overwhelming urge to make a 'scholarly' aside, I will resort to a footnote.

In many senses feminist postmodernism has become 'The New Way' to approach feminist research, pedagogy and politics. However, when one takes this new way, one confronts many confusions, difficulties, dilemmas and dangers. Here I will discuss postmodernism in a metanarrativizing way fully anticipating a reaction of incredulous 'othering' from the mini narrativists who read it. In postmodernist terms what I am about to do is scandalous. I will talk of postmodernism as IT not ITS, as singular not plural. Can I get away with this if I say that what I am discussing is the cultural logic of late postmodernism? (Just a little intertextual joke there.[6])

Postmodernism tells us that all that we once thought was solid has 'melted into air'[7]

- all certainties are to be replaced by uncertainties,
- all stabilities are to be replaced by instabilities.

That's what it *definitely* says! It has ordered us to recognize the disorderly.

Postmodernism talks to us, with great *authority*, about endings and death

- the death of the author;
- the death of the subject;[8] and
- the end of the Enlightenment project.

It has discursively either killed off or at least seriously wounded all epistemologically and politically incorrect (PI) 'isms' such as

- structuralism;
- functionalism;
- humanism;
- realism;
- binarism;[9] and
- essentialism.[10]

It has killed off all metanarratives to allow difference and plurality to thrive.[11] It has made way for the 'return of the repressed'.

It has voiced the 'unvoiced' but then it made problematic their voices and, indeed, the notion of 'voice'.

When, subsequently, the 'unvoiced' tried to speak, or to unvoice the voiced, (including the poststructuralist voice), postmodernism pointed to the problem of authority and to their multiple subjectivities/positionalities and therefore to the impossibility of their politics of identity and location.

Indeed, postmodernism has told us all that we can have no political home; it has sent us into exile, named us nomads, dubbed us diasporic. But, ironically, at the same time it talks up prime real-estate theory and almost fetishes position, position, position.

Postmodernism is, indeed, anti-structure but it is terribly interested in the spacial

- in centres and margins and boarders,
- in decentring and recentring; and
- in being central, i.e., in being 'The Theory' which positions all other theories as 'other'. (Doing as well as recognizing 'othering' is an 'essential' skill of the postmodernist.)

Despite postmodernism's 'lack' of support for a politics of location, it will support a politics of affinity. Indeed, it has a strong affinity with the building industry — hence its obsession with construction and deconstruction, fixing and unfixing, and bricollage spelt brick etc.

The Federated Union of Postmodernists will nail you to the wall and 'other' your very foundations if you talk about truth of any kind except the truth that postmodernism tells about no truth and other related non-truths.

Postmodernism tells us not to try to tell the truth. It tells us that as soon as we become a truth teller we become a power monger — and authoritative/ authoritarian author who is by no means as dead as we should be. While postmodernism believes in the freedom and playfulness of the signifier and the lively reader — in general (but not in a metanarrativizing way, of course), it also believes that power mongers' signifiers are much less playful than those of their 'others'.

Amongst such power mongers are university teachers/researchers — those who are supposedly employed, in part, to seek the truth, test the truth and tell the truth to those who

- won't pass the Course without it;
- want it;
- need it;
- deserve it;
- pay for it; or
- get it anyway (because they bought the book in a hurry and didn't read the blurb on the back cover).

For some university teachers/researchers, the postmodernist 'truth' is a non event, a perverted nonsense, an intellectual wank, a lie — a silly lie.

They ignore it, ridicule it in the newspaper or at parties or spend a lot of effort telling their own truths about postmodernism; preferably, of course, in referred journals or well reviewed popular but scholarly books. Deconstructing deconstruction is a popular game amongst some aspiring and expired academics. It allows them to show off, to appear to be cutting at the cutting edge.[12]

For other academics, hearing the 'truth' about 'truth' is a very disturbing experience. No longer feeling the bearable rightness of being an academic, they recognize 'the unbearable lightness of being' an academic. They wonder what to do. They search for a purpose in the now purposeless world of the academy.

Some find their comfort in posing as simulacra (now that is tricky), or in untruthing others; in pigging out on incredulity, deconstruction and genealogy.

Piously hexing and vexing the text (and there is no such thing as a text-free zone — that *is* 'all there is', tell Peggy Lee) or textual terrorism is their new academic purpose. This sometimes involves a lot of self-righteousness and sneering and has led some other people (i) to consider the development of a post-Marxist theory of alienation which will help to explain why poststructuralists can be such a turn off at times (well, to be honest, lots of the time) and (ii) to refuse to watch TV with them because they won't let them enjoy such 'simple' pleasures like *Roseanne* without hexing and vexing and speaking in tongues (to please Donna Harraway).

The incredulists get a great deal of pleasure out of deconstructing pleasure — which means they are not much fun to be around — unless you are one of them. And sometimes, even then, they're not much fun. You now hesitate to show your writing to your postie friends because, too often in the past, their pleasure in deconstruction has become your work's unpleasant destruction. You cringe at the memory of rereading your writing after their friendly (read terroristic) 'look at it for you'. How did you miss its residual humanism, its subtle but oppressive binary logics and its embarrassing shades of essentialism? But, after all, what are friends for if not to save you from your 'self'?

(Of course you don't have a 'self', at least not a stable self, certainly not now anyway; not after what they said about your book draft which has also melted into air — cyber-space actually!)?

Yet other academics, often those with a politically incorrect socialist feminist background, which, through guilt, they attempt to repress, try to divest themselves totally of authority, voice, reason and all P.I isms.[13]

They search for new ways of continuing to work as feminist teachers and researchers. (After all they have mortgages on more than exposing 'truth').

These people tell tales, and tales about tales. They get into performance, parody, and pastiche.[14]

Through these means they seek to disrupt, destabilize, and unsettle.

They seek to be seriously mischievous, naughty but nice, playful but political and most of all pure and correct — good, fun, poststructuralist feminists who even in their dreams never have an essentialist moment and who couldn't possibly even ask their daughter to tell the truth about where she has been till four o'clock in the morning and why is she coming in looking like *that*! (Indeed, for mothers of adolescent daughters who might like to have a little order in their lives, exert a little authority, clarify a few matters, like for instance 'what happened to my shirt that you borrowed two weeks ago?', postmodernism does not hold out much possibility or hope. But postmodernism is not 'into' hope, not really. Certainly it is not into making 'hope practical' but it thrives on making 'despair convincing' — as if we needed help in this respect.[15])

Yet others say 'Hang on a minute, if I'm to live up to the paradoxes inherent in postmodernism, if I am to have any useful relationship to contemporary emancipatory movements then I can't simply obey its imperatives. But at the same time, I can no longer think the way I once thought or work the way I once worked'.

These people tend to do one of two things. They either leave the University, lock themselves in a dark room and wait for Foucault and Derrida to re Kant, or refuse the

- deathism;
- endism;
- pessimism;
- negativism;
- relativism;[16] and
- authoritarian anti-authoritarianism

of postmodernism and start exploring post, post ways of thinking and doing epistemology, methodology, pedagogy and their associated politics. They look back but only to help them to look forward. Scavenging carefully through the mess and clutter of postmodernism and its critical predecessors, they salvage that which will help them to think anew and renew their work for change. They try to work 'with and out of' (Yeatman 1994, p. 3) through and beyond postmodernism.

Spelling out an adequate feminist postmodernist politics for/in education is clearly not an easy or unambiguous task. And, it is a task easily avoided or rejected on the grounds that to undertake it would be to go against the central tenets of postmodernism. However, it is just this sort of faint-hearted response to the challenge which becomes dangerous for feminism and other emancipatory movements in the difficult times we are going through. Fortunately for feminism, not all feminists subscribe to this form of postmodern paralysis. Let me now note some ways in which the thought of the not so faint-hearted is proceeding.[17]

In my view, materialist feminists are first past the post by a long way when it comes to explicating the political. (I include under this title Donna Haraway, Anna Yeatman and Rosemary Hennessy. Whether they would all agree to this is another matter.) Materialist feminists try to identify and clarify what it means to undertake what Yeatman (1994) calls 'postmodern emancipatory politics' *in the postmodern age*. They are concerned to 'rewrite feminism for and in the postmodern moment confronting its contradictory positionality under late capitalism and in relation to an array of oppositional knowledges' (Hennessy, 1993, p. 13). They are interested in the mechanics *and the politics* of signification and subjectivity. They are concerned about the social effects of the modes of intelligibility offered by various aspects of postmodern theorizing. They are concerned to remap the postmodern in order to clarify its political implications — to criticize and extend it.[18] This remapping almost invariably involves some discussion of the relationship between modernism and postmodernism, for the two come together in materialist feminism. And, as I will go on to explain, materialist feminism is in some very real sense past the post. Of course this raises the obvious question about the meaning of the term 'post' which to some implies total rupture and discontinuity — even antagonism, and to others implies continuity but difference. In this instance it implies the latter. As Yeatman points out she is not 'anti but post'.

Materialist feminist politics revolves around the interplay of difference and dominance. To Yeatman, such politics (which she calls critical, postmodern/feminist) are about 'a democratic politics of voice and representation where the ideal state is not the overcoming of domination once and for all but ongoing imaginative and creative forms of positive resistance to various types of domination' (p. 9). Yeatman makes the important point that such a form of politics does not 'abandon modern universalism and rationalism but enters into a deconstructive relationship with them' (vii). Indeed, she goes so far as to say that 'The kind of emancipatory politics of difference which critical postmodern/feminist theorising pursues is weakly developed unless it understands its dependency on the values of modern universalism, rationalism, justice and individualism.' (x) and more specifically with 'the modern tradition of emancipatory discourse', (p. 10). She continues

> it concerns the authority and nature of reason. Where moderns turn
> their enquiry on the question of the conditions of right reason,

postmoderns interrogate the discursive economies of the different versions of right reason that we have inherited. Postmoderns insist on the exclusions which these different economies effect. They desacralise reason, they do not reject it. Specifically, they attempt to work reason and difference together. (Yeatman, 1994, pp. vii–iii)

Like other materialist feminists, Yeatman is not frightened to explore the extent to which feminism still needs to claim normative grounds in order to stake out its emancipatory politics. As Hennessy says 'holding on to normative grounds does not mean embracing master narratives or totalising theories. But it does mean rewriting them' (1993, p. 3). While postmodernism has made notions of authority, accountability, vision and emancipation problematic this does not necessarily mean their abandonment. Rather what it means is their reinvention after having interrogated such concepts with a view to unmasking their particular 'economy of inclusions and exclusions' (Yeatman, 1994, p. ix).

This view of politics moves clearly beyond the notion that negative struggle or play can be the only form of struggle. That such a view of contestation is limited is increasingly being recognized. For example, Biddy Martin (1988), argues that, while acknowledging the limitations of modernist feminisms, they must also be recognized as providing certain conditions of political possibility. She points out that feminism faces something of a paradox which she characterizes as the historical and political necessity 'for a fundamentally deconstructive impulse and a need to construct the category woman and to search for truths, authenticity and universals', thus necessitating a 'double strategy'. In so saying, she asks; 'How do feminists participate in struggles over the meaning(s) of woman in ways that do not repress pluralities without losing sight of the political necessity for fiction and unity?' How do we avoid establishing 'a new set of experts who will speak the truth of ourselves and our sex in categorical terms, closing our struggle around certain privileged meanings and naturalising the construct woman?' She concludes by saying: 'We cannot afford to refuse to take a political stand "which pins us to our sex" for the sake of an abstract theoretical correctness, but we can refuse to be content with fixed identities or to universalize ourselves as revolutionary subjects' (pp. 13–18).

Other feminists also emphasize the importance of being practical. They too reject the claims by some postmodernist feminists that negative critique, deconstruction or parody is the best we have to offer and note the importance both of feminist utopias and visions and of political mobilization. However, they also point to the necessity for organizations, strategies and visions which, as Sawicki (1991, p. 12) puts it, are 'sensitive to the dangers of authoritarianism, ethnocentricism and political vanguardism'. With regard to political mobilization dialoguing across difference becomes the strategy to adopt with a view to reaching what Yeatman calls a 'negotiated and provisional settlement; one which, draws on, deconstructs and reinvents according to the circumstances, concepts associated with modernist emancipatory projects, rights, democracy, justice and so forth'.

Let me expand this point a little by looking at the issue of difference. Drawing from the work of Audre Lorde, Sawicki invites us to explore the many dimensions of difference. She asks us to consider 'How power uses difference to fragment opposition and to divide individuals within themselves' (p. 18). But she also insists that we must uncover the distortions in our understandings of each other and in the process, both redefine what differences mean and seek to preserve them. Further, she says we must search for ways of utilizing difference as a multisource both of resistance to various modes of domination and of change. In this sense, then, feminism becomes a broad-based, diverse struggle which combines an 'appreciation of the limits of individual experience' (p. 12) with an appreciation of our commonality. But of necessity part of this struggle is to redefine and learn from our differences. In this regard, Sawicki makes the case for radical pluralism and coalition politics built on shifting allegiances and interests, rather than on the ahistorical illusion of stable coalitions. The benefit of this approach to difference is that it does not slip into the vapid celebration of difference for its own sake but it locates its systems of exclusion and exploitation.

As I see it, this way of thinking about difference has important implications for feminist teachers in universities, for curriculum and pedagogy. Rather than implying the necessity of abandoning certain modernist feminisms, it implies the need for an education in different feminisms, for an exploration of their different weaknesses and strengths in particular circumstances in educational institutions and beyond, and for a view of them as strategies rather than truths for pedagogy. Feminist university teachers could help students to see different feminisms as strategies for change to be selectively and judiciously deployed. They could then also help students to see that feminism itself is a discursive field of struggle, not only with different 'horses for different courses' but also with different dividends for different punters. This is not by any means a call for a pluralist view of feminisms, rather it is a recognition of the strategic merits of different feminisms but one which should not blind teachers to their dangers. A feminist politics of difference has alerted other feminisms to their particular dominating tendencies; to their potential dangerousness, as Foucault would say.

Another feature of a materialist feminist politics is its insistence not so much on the materiality of discourse but that discourse has material effects; that discourse constitutes and is constituted by wider social power dynamics. It recognizes that the politics of discourse is often overdetermined by the power relationships which exist beyond the moment and the specific locality, indeed that times and places cannot be isolated from their wider contexts. As Sawicki (1991) and others point out, the postmodernisms which arise from Foucault do not necessarily deny broad patterns of domination and subordination. What they do deny, however, is that one theory fits all situations. To be more specific, they deny that all power is possessed by one particular group or set of institutions, that it is dispersed from a centre, and that is primarily repressive. Their focus however, is on the 'myriad of power relations at the micro level of society' (Sawicki, 1991, p. 20). When they do widen the lens they nonetheless show the ways in which the micro-physics of power contribute to more widescale sets of relationships. However, for Foucault, understanding the local is what is important in developing strategies of resistance, which, he feels, of necessity, must also be local.

Along with other materialist feminists such as Rosemary Hennessy and Nancy Fraser I do not entirely agree with Foucault on these matters. Indeed, the distinguishing feature of materialist feminism is that it articulates important insights from postmodernism with an analysis of social totalities. It articulates an analysis of struggles over meaning with an analysis of struggles over other resources. From postmodernism it draws on ideas about signification, textuality, subjectivity and difference. It also insists that 'modes of intelligibility [including theory] are closely tied to economic and political practices' (Hennessy, 1993, p. 8). It stresses materiality and historical specificity — including the historical specificity of its own theories. It also articulates a commitment to the possibility of transformative social change. (Call it old fashioned or maybe the new fashion.)

I find it useful, despite their differences, to use Antonio Gramsci alongside Foucault, for it was Gramsci (1971) who, through his notion of hegemony, developed a most persuasive account of the ways in which social groups and collective identities and sociocultural hegemonies are formed and reformed through discourse (see further Kenway, 1988; Fraser, 1992). As Nancy Fraser (1992) explains:

> The notion of hegemony points to the intersection of power, inequality and discourse. However, it does not entail that the ensemble of descriptions that circulate in society comprise a monolithic or seamless web, nor that dominant groups exercise on absolute top–down control of meaning. On the contrary, 'hegemony' designates a process wherein cultural authority is negotiated and contested. It presupposes that societies contain a plurality of discourses and discursive sites, a plurality of positions and perspectives from which to speak. Of course not all of these have equal authority. Yet conflict and contestation are part of the story. (Fraser, 1992, p. 179)

The concept 'hegemony' has the benefit of helping us to recognize the unruly but patterned nature of systemic and widescale assymetrical power relations. It allows for a recognition of social totalities without abandoning a recognition of their specific manifestations in different places and times and their different implications for the positionality of different women. Or, as Hennessy (1993) says in developing an argument for systemic analysis,

> it makes it possible to acknowledge the systematic operation of social totalities . . . across a range of interrelated material practices. These

totalities traverse and define many areas of the social formation — divisions of labour, dimensions of state intervention and civil rights, the mobility of sites for production and consumption, the reimagination of colonial conquest, and the colonisation of the imagination (Hennessy, 1993, p. xvii).

The social totalities Hennessy refers to are capitalism, patriarchy and colonialism.

Of course Gramsci developed his theory of hegemony during what has been dubbed the historical period of modernity and any discussion of hegemony these days needs to take into account the particularities of what is often called the postmodern age or postmodernity. And here we meet another distinguishing feature of materialist feminism which as I suggested above locates itself firmly within the historical period of postmodernity which requires a little explanation beginning with a few quick qualifications.

Firstly, when I talk of postmodernity in the next few paragraphs, I am focusing on broad material, social and cultural shifts and conditions. I am not focusing on the philosophical/intellectual shifts I have called postmodernism and parodied earlier in this chapter. Nor am I referring to the artistic/cultural products defined as postmodernist or postmodern. Of course these are not unrelated although exactly how and why is difficult to specify. Secondly, I acknowledge that as a descriptor of current times postmodernism or the postmodern age are highly contentious and contested terms, particularly when used to imply a sharp distinction between the historical periods of modernity and postmodernity, a global applicability without different implications for different regions, and when they suggest that all the defining characteristics are historically unique. As Featherstone (1991, p. 3) points out 'the postmodern is a relatively ill-defined term as we are only on the threshold of the alleged shift, and not in the position to regard the post-modern as a fully fledged positivity which can be defined comprehensively in its own right'. In this sense then, postmodernity emerges from or 'feeds off' (p. 6) rather than dramatically breaks with modernity. While I acknowledge a certain discomfort in using the concept, I nonetheless find it useful as a shorthand which points to the 'cultural logic' or 'cultural dominant' (Jameson, 1984) or to key features of contemporary times in the 'first-world' countries of the West — features which clearly also have an impact on 'third-world' countries. So what am I referring to here and why is it pertinent to education?

The key 'logics' or features of postmodernity include the techno-scientific and communications revolutions, the production of what can be called 'techno' or 'media' culture, the development of a form of techno-worship, the collapse of space and time brought about by the application of new technologies, the cultural dominance of the commodity and the image, the internationalization and postindustrial technologization of the economy (at least in western economies), and an identity crisis for nation states accompanied by the decline of the welfare state and the intensification of state-inspired nationalism. And, of course all of this has implications for human relationships and subjectivities and for cultural 'sensibilities' or 'moods' as do the new social movements and philosophical and artistic/cultural trends which are part of postmodernity and which are also under discussion in this chapter (see further Hinkson, 1991).

A particular feature of postmodernity is the development of what can be called the global economic and technological village. Significant changes in international economies, including the growth of world trading blocks and supernational corporations, the internationalization of the labour market and the money market and the rapid growth, and, again, the extensive application of new information and communications technologies have facilitated these 'developments'. The mode of production associated with this 'village' has been called post-Fordism and post-Fordism commonly, although not unproblematically, refers to an unevenly emerging movement away from the mass manufacturing base and assembly line practices of the Fordist era towards 'flexible' and decentralized labour processes and patterns of work organization brought about by the rapid growth, development and application of new information and communications technologies.[19] This is accompanied by 'the hiving off and contracting out of functions and services; a greater emphasis on choice and product differentiation, on marketing packaging and design, on the 'targeting' of consumers by lifestyle, taste and culture, . . . a decline in the proportion of the skilled, male, manual working class, the rise of the service and white collar classes and the "feminisation" of the work force' (Hall, 1988, p. 24).

These changes are said to have resulted in crises both for the nation-State which loses much of its capacity to control its economy and culture and for certain segments of capital which seek out new and often very exploitative ways to survive in times which threaten their annihilation. Needless to say, as the unemployment figures and the attack on unions indicate, these changes have in many instances been disastrous for workers (see Levidow, 1990). The Australian government's particular approaches to addressing these crises and gaining some control over its economy and culture can be seen to arise from the profoundly successful discursive and interdiscursive work of disparate but powerful social and political groupings who have reshaped public and political opinion in favour of economic rationalism (see Pusey, 1991), corporate managerialism (see Yeatman, 1990) and market forms in public services and vocationalism in education (see Kenway with Bigum and Fitzclarence, 1993). As a result all sectors of education have been dramatically restructured leading, in the worst cases, to the sorts of vandalism of the education system that I described at the beginning of this chapter.

Universities are certainly being redefined by the postmodern condition. Here is how Hennessy understands this process.

Computer technology has intensified capitals reach, proliferating opportunities for investment, speeding up shifts in production and refining divisions of labour. The accompanying fragmentation and dislocation of communities and the increasingly anonymous corporate structure have made the operations of exploitation in the age of information ever more insidious even as inequalities between women and men, minorities and dominant racial and ethnic groups have intensified. As the terms of economic power veer more and more towards control over information, knowledge is being stripped of its traditional value as product of the mind making it a commodity in its own right whose exchange and circulation helps multiply new divisions of Labor and fractured identities. Politically the 'ruling class' is being reconfigured as a conglomerate of corporate leaders, high level administrators and heads of professional organisations. An accompanying reinscription of the bourgeois 'self' as a more complex and mobile subjectivity inextricably bound up in myriad circuits of communication is unfolding in multiple cultural registers. One of them is the academy. (Hennessy 1993, p. 10)

Indeed it is becoming unavoidably obvious that universities are reorienting themselves more and more in line with the demands of the corporate State and, in turn, with the needs of the service-based economy, capital's expanding global markets and consumer culture. Universities now increasingly concentrate on providing both scientific and technological information tailored to the needs of multinational capitalist production and professional training for middle-level managers and the professions. It is important to note here though that at the same time, this historical moment has produced other political discourses which also have had an impact on the knowledge taught in the academy hence the rise of those subordinate knowledges associated with new social movements such as feminism and multiculturalism, and with new media forms such as cultural studies. And as many commentators observe, the extent to which these knowledges perform a counter-hegemonic function or become neutralized and sabotaged within the academy remains open to question. Meanwhile I will briefly note the ways in which materialist feminists are attending to the postmodern condition.

According to Hennessy (1993) feminist politics today require a systemic, critical, 'global analytic'. This, she argues, attends to multinational capital with its 'dense grid of information and highly refined international divisions of labor' (p. 15) and insists on a systematic reading of the global. This involves an attempt to delineate the relations between the highly fluid ideological processes and economic and political arrangements which characterize the complex social arrangements of postmodernity. It understands the social in terms of 'systems and structures of relations' (p. 16) and multiple registers of power. These are the sorts of matters which Hennessy believes should come under scrutiny here: shifting centres of production, the formation of new markets through colonization, the relationship between political alliances, state formations and disciplinary technologies and the global power relations that local arrangements sustain and vice versa. More generally, she is concerned with the ways in which postmodernism produces new 'material conditions of alienation and exploitation', 're-scripts systems of domination and opens up new frontiers for capitalism, patriarchy and colonisation' and reforms subjectivities. Let me say a few words on the question of postmodern subjectivities.

Materialist feminism both draws on and extends the postmodern conceptualization of subjectivity. It recognizes the subject as fragmented, dispersed and textualized but draws attention to the fact that this occurs within the workings of globally dispersed and state controlled multinational capitalism and consumer culture. As Hennessy (1993, p. 6) says, 'In the "age of information", cybernetics, instantaneous global finance, export processing zones, artificial intelligence and hyper-realities an atomised socius affords an increasingly fluid and permeable capital its products, its work-force and its new markets.' Donna Harraway offers the cyborg as metaphor for women's subjectivity in the conditions of postmodernity. Focusing on the informatics of domination and the polyvocal information systems which characterize these times, she gives us the cyborg as an 'ironic myth which is faithful to feminism, socialism and materialism' (p. 65) — a myth both produced through technocratic domination and scientific discourses and also through the politics of counter identity.

From what I have said it should be clear that the crisis of knowledge in the academy is the complex result of both postmodernity and postmodern philosophy (postmodernism). Equally, students in the postmodern university are the subjects of postmodernity and postmodern philosophy. Feminists who focus on one side of the coin without the other, fail to understand their own historical location and equally, again, they fail to help students reach an understanding of the ways in which their identities are structured through their engagement within global relationships of difference and dominance. This is only one of the issues at stake here and I will now briefly pick up on some others pertinent to my parody later.

Clearly postmodernism has destabilized the professional authority of feminist teachers and researchers in universities and clearly this is a good thing to the extent that such authority made sweeping unsustainable claims and unvoiced the unvoiced in the name of feminism. However, as I implied above, some now seem to believe that this gives them permission to simply wave away their professional authority by either denying or playing with it. To do so, in my view, is to ignore many important 'what next?' questions associated with the relationship of feminist academics both to the politics of the state (as I implied above) and to feminists in associated fields outside the academy, not to mention their wider constituencies who are particular groups of women and girls and women and girls in general. As I see it, three key questions are as follows; firstly 'What is the nature of such professional authority after postmodernism?', secondly, 'How are feminists to be accountable?' and thirdly 'To what purpose do feminists participate in the politics of the state?' In what remains of this chapter, I will begin to address these questions.

Let me begin with the question of knowledge and authority. The point to be made here is that postmodernism does not require that feminists stop making knowledge claims or asserting truths. Indeed, participating in the politics of discourse, i.e., in the disarticulation and rearticulation of meaning without recourse to closure, is at the heart of postmodernist feminism and materialist feminism. Yeatman (1994, p. 14) makes the case that 'there is no privileged position "outside" the semiosis of a particular representational formation. Contestation, thus, does not explore an autonomous alternative representational space. Instead it works with the contradictions, heteroglossia, and historically contingent features of a specific representational or discursive formation.' However, a condition of such participation in the politics of discourse, is that knowledge claims are recognized, always, as embodied and particular. Yeatman talks about perspectival and positioned views of knowledge, which are 'governed by the view of those who are the knowers', and are 'historically variable and specific' (p. 19). Harraway talks similarly of 'situated knowledges', of 'partial, locatable and critical knowledges'. She notes Sandra Harding's 'multiple desire' for both a 'successor science project and a post-modern insistence on irreducible difference' and for 'a radical multiplicity of local knowledges' and points out that 'All components of the desire are paradoxical and dangerous and their combination is both contradictory and necessary' (Haraway, 1991, p. 187). Hennessy (1993, p. 25) argues that 'claims to truth are historical and inescapably inscribed in theoretical frameworks'.

It is in the context of these qualifications that it becomes possible to talk of feminist versions of authority and accountability. Indeed, Yeatman insists on the 'provisional exercise of authority'. She develops a notion of accountability which is tied to the work of what she calls subaltern intellectuals — those who develop an intellectual 'narrative which is ordered by metaphors of struggle, contest, forced closure, strategic interventions and contingent openings of public spaces for epistemological politics' (p. 31). She notes how such intellectuals are positioned across complex lines of intellectual and political authority and accountability which have the potential to result in them both mediating and domesticating the claims of their constituencies outside of the academy. This contradictory set of demands for accountability do make her authority problematic and challenge her to self-consciously negotiate them. Yeatman continues,

> Subaltern intellectuals are positioned in a contradictory relationship to intellectual authority. As intellectuals and as evidenced especially when they are directing their intellectual claims upwards, as it were to the ruling elites of academy they are drawn within the culture of intellectual authority and use its conventions unproblematically. At the same time as subaltern intellectuals they are not only positioned as outsiders in respect of these ruling elites, which can foster a tendency to call into question the reliance of these elites for their status on intellectual authority, but they are positioned with loyalties and ties both to

fellow subaltern intellectuals . . . and to subaltern non intellectuals. (Yeatman, 1994, p. 35)

In a similar vein, Hennessy (1993) points to the responsibilities of the oppositional intellectual. Drawing on Stuart Hall she talks of the 'alienation of advantage', of identifying the ways in which knowledge, and indeed the knowledge we use as intellectuals, supports unfair advantage. To her, the responsibility of the oppositional intellectual is to put a hegemonic system of knowledge in the service of counter-hegemonic projects and to help the non-dominant to develop counter-hegemonic knowledges.

Social institutions such as universities and schools and education bureaucracies, cultural products such as curriculum texts, and interpersonal processes such as pedagogy (teaching–learning) are made up of many different and often contradictory discourses and discursive fields. Some of these are dominant, some subordinate, some peacefully coexisting, some struggling for ascendancy. Universities and schools can be seen to consist of fragile settlements between and within discursive fields and such settlements can be recognized as always uncertain; always open to challenge and change through the struggle over meaning, or what is sometimes called the politics of discourse; that is, interdiscursive work directed towards the making and remaking of meaning. Materialist feminists participate in this struggle over meaning but recognize more fully than do postmodernist feminists that this struggle is overdetermined by the distribution of other resources. It is neither naive nor voluntaristic.

What is important is to what end and *how* feminists practise their authority as intellectuals, whether they make it problematic to themselves and others and whether and how they make themselves accountable and to whom. The question about accountability to whom leads back to the point that feminists in universities are split across contradictory lines of accountability. Their work has many different audiences. As Yeatman notes these include the academic world, students generally and female and feminist students particularly and women generally. For those in professional faculties they also include service-delivery practitioners (such as teachers, bureaucrats and policy makers) generally and oppositional service-delivery practitioners particularly. Clearly the feminist academic's position is highly ambiguous but this does not mean that she should abandon her authority which for various reasons and in various ways can play a powerful supportive role for the non-dominant. Indeed, in some senses the feminist academic should 'hold onto her authority as an intellectual and place it in the service of the non-dominant' (Yeatman, 1994). A similar point applies to her relationship with oppositional service-delivery practitioners who to some extent depend on her authority and expertise for the legitimacy and development of their own projects. The ironical twist here is that those who are on the receiving end of such service delivery may well need some protection from it and again the role of the independent subaltern intellectual comes into play if, through independent research, he or she is in the position to respond to the voices of non professionals and feed it back into

the process of policy development. So, in discussing the professional authority which accrues to feminist academics by virtue of their institutional location, Yeatman argues that this should not be surrendered; that 'feminists should
not abandon too readily the authority which resides in scholarly erudition and
expertise'.

However, to Yeatman the notion of public or audience is crucial and she
insists that feminist academics examine the ways in which they construct their
actual and potential audiences — their 'strategies of public address' — so as to
'avoid deauthorising the voice of less credentialled feminists and nonfeminist
others'. Haraway (1990) talks of the political and strategic necessity for the
development of webs of communication called solidarity in politics, . . . 'shared,
power sensitive conversations' and for a 'positioning which implies responsibility for enabling practices'. She argues that this become a basis for 'making
rational knowledge claims in feminist terms'.

Returning to the subject of my *angst*, and in conclusion let me say that
it is a fascinating paradox that postmodernism has assumed such a hegemonic
status amongst feminists in universities; a new and sneaky disciplinary technology which, by handing around the tools for its own dismantling, reasserts
its discipline. (Audre Lorde you got it right about 'the masters' tools'!) Clearly
moving past this post is a very difficult and risky business. But, in my view
it is necessary if feminism is to remain a viable force for change in the
postmodern university, in the postmodern State and in the postmodern age.

Notes

1 I am aware that feminism is best discussed in the plural and I am also aware that,
   despite the addition of an 's', feminism/s is/are still undergoing an identity crisis
   with regard to who to be, how to be and what to value. Too soon, in my view,
   the addition of an 's' lost its radical potential and became a lazy way of being
   inclusive.

2 In education policy circles this has taken the form of a boys' movement which,
   by and large seeks to reign in the feminist policy agenda. Proponents of the boys
   make the case that boys' education has been neglected and that boys have been
   disadvantaged as a result of policies directed towards the education of girls.

3 Being unsettled and disturbed by certain directions in feminism in education is by
   no means unusual for me, particularly with regard to dominant directions in
   feminist policy and curriculum (see for example Kenway *et al.*, 1994).

4 For the rest of this chapter I will use the term 'postmodernism' to include
   poststructuralism. It seems to be the case that a great deal of the education literature in the US collapses the two and for the sake of space and convenience I will
   do so here. However, like Roman (1994), I do not think this is good enough and
   I refer readers to her excellent paper given at the American Association for Research in Education conference in 1994 for a discussion of the conceptual and
   political differences.

5 I refer here to a research project I am conducting with some colleagues called

'Marketing Education in the Information Age' (see further Kenway, with Bigum and Fitzclarence, 1993).

6 Jameson got away with it when he talked about 'Postmodernism or the cultural logic of late capitalism' (Jameson, 1984) or the 'cultural dominant', i.e., the key features of contemporary times.

7 Actually, it was Marx who developed this metaphor.

8 It is interesting to speculate about the genealogy of this focus on endings and death. In more sociological terms it relates to the decline in popularity of causality theses and to the shift from theories which focus on social and cultural production to those which focus on social and cultural reception. Exploring these shifts in the historical context of the life of intellectuals would be an interesting and no doubt revealing project.

9 Spotting dualisms and naming them as hierarchical and oppressive has been fashionable in certain educational circles for some time. However, it has not usually been the case that the relationship between the two sides of the binary has been well theorized. Yeatman (1994) offers a useful discussion of the ways in which binary differences both divide and unite or as she says 'exist within each other' (pp. 17–18). Drawing on Trinh Minh-ha's notions of outsider on the inside and insider on the outside she points to the implications of this insight for a politics of difference *and* commonality thus leading to the notion of hybridized identity and to the possibility of affinity politics which accommodate differences.

10 Diana Fuss (1989) wrote an excellent genealogy of the essentialism debate at the beginning of which she pointed to the often mindless and politically unhelpful demonizing of essentialism.

11 Hennessy (1993, p. 7) makes the point that 'it is increasingly important for feminists to come to terms with the difference between theory as a mode of intelligibility and theory as a totalizing or master narrative'.

12 Brodribb, 1992, is an annoying feminist example of this.

13 It is this particular strand of postmodernism of which I am most critical. In my view it has shades of nihilism and contributes to a form of anomie that takes us nowhere fast.

14 Yeatman (1994, p. 3) argues that such a position is 'a more or less ironically inflected, sceptical, playful but fundamentally quietistic relationship to the postmodern condition'. She calls it a 'positivistic' relationship.

15 Thanks to Raymond Williams for these turns of phrase.

16 Postmodernism is commonly accused of relativism and in some instances it is an easy target and in others not so Liz Grosz (1988, p. 100) makes a useful distinction between relativist theories of knowledge in feminism and relational theories which she sees as those that are connected to other practices rather than being free-floating and available to any subject. But there is a further point to be made here. As Yeatman (1994, p. 30) points out, relativism develops an 'ideological fiction of a horizontally integrated community of differently valued-oriented intellectuals'. It thus fails to attend to the assymetrical relationships of power within which different knowledges are intricated.

17 If I had more space here and time in my life I would do more than 'note'. A more elaborated discussion will have to wait.

18 A number of political cartographies of the postmodern have emerged from feminists (and others) in recent times. See for example Ebert, 1991 a and b. Interestingly,

these almost invariably map the postmodern along a positive (i.e., critical, resist-ant)/negative grid.

19 For an extensive discussion both of post-Fordism in its different variations, and of its implications for education see Kenway, 1993.

References

ALCOFF, L. (1988) 'Cultural feminism versus post-structuralism', in MINNICH, E. O'BARR, J. and ROSENFIELD, R. (Eds) *Reconstructing the Academy: Women's Education and Women's Studies*, University of Chicago Press, Chicago.

BRODRIBB, S. (1992) *Nothing Mat[t]ers: A Feminist Critique of Postmodernism*, Spinifex Press, North Melbourne, Victoria, Australia.

DE LAURETIS, T. (1990) 'Eccentric subjects: Feminist theory and historical conscious-ness', in *Feminist Studies*, 16, 1, Spring.

EBERT, T. (1988) 'The romance of patriarchy: Ideology, subjectivity, and postmodern feminist cultural theory', *Cultural Critique*, 10, pp. 19–58.

EBERT, T. (1991a) 'The (Body) politics of feminist theory', *Phoebe*, 3, 2, pp. 56–63.

EBERT, T. (1991b) 'The "difference" of postmodern feminism', *College English*, 53, 8, pp. 886–904.

FEATHERSTONE, M. (1991) *Consumer Culture and Postmodernism*, Sage Publications.

FOUCAULT, M. (1977) *The Archaeology of Knowledge*, Tavistock, London.

FRASER, N. (1992) 'The uses and abuses of French discourse Theories/or feminist poli-tics', in FRASER, N. and BARTKY, S.L. (Eds) *Revaluing French Feminism: Critical Essays on Difference Agency and Culture*, Indiana University Press, Bloomington and Indianapolis.

FUSS, D. (1989) *Essentially Speaking: Feminism, Nature and Difference*, Routledge, New York.

GRAMSCI, A. (1971) *Selections from the Prison Notebooks*, HOARE, Q. and NOWELL-SMITH, G. (Eds), International Publishers, New York.

GROSZ, E. (1988) 'The In(ter)vention of feminist knowledges', in CAINE, B. GROSZ, E. and DE LEPERVANCE, M. (Eds) *Crossing Boundaries: Feminisms and the Critique of Knowledge*, Allen and Unwin, Sydney.

HALL, S. (1988) 'Brave New World', in *Marxism Today*, October pp. 24–9.

HARAWAY, D. (1990) 'The actors are cyborg, nature is coyote and the geography is elsewhere: Postscript to "Cyborgs at Large"', in PENLEY, C. and ROSS, A. (Eds) *Technoculture*, Oxford, University of Minnesota Press, Minneapolis.

HARAWAY, D. (1991) *Simians, Cyborgs and Women: The Reinvention of Nature*, Free Association Books, London.

HENNESSY, R. (1993) *Materialist Feminism and the Politics of Discourse*, Routledge, Chapman and Hall, New York.

HINKSON, J. (1991) *Post-modernity, State and Education*, Deakin University Press, Vic-toria, Australia.

JAMESON, F. (1984) 'Post-modernism, or the cultural logic of late capitalism', *New Left Review*, 146, pp. 53–93.

KENWAY, J. (1988) *High Status Private Schooling in Australia and the Production of an Educational Hegemony*, PhD thesis, Murdoch University, Western Australia.

KENWAY, J. (1993) *Economizing Education: The Post-Fordist Directions*, Deakin Univer-sity Press, Geelong Victoria.

KENWAY, J., BIGUM, C. and FITZCLARENCE, L. (1993) 'Marketing education in the post-modern age', in *Journal of Education Policy*, 8, 2, pp. 105–23.

KENWAY, J., WILLIS, S., BLACKMORE, J. and RENNIE, L. (1994) 'Making hope practical rather than despair convincing: Feminism, post-structuralism and educational change', in *British Journal of the Sociology of Education*, 15, 2, pp. 187–210.

KENWAY, J. and WILLIS, S. with Education of Girls Unit, SA (1993) *Telling Tales: Girls and Schools Changing Their Ways*, Australian Government Publishing Service, Canberra.

LEVIDOW, L. (1990) 'Foreclosing the Future', in *Science as Culture*, 8, pp. 59–79.

MARGINSON, S. (forthcoming) *Schooling What Future?: Balancing the Education Agenda*, Deakin Centre for Education and Change, Deakin University, Geelong, Australia.

MARTIN, B. (1988) 'Feminism, criticism and Foucault', in DIAMOND, I. and QUINBY, L. (Eds) *Feminism & Foucault: Reflections on Resistance*, North Eastern University Press, Boston.

PUSEY, M. (1991) *Economic Rationalism in Canberra: A National Building State Changes Its Mind*, Cambridge University Press, Sydney.

ROMAN, L. (1994) 'Postmodernism Relativism and Feminist Materialism as Issues of Importance to Science Education', Paper given at the American Association for Research in Education conference, New Orleans.

ROSENAU, P. (1992) *Post-modernism and the Social Sciences*, Princeton University Press, New Jersey.

SAWICKI, J. (1991) *Disciplining Foucault: Feminism, Power and the Body*, Routledge, New York.

YEATMAN, A. (1990) *Bureaucrats, Technocrats, Femocrats: Essays on the Contemporary Australian State*, Allen and Unwin, Sydney.

YEATMAN, A. (1994) *Postmodern Revisionings of the Political*, Routledge, New York.

4 After Postmodernism: A New Age Social Theory in Education

Philip Wexler[1]

The foundation of a sociology of presence is first, in a rereading of social theory from a new, strategic vantage point that identifies the precursory elements of a new synthesis. Second, as the transition out of Puritan, Enlightenment sociology is described within a cultural movement, a new synthesis is also part of a wider cultural process, which requires some description; the culture which feeds emergent academic theory is itself part of a new historical age. Third, in such new circumstances, and with a strategic rereading of social theory, I try to outline the basic interests and direction of a sociology that goes beyond representation of the transition called 'postmodernism', into a new age and I explore what such a transfigured social theory might mean for theory and practice of education.

In the last seventy-five years, each generation has had its version of 'classical sociology'. But, I don't think that we have yet had ours, unless the revolt of 1968 is going to count as a mature statement, rather than as either the expression of an earlier generation of sociologists, or as a preliminary voice of this one. The politicized, so-called 'radical' reading of sociology never undid the postwar methodological positivist, progressive Enlightenment, anti-Marxist interpretation of the sociological pillars.

The 'strategy' with which I read is to now surpass the critical analysis which once helped to defend against the long shadow of the 1950s. That critical social analysis attacked methodologicalist pretenses to antiseptic, certain, ritually secured knowledge, and behind that, to what Gouldner aptly called its 'background assumptions', about the good and happy life. Critical social analysis was a negation, an opposition to an ahistorical, decultured sociology, and to its denial of widespread social inequality and immiseration. It was indeed a 'hermeneutic of suspicion', as Ricoeur characterized critical theory; a suspicion of scientist and moral pretenses in the face of evident suffering and impoverishment, public corruption and distortion of private lives.

Critical social analysis pulled the rug from what had been swept under it — not simply inequality and exploitation, but commodification of all social spheres, and its most general human effect in stultification of human potential, or, more broadly, 'alienation'. Marxism and its tributaries was the main theoretical resource for the New Left, sociological generational negation. Methodologism and social conservatism successfully claimed Durkheim and Weber, while depth psychologies and secular and religious existential philosophies were cordoned off to a highbrow, though marginalized, general culture beyond the pale of social theory.

In education at least, social theoretical work went directly from the 'radical' negation of the certain knowledge/happy life regime of the 'mainstream', to a bibliophilic celebration of borrowed grand anti-theories of postmodernism, which, as I have argued earlier, belong to a decadent and disintegrative cultural phase — when they are not simply masquerading traditional liberal pluralism. Neither the historically important negation of critical theory, nor the more doubtful aestheticization of postmodernism and poststructuralism succeeded in providing a fundamentally different alternative to the regime of positivity that they claimed to negate or dissolve.

There has not been a strong or coherent tendency toward an 'affirmative negation' — which is simultaneously a rejection of positivity, the falsely naturalized world of commodification, extreme rationalization, and its analogous culture of scientific rationalism, and the establishment of an ideal state of individual and collective being. Of course, academic western Marxism wanted to make that claim. But history has shown what the dissenting cultural edge of the New Left suspected: that even the utopian critics and avatars of negation were unable to break through the social-psychological formations of repression which limited and canalized not only the character of their hopes for 'liberation', but also the conceptual paths by which to grasp the present and to transform it. Both the conception of the negating critique and the forms of life which drove it only went part of the way, analytically demystifying the naturalized repressive social order, without reaching and unleashing another form of life and the social understandings carried within it.

My claim is that beginning has now been carried further by a changed set of social and cultural circumstances. Postmodernism is a cultural sign of a disintegrative phase of positivity's regime. After it, but already within it, a new culture emerges that carries socially transformative hopes over the boundaries that repression formerly set for them. A new culture means new ideals and also new ways of thinking about social and individual life. In its reflective aspect, traditions are brought forward and renewed, precursors and antecedents are rediscovered. For me, those precursors are in the cultural revolts of the 1960s and 1970s, and even more in the incipient social analyses that diagnosed the repression to be overcome, but were still unable to live and think beyond that regimes's hegemony. That is why, for example, I have described 'new sociology of education' as always bound to the mainstream that it criticized. The antecedents are not only in the culture and critical social thought of the 1960s and 1970s, or, ultimately, in the great core world civilizational cultures, but also in the turn of the century sociological canon.

The new culture is the culture of the new age. Its ideal state is one that Erich Fromm referred to in his introduction to the Bottomore and Rubel

(1956) Marx reader as 'de-alienation'. This state or ideal of being is the driving point not only for Marx, but also for Durkheim and Weber. Dealienation involves in every case the collective production or release of socially bound energies that in their unrealized condition are the source of individual and collective distortion, disease, and historical blockages to the realization of higher evolutionary potentials. For the radical Freudians like Wilhelm Reich and Erich Fromm, and for the sociological existentialists like Martin Buber, the overcoming of socially organized life repression releases collective energies which become reorganized as new modes of individual and collective being.

The social theory of the new age is always, in the first instance, beyond negation; theorizing, as Norman O. Brown put it, 'the way out', surpassing repressed, commodified, rationalized social existence to the attainment of an ideal state of 'nirvana' (Marcuse, 1955), 'resurrection' (Brown, 1959), 'orgasmic potency' (Reich, 1949), 'acosmic brotherliness' (Weber, 1946), or largely feminine 'intersubjective mutuality' (Benjamin, 1989). Second, while it takes multiple forms, I believe that there is an underlying common commitment to a theory of social energy, an energy which is biopsychological, but collectively shaped, inhibited and released. Third, the generation of this energy — whether as 'libido' or 'bion', 'effervescence' or 'charisma' — has its primal force in cultural creation, but even more particularly, in the religious experience and articulation at the fount of culture and society.

New-age social theory is about: the conditions for the creation and freeing of this social energy; the description of its precise character; its working simultaneously at the collective and individual levels; processes of its regeneration and flow; its meaning and linkage in body, mind and soul; and, in a return to the initial 'de-alienated state', how social energy either leads to, or is inhibited from, paths of redemption, salvation and a messianic time that is beyond the regime of positivity, beyond the intense struggling phase of negation and beyond the decadent phase of dissolution. Education, while it is now at the pinnacle of a technocratic movement, is the site for the clearest articulation of new-age social theory. In part, that is because education works through identity or self, which is now the central locus of a cultural transformation into a new age.

Preliminary Rereadings

Although Durkheim is typically taught as the exemplar of scientific rationalism in sociology and exponent of individualism, his later essays make clear that 'the cult of the individual' is a compromise with individualism, as the historically workable cult, a compromise designed to favour collective ritual and not individualism. The 'cult of the individual' is a transitional commitment, an acknowledgment of the end of the old order, and extraction of all that is valuable in a more centrifugal society.

Durkheim's hope, however, is evidently, not for his time of 'moral cold', but for a 'warmer' social existence, in which a collective religion energizes the moral life, which in turn enables both generative collective representation and the motivational discipline required for a restrained balancing of what are otherwise unlimited individual passions. Robert Bellah (1973) notably reads the passionate Durkheim of collective energy and religion as the crux of social and individual life. Bellah writes of Durkheim:

> Repeatedly during his later years he hopes for a revival of the pro-found collective experience, the experience of fusion and ecstasy, which is the essence of primitive religion and the womb out of which the renewal of society at any period can take place. (Bellah, 1973, p. xlvi)

And further on, Bellah adds:

> In Durkheim there is to be found a moral vision, *a return to the depths of social existence* [my emphasis], which is in some ways more radical than that of his rivals. There are some significant parallels with Freud, since Durkheim was trying to understand the unconscious sources of social existence as Freud was the unconscious sources of personal existence. (Bellah, 1973, p. liv)

From our vantage point, Durkheim is not a 'happy' modern, but rather one who anticipates the dawning of a new culture, a new age. What gives this anticipatory hope interpretive power is Durkheim's understanding of society as a field of forces, of creative social energy generated in the religious origins of collective life. On a new age, he wrote:

> The old ideals and the divinities which incarnate them are dying be-cause they no longer respond sufficiently to the new aspirations of our day; and the new ideals which are necessary to orient our life are not yet born. Thus we find ourselves in an intermediary period, a period of moral cold which explains the diverse manifestations of which we are, at every instant, the uneasy and sorrowful witnesses.
>
> But who does not feel — and this is what should reassure us — who does not feel that, in the depths of society, an intense life is developing which seeks ways to come forth and which will finally find them . . . a center of crystallization for new beliefs.
>
> All that matters is to feel below the moral cold which reigns on the surface of our collective life the sources of warmth that our societies bear in themselves. (Durkheim, quoted in Bellah, 1973, p. xlvii)

Durkheim's language of explanation for collective life shows how much underlying images of cold and heat, there is a view of 'currents of energy' and forces. This social energy is generated in religious activity, and it is the renaissance of such activity, following Bellah (and later, Alexander, 1988), which incurs the new age

> In a word, the old gods are growing old or already dead, and others are not yet born . . . A day will come when our societies will know again those hours of creative effervescence, in the course of which new ideas will arise . . . (Bellah, 1973, p. xlvii)

Against moral 'stagnation', Durkheim looks toward the 'spiritual' as the 'ways that social pressure exercises itself' (1973, p. 171). Religion is a 'force' for occasions of 'strengthening and *vivifying* (my emphasis) action of society'. There is a reciprocal flow of energy between individual and collective that is most evident during intermittent social states of effervescence. For the individual, at such times . . . he feels within him an abnormal over-supply of force which overflows and tries to burst out from him . . . this exceptional increase of force is something very real . . . (1973, p. 173).

Further, in the same section of *The Elementary Forms of Religious Life*, he notes, significantly:

> But it is not only in exceptional circumstances that this stimulating action of society makes itself felt; there is not, so to speak, a moment in our lives when some current of energy does not come to us from without . . . this is the moral conscience, of which, by the way, men have never made even a slightly distinct representation except by the aid of religious symbols. (op. cit., p. 174)

And again, the religious basis of social energy:

> . . . the forces that move bodies as well as those that move minds have been conceived in a religious form. (op. cit., p. 186)

So as to leave no doubt about the primacy of religion in a social life based in 'currents of energy', Durkheim declared in the journal, *L'Année Sociologique*:

> This year, as well as last, our analyses are headed by those concerning the sociology of religion. The according of the first rank to this sort of phenomenon has produced some astonishment, but it is these phenomena which are the germ from which all others — or at least almost all others — are derived. Religion contains in itself the very beginning, even if in an indistinct state, all the elements which in dissociating themselves from it, articulating themselves and combining with one another in a thousand ways, have given rise to the various manifestations of collective life . . . At any rate, a great number of problems change their aspects completely as soon as their connections

with the sociology of religion are recognized. (Durkheim, 1960, pp. 350–1)

If religion is the 'primordial' source of ideas, of collective representations, it is only because it is the source of social energy. Of the religious source of energy, he writes:

> To consecrate something it is put in contact with a source of religious energy, just as today a body is put in contact with a source of heat or electricity to warm or electricize it; the two processes are not essentially different. Thus understood, religious technique seems to be a sort of mystic mechanics. (op. cit., p. 192)

The language of mechanical energy is more than a convenient metaphor:

> in fact, we have seen that if collective life awakens religious thought on reaching a certain degree of intensity, it is because it brings about a state of effervescence which changes the conditions of psychic activity. Vital energies are over-excited . . . (op. cit., p. 195)

Although Durkheim may now be seen as having been an opponent of Henri Bergson and his vitalist thought, the power of society for Durkheim is that 'it is life itself which has a creative power which no other observable being can equal' (op. cit., p. 222).

Weber also felt the necessity of a new age, but tentatively and with a deeply reserved sense of anticipation. For Weber too, religion is the source of social energy. Compared to Durkheim, his language and social analysis is less recontextualized to either a secular or more abstract and general theoretical plane; he is openly working out the sociocultural and individual consequences of various paths of religious action. His observations are historical, and the determinative social force of religion is culturally specific, and full of unforeseen and in the case of Puritan Protestantism, undesirable cultural and individual effects. Religion may be the basic force. With characteristic ironic understatement, Weber wrote:

> The modern man is in general, even with the best will, unable to give religious ideas a significance for culture and national character which they deserve. (Weber, 1958, p. 183)

Yet, the early rationalization of religious activity, 'demagification' — despite the contradictory social effects of the rationalization of magic to prophetic religions — leads to the deadening closure of bureaucracy. That is the social organizational apparatus of a rationalized culture which destroys culture, produces only *ersatz* or fake prophecies, and dead-ends by locking the original creative energies of religion in an 'iron cage'.

The culture of the present age links its collective religious origins with a deformed, 'alienated' individual way of life or social character:

> For when asceticism was carried out of monastic cells into everyday life, and began to dominate worldly morality, it did its part in build- ing the tremendous cosmos of the modern economic order. This order is now bound to the technical and economic conditions of machine production which to-day determine the lives of all the indi- viduals who are born into this mechanism . . . Perhaps it will so de- termine them until the last ton of fossilized coal is burnt. In Baxter's view the care for external goods should only lie on the shoulders of 'the saint like a light cloak, which can be thrown aside at any mo- ment.' But fate decreed that the cloak should become an iron cage . . . To-day the spirit of religious asceticism — whether finally, who knows? — has escaped from the cage. But victorious capitalism, since it rests on mechanical foundations, needs its support no longer. The rosy blush of its laughing heir, the Enlightenment, seems also to be irretrievably fading, and the idea of duty in one's calling prowls about in our lives like the ghost of dead religious beliefs. (Weber, 1958, pp. 181–2)

'Mechanism' and the deadness of a 'rationalist way of life' (op. cit., p. 240) leads to the 'personality type of the professional expert', who supplants 'the cultivated type of man'. In terms directly reminiscent of Marx's description of alienated being, Weber explains the consequences of the 'mechanization and discipline of the plant' as those in which:

> . . . the psycho-physical apparatus of man is completely adjusted to the demands of the outer world, the tools, the machines — in short, to an individual 'function'. The individual is shorn of his natural rhythm as determined by the structure of his organism. (op. cit., pp. 261–2)

And, in the 'universal rationalization and intellectualization of culture' (op. cit., p. 344), 'The total being of man has now been alienated from the organic cycle of peasant life . . .' The social apparatus of bureaucratic special- ization, which increases precision, speed, calculability and profit, also destroys the 'cultivated man', and deadens or 'petrifies' life in an 'iron cage'.

Weber's new age is a nebulous possibility because rationalization, for whatever scientific clarity it has brought — which he defends in 'Science as a Vocation' against romantic academic ideologizing — has destroyed the spirit, which is the well-spring of cultural life:

> No one knows who will live in this cage in the future, or whether at the end of this tremendous development entirely new prophets will arise, or there will be a great rebirth of old ideas and ideals or, if

neither, mechanized petrification, embellished with a sort of convulsive self-importance. For the last stage of this cultural development, it might well be truly said: 'specialists without spirit, sensualists without heart; this *nullity* (my emphasis) imagines that it has attained a level of civilization never before achieved'. (op. cit., p. 182)

Against the life-destroying petrification of social mechanization in rationalized specialization, there is an antipodal force that has asserted itself historically to '. . . *transcend* the sphere of everyday economic routines' (Weber, 1968, vol. 3, p. 111). That is 'charisma', the 'strongest anti-economic force' which 'transforms all values and breaks all traditional and rational norms' (op. cit., p. 1115). Against rationalization, charisma is 'the specifically creative revolutionary force of history'. 'Charismatic belief revolutionizes men "from within" and shapes material and social conditions to its revolutionary will.'

Like Durkheim's model of social energy in the dynamic density of 'collective effervescence', charisma '. . . arises from collective excitement produced by extraordinary events and from surrender to heroism of any kind.' (op. cit., p. 1121).

But charisma is inherently unstable because of the 'desire to transform charisma and charismatic blessing from a unique, transitory gift of grace of extraordinary times and persons into a permanent possession of everyday life'.

Despite the inevitable instability of charisma and the flourishing of '*ersatz* prophecy', Weber does seek a way out of the iron cage by a re-examination of asceticism and mysticism (Weber, 1946, pp. 323–59). Asceticism tends toward rationality and is sublimated in knowledge. Mysticism, with its emphasis on unity and ecstasy, has '. . . always inclined men towards the flowing out into an objectless acosmism of love . . . But its ethical demand has always lain in the direction of universal brotherhood . . .' (p. 330). This tendency conflicts with the other sociocultural spheres of aesthetics and eroticism. These spheres, which are '. . . like a gate into the most irrational and thereby real kernel of life, as compared with the mechanisms of rationalization' (p. 345), are in tension with the 'ethic of religious brotherliness'. Ultimately though, it is the 'vocational workaday life, asceticism's ghost, which leaves hardly any room' (p. 357) for 'the cultivation of acosmic brotherliness'.

Charisma, grace and gratitude, magic, spirit, ecstasy, care and love were harnessed by intellectualization in prophecy and rationalization in an evermore centralized, specialized, scientific and precisely calculable social apparatus. Yet, despite the unintended deadening effects of the 'disenchantment (the demagification) of the world', the 'irrational' 'real kernel of life' struggles for reappearance on the collective historical stage as the 'revolutionary' of a personal grace that, like Durkheim's effervescence, flows between the individual and the collective as excitement of 'particular states'. 'Pianissimo', in everyday life, the mystical drive toward union and ecstasy and its implied ethic of acosmic love, struggle, in an inner tension with estheticism and eroticism, to reclaim the force or energy of 'the transformation from within'.

Charismatic energy, ecstasy and love are the life which is opposed to the apparently triumphant death of 'mechanized petrification'. Either through the fusion of energy in mystical union, or its di-fusion in 'caritas' interpersonal love, there are ways out, though they are, in Weber's early twentieth-century world, inaccessible, 'unless it is among strata who are economically carefree'. (Weber, 1946, p. 357).

Mid-twentieth century social thought continues to articulate the conflict between a deadening civilization and life-affirming cultural and personal forces. However, this 'dialectic' is played out increasingly less within either mainstream or radical sociology, nor, later, in rationalized postmodernism. Instead, it is found among religious existentialists like Martin Buber, and dissident theorists and practitioners of psychoanalysis like Wilhelm Reich, Norman O. Brown, Erich Fromm and others (Marcuse, 1955; Benjamin, 1989). In reading Buber, for example, I juxtapose his emphasis on the sacred as one of integration rather than the differentiation of sacred and profane which Durkheim made fundamental in his religious sociology, and, which I have argued (Wexler, 1993), Basil Bernstein secularized and recontextualized in a sociology of education premised on the rules of differentiation.

In modern Judaism, Martin Buber clearly sets himself against what he sees as the dualism and rationalism of the historic Jewish mainstream. Not differentiation, but integration and unity are the hallmarks of Judaism, according to Buber (1967). Not religion, but 'religiosity' — the state of experience, in James' and Weber's terms — is what needs to be understood, and lived. Against collective practices and interdicting laws and rites of differentiating structures and spheres of activity, Buber proposes *der Helige Weg*, the 'holy way' of unified existence. Unlike Durkheim, who sees a separation, or insulation, of the sacred and the profane as religion's defining aspect, Buber quests for integration and unity, by sanctifying everyday life, ending the dualism, sacred–profane. The Hebrew couplet that begins with 'The Lord differentiates between the sacred and the profane' is followed by, 'All our sins will be erased by Him'. In other words, *havdalah* (differentiation) is a preface to salvation or redemption.

On this path, Buber carries forward to modernity a sociology of the *zwischenmenschliche*, the intersubjective, as Eisenstadt has translated it (Buber, 1992), and of the utopian (1949). His modern reading of Hasidism places this work within the long tradition of Jewish alternative movements, that have been broadly referred to as 'mystical' (see, for example, Scholem, 1946).

Buber's analyses and language fuse social understanding and religious partisanship, particularly critique of the Jewish mainstream:

> I shall try to extricate the unique character of Jewish religiosity from
> the rubble with which rabbinism and rationalism have covered it.
> (Buber, 1967, p. 81)

What he wants to uncover, is a religiosity of the Orient rather than of the West, a religion like Taoism and Buddhism, which offers 'a way' or 'path' aimed at a redeemed life for both the individual and the collective. Religiosity is not only an object of social study, but above all, a lived experience, articulated in the deed as well as the word. The experience striven for, as in mysticism generally, is of unity, although Buber argues for a strong particularly Jewish orientation to the attainment of unity:

> But wherever one opens the great document of Jewish antiquity . . . there will one find a sense and knowledge of disunion and duality — a striving for unity.

> A striving for unity: for unity within individual man; for unity between divisions of the nation, and between nations; for unity between mankind and every living thing; and for unity between God and the world. (Buber, 1967, pp. 26, 27)

Buber's emphasis on *unity* is as great as Durkheim's and Bernstein's on separation and insulation. 'And it is stated with still greater emphasis: "Only when you are undivided" (that is, when you have overcome your inner dualism by your decision) "will you have a share in the Lord your God."' (1967, p. 82). What he writes of as '. . . the tendency to realize undivided life in the world of man, in the world of being with one another', (p. 126) aims to overcome the sacred profane distinction. Buber was a critic of nationalistic Zionism as much as of rabbinism, although he sought a utopian possibility within the Zionist movement. In writing about ancient Judaism and its relation to Zionism, Buber underlines his ideal of overcoming the sacred–profane dualism, and its boundaries, by calling for a transformation of everyday life through an infusion of the sacred impulse to the profane:

> We must choose in this tradition the elements that constitute closeness to the soil, *hallowed worldliness*, [my emphasis] and absorption of the Divine in nature; and reject in this tradition the elements that constitute remoteness from the soil, detached rationality, and nature's banishment from the presence of God. (Buber, 1967, p. 145)

Unity, hallowing the everyday, is the path, through individual consciousness and decision, to redemption of the individual 'the turning', and collective utopia:

> Unified, unifying, total man, free in God, is the goal of mankind's longing that is awakening at this hour. (p. 170)

> . . . must perceive how the Jewish people's old religious fervor still endures among them, though in distorted and occasionally degraded form, and how there burns within it the desire, as yet unstilled, to hallow the earthly and to affirm the covenant with God in everyday

life . . . along with those of decadence it carries within it the elements of purification and redemption. (p. 172)

. . . the duty of realizing the divine truth in the fullness of everyday life, by side-stepping into the merely formal, the merely ritual . . . (p. 195)

All these principles can be summed up by the watchword: from within . . . (p. 146) . . . Everything is waiting to be hallowed by you. (p. 212). (Buber, op. cit.)

While Buber may be seen as the avatar of a mystical, utopian Judaism of unity and redemption, the so-called 'mystical' tradition may offer more generally, a dialectic that combines unity or integration with differentiation. Adin Steinsaltz (1992), in his contemporary 'discourses on Chasidic thought', interprets Kabbalah to speak of the power of division, as well as unity. 'Creation' is his textual basis for a kabbalistic dialectic of difference that begins with a 'separation' or 'sawing' of the first androgynous person into male and female:

This sawing in two creates a real separation, a distance between the parts of that which was once one and the subsequent problematics of two different personalities. It also creates a new tension, something new that had not existed before. This tension between the two who had once been a unity corresponds to the entire system of Creation; spirit and matter, higher world and lower world, direct light and returning light, and so on. These opposites reflect the fact that even though a unified world undoubtedly has great advantages, it is rather static and perhaps even uninspiring in its inability to get beyond itself, whereas a divided world is much more dynamic and capable of change . . . this breaking up or sawing apart of wholeness in order for something new to come into being. (Steinsaltz, 1992, pp. 41–2)

These dynamics of unity and difference, of polarities, are of course central in other religious traditions, notably, Taoism, Buddhism, and Yoga. It is to these traditions that I believe we will ineluctably continue to turn as postmodern culture reveals no world-redeeming alternative to the European Enlightenment and its tributaries like 'classical' sociological theory and its applications. Future 'misreadings' will have to challenge also the religious discourses which I suggest are foundational of contemporary social understanding, as we strive to discover a cultural ethos that makes effective claims on subjectivity and intersubjectivity. To have also the 'evolutionary' value that Weber hoped — to be collectively redemptive — such a culture will have to 'stand in the face of' all the current orders, and in that sense, be not reproductive, but revolutionary.

Like Weber, and in this regard, like Durkheim, Buber overcomes alienation by proposing an ideal 'state', which he calls 'the-between-people'. In this state, transcendental energies, which originate in a direct personal creative religious encounter, flow over into intentional self and social regeneration through a social presence that simultaneously represents both mystical union and care for a personal other. It is a 'living' humanism that combats what Buber sees as the inertness both of religion and society. Energy is created in encounter, in the 'meeting'. Here too, there is a sociology of presence and energy, which begins with religious experience, overcomes dead or 'I–it' social relations, to find and generate social and individual life energies — a path of renewal, regeneration and creativity.

Brown derives the struggle of 'life against death' not from a combined Simmelian sociology of urban alienation and Jewish mysticism as does Buber, but from a Romantic, Christian reinterpretation of Freud's 'libido' as more a life than, in Freud's terms, a 'love force'. The alienated state is repression, and, writes Brown: 'Therefore the question confronting mankind is the abolition of repression — in traditional Christian language, the resurrection of the body' (1959, p. 307). In opposition to Freud, who saw repression as an individual and civilizational necessity, Brown calls for the elimination of all repression, in a liberation of the body: 'The life instinct also demands a union with others and with the world around us based not on anxiety and aggression but on narcissism and erotic exuberance.'

Brown also looks to religion — particularly 'western mysticism' — as a channel through which repression/alienation can be overcome. 'So seen', he writes (op. cit., p. 310), 'psychoanalysis is the heir to a mystical tradition which it must affirm.' Mysticism and Romanticism (the later of which Freud did acknowledge as the precursor to his theory of the unconscious) 'stays with life', and surpasses the critical negation of analysis with affirmation of the 'spiritual', energetic and perfectible body:

> Modern poetry, like psychoanalysis and Protestant theology, faces the problem of the resurrection of the body. Art and poetry have always been altering our ways of sensing and feeling — that is to say, altering the human body. And Whitehead rightly discerns as the essence of the 'Romantic Reaction' a revulsion against abstraction (in psychoanalytical terms, sublimation) in favor of the concrete sensual organism, the human body. (Brown, op. cit., p. 312)

And then quoting the poet Blake, 'Energy is the only life, and is from the Body . . . Energy is eternal Delight.'

The return of the concrete, the body as the locus of energy, and its deeper source in mystical religion, all leads to a view of social theory itself as part of the apparatus of repressive alienation or, in this language, neurosis of civilization:

> Contemporary social theory (again we must honor Veblen as an exception) has been completely taken in by the inhuman abstractions of

67

the path of sublimation, and has no contact with concrete human beings, with their concrete bodies, their concrete though repressed desires, and their concrete neuroses. (op. cit., p. 318)

For Reich, the 'de-alienation' or undoing of the repressed body is not a mystical, but a material, 'vegetative system' process that can be experimentally traced to the cellular or 'bion' level. Psychoanalytic work in the 'talking' therapy led him first to a recognition of the embodiment of neurosis in the entire musculature in a process of defense against anxiety that creates 'armor' which is fully physical as well as psychological. This armor binds and blocks and dams up the natural flow of bio-energy, causing deformation and disease. The natural flow of energy is realized through the expression, following the Freudian model of psychosexual development, in genitality, in orgasmic sexual interaction (Reich, 1949).

Full genitality makes transparent the flow or 'streamings' of body energy which are repressed in character armors that ultimately derive from the social pathologies of an authoritarian, patriarchal, anti-sexual, repressive social order. By understanding both sex-pol — the sociopolitical formation of sexuality and the sex-economy of body and interpersonal energy dynamics, a genitality of the unrepressed streamings releases body energy for individual and collective creative self-transformation. Mann and Hoffman (1980) recount the path of Reich's development, from radical sex-pol psychoanalysis to an holistic body therapy of energy, to a simultaneously more materialist theory of energy field in self and environment on the one hand, and on the other, toward a more 'religious', or, as they describe it, 'spiritual reawakening'.

Reich is an important precursor, although he stands quite outside the sociological canon. His energy theory represents a therapeutic and political commitment to an unalienated state and to a social psychology of presence. Social pathology is represented in individual psychology and biology. The bio-dynamics of the body offer a de-alienated state from which to counter repression, first at the individual interactive, sex therapeutic, holistic health level, and then, from there, in a broader social reform — especially through sex education, but also in a model of self-regulation of children (A.S. Neill of Summerhill fame was a disciple of Reich's). If it is Romanticism, it is of a materialist, even experimental variety. Like the classical sociologists, for Reich, energy is real, culturally shaped and individually embodied. Toward the end of his life, it appears that 'the way out' (in fact Reich died in prison, in Lewisburg, Pa.) recognized an interaction of the spheres of the body, mind, social organization and spiritual as both the path of understanding and practice by which life energies could overcome the socially induced living death that Reich had repeatedly observed in his clinical practice. Like Brown, the purpose of practice and analysis is the resurrection of life against a culture of death.

More than anyone else, Fromm made the affirmation of life an explicit foundation of his social theory. Nathan Gover (1984) calls him a 'biophile'.

Unlike the classical sociologists and Reich, he openly derived a counter-alienation social theory through a close textual reinterpretation of religion. Fromm's 'radical interpretation of the old testament and its tradition' (1966) sees the paradigmatic case of alienation as equivalent to death in the biblical struggle against idolatry. The key point about idolatry, for Fromm, is not the jealousy of a monotheistic god, but that idolatry, which he sees as 'the main religious theme', represents death against life: 'The idol is a *thing*, and it is not alive. God, on the contrary, is a *living God.*' (1966, p. 37). 'He quotes the Psalm 115: 'They (idols) have hands, but do not feel; feet, but do not walk; and they do not make a sound in their throat. Those who make them are like them.' (op. cit., p. 38).

Alienation is a preface to its overcoming, which is signified by the concept of 'the messianic time'. In this time, writes Fromm:

> . . . he returns to himself. He regains the harmony and innocence he had lost, and yet it is a new harmony and a new innocence. It is the harmony of a man completely aware of himself, capable of knowing right and wrong, good and evil . . . In the process of history man gives birth to himself . . . that man would become like god himself. (op. cit., p. 97)

There is of course, the crucial encounter with the divine, described in the paradox of the burning bush: the bush symbolizes the paradox of all spiritual existence, that in contrast to material existence its energy does not diminish while it is being used. (p. 75).

In addition to eternal energy and the messianic time, which is the template for a 'universal historical transformation which forms the central point of the prophetic messianic vision' (p. 109), it is the life principle and its affirmation that Fromm carries away from his old testament encounter; what he refers to as 'the affirmative attitude toward life' (p. 141). This principle is worth quoting at greater length:

> Life is the highest norm for man; God is alive and man is alive; the fundamental choice for man is between growth and decay.

> One might ask how man can make a choice between life and death; man is either alive or dead, and there is no choice, except if one were to consider the possibility of suicide. But what the biblical text refers to is not life and death as biological facts but as principles and values. To be alive is to grow, develop, to respond; to be dead (even if one is alive biologically) means to stop growing, to fossilize, to become a thing . . . to choose life is the necessary condition for love, freedom and truth. (op. cit., p. 142)

Fromm's social solution is '. . . to recognize this danger and to strive for conditions which will help bring man to life again'. (p. 180). For him, that means a 'renaissance of humanism that focuses on the reality of *experienced* values rather than on the reality of concepts and words [my emphasis]'.

Experienced values have their origin in the realization of the 'interpersonal fusion' which is 'the most powerful striving in man' (1956, p. 18) and the replacement of God as father with the principle of God. Ultimately, monotheism leads to mysticism, and theology disappears in favour of the experience of mystical union, a union which addresses the human need for transcendence and overcoming the separation and aloneness of individual being. In terms of our discussion of Weber's struggle for freedom out of the iron cage by examining the cultural, and particularly religious 'spheres', here too, there are ways out in both mystical union and love.

Fromm takes the interpersonal fusion of love, not as an abstract concept, but as an 'experienced value'. That means love becomes a practice, an art, a virtue that can be described and actualized. Unlike Brown, narcissism is not the answer (and, as we shall see, the dialectic of narcissism is a crucial crossroads for transformative paths in the New Age), but a sleep from which one needs to wake to the humility required for the practice of reason and objectivity. In *The Art Of Loving*, Fromm argues through the steps of an existential practice that can overcome human separateness along the interpersonal path. The road is winding, but leads away from idolatry of self and other (masochism) toward a 'rational vision' of faith grounded in courage and, ultimately, human 'productiveness'.

The practice of love shows how traditional humanistic values are justified experientially as a 'path', and intentional 'right way of living', a 'Tao' or 'Halacha'. The practice creates life; by developing the elements of the capacity to love, it then '. . . demands a state of intensity, awakeness, enhanced vitality . . .' (1956, p. 129) Fromm specifies what his solution means as a social practice — that people should 'become as Gods', and so reverses Marx's original model of God's disempowerment and reduction of human being. Ultimately, it is the capacity to love which recreates the energy of life.

Unless social and cultural circumstances prevail which make these rereadings real, they remain utopian, with at best an analytical interest in the study of culture, society and individual — as religiously, interpersonally, and biologically driven energy systems who can, with right practice, revolutionize and transform the historical tendency toward their repressive alienation and death embodied in the current cultural order.

New Cultural Age

The quest for a sociology of presence with an analytical interest in a theory of social energy and a transformative interest in a life-affirming practice leads through a strong Romantic thread in classical sociology, psychoanalysis, and existentialism. But, the social theorist who most self-consciously heralds a new age, and tries to derive its arrival empirically and theoretically, stands outside of western European Romanticism: Pitirim Sorokin.

Sorokin's analysis of social and cultural dynamics (1957) is a phase or wave theory of European civilization. Empirically, cultural and social forms are characterized in a chronological periodization of sensate, ideational and idealist cultures. Each culture has its own 'mentality', that structures all the predominant social forms and values. There is a certain tendency to coherence in cultural systems, and an evolution immanently, by a system reaching its limit and beginning a disintegrative phase. The two types of polar cultures are the ideational and the sensate. Ideational culture assumes an ultimate supersensate, immaterial, spiritual reality. As Sorokin puts it: 'In brief, the Sensate culture is the opposite of the Ideational in its major premises.' (1957, p. 28)

The first part of Sorokin's encyclopedic cultural inventory is a classification of cultures and a discussion of subtypes, as well as the rules of integration and disintegrative succession of mentalities. The second part, is a diagnosis of 'the crisis of our age', which is, of course, for Sorokin, the decline of the 600-year-old wave of the sensate culture, and the emergence of either an ideational or idealistic (a mixed genre) culture. We are now living, he wrote in the 1930s, in a painful transitional stage in which the sensate culture is dying:

> We are seemingly between two epochs: the dying Sensate culture of our magnificent yesterday, and the coming Ideational or Idealistic culture of the creative tomorrow. We are living, thinking, acting at the end of a brilliant six-hundred year-long sensate day. (op. cit., p. 625)

Sensate culture is now 'in agony':

> . . . when through its achievements it has given into man's hands terrific power over nature and the social and cultural world, without providing himself with self-control . . . it is becoming increasingly dangerous.

> This control is impossible without a system of absolute or universal and perennial values. (op. cit., p. 628)

A Sensate culture cannot provide that because of its expedient and hedonistic character. As a result, we are 'at the end of the road', although there is a slow emergence of an alternative. Interestingly, Sorokin's description of the current phase of sensate culture seems apt for postmodernism, with its 'syncretism of undigested elements, devoid of a unity or individuality' (which postmodernism celebrates). The crisis precedes an ensuing catharsis of suffering, by which culture will be '. . . brought back to reason, and to eternal, lasting universal, and absolute values.' This suffering is, in Sorokin's terms, followed by a period of charisma and resurrection, and the 'release of new creative forces'. (op. cit., p. 702).

If we are at such a transitional time, alternate cultural premises appear in the 'bazaar', including those which call for a rejection of the mechanist philosophy of Enlightenment in favour of a revived, holistic 'vitalism'. Only during such a time should we expect a revival of interest in Bergson, and a reader on the 'crisis in modernism' (Burwick and Douglas, 1992) which re-examines vitalism. In his essay on vitalism and contemporary thought, Chiari reasserts an anti-mechanistic life philosophy:

> In one form or another, whatever the name, some type of energy, essence, or 'entelechy' of life cannot be done away with or declared dead, for it is inherent in life . . . Life is above all becoming . . . the elan vital is creative freedom, in the image of God, not confined to the biosphere . . . It is the dynamic energy which guides the evolution of the living. (op. cit., pp. 245–73)

And finally, 'the notion of oneness of life as self regulating creativeness . . .' The return of what McDermott calls 'esoteric philosophy' (1993, p. 267) is part of the bazaar in which the western philosophical canon is broadened to a global and esoteric or dissenting traditions perspective. McDermott quotes Whitehead that:

> . . . modern scholarship and modern science reproduce the same limitations as dominated the by gone Hellenistic epoch, and the bygone Scholastic epoch. They canalize thought and observation within pre-determined limits, based upon inadequate metaphysical assumptions dogmatically assumed. The modern assumptions differ from the older assumptions, not wholly for the better. (McDermott, 1993, p. 284)

At this level of generality, talk of a new cultural age is hypothetical and apparently removed from the traditions of empirical social science. What is, I think, interesting, is the extent to which survey analyses of the hegemonic, so-called 'baby-boom' generation reveal at the concrete level of individual lives and opinions, the same sort of shift in assumptions. Notably, in his recent book (1993) Wade Clark Roof reports survey results on what he refers to as a 'generation of seekers'. According to Roof:

> They are still exploring, as they did in their years growing up; but now they are exploring in new, and, we think, more profound ways. Religious and spiritual themes are surfacing in a rich variety of ways-in Eastern religions, in evangelical and fundamentalist teachings, in mysticism and new age movements, in Goddess worship and other ancient religious rituals, in the mainline churches and synagogues, in Twelve Step recovery groups, in concern about the environment, in holistic health, and in personal and social transformation. [And further] . . . baby boomers have found that they have to discover for

themselves what gives their lives meaning, what values to live by. (Roof, 1993, pp. 4–5)

What Roof foresees for the 1990s is a 're-emergence of Spirituality'. Indeed, against the conventional wisdom of this as the political, radical generation, he observes: 'The generation may well be remembered, in fact, as one that grappled hard in search of a holistic, all-encompassing vision of life and as a spiritually creative generation.' (p. 243).

While there is a postmodernism in this 'pastiche-style of spirituality', it is also a search for postmaterial values, although the commitment to the search is through an emphasis on self. Indeed, like Norman O. Brown, Roof raises the possibility of a two-sided narcissism, in which baby-boomer narcissism is 'compatible with the positive, reinforcing role of religion: a person's need for affirmation, for encouragement, for support, for expressiveness'.

He continues: '. . . a transformed narcissism is not only compatible with a religious orientation but may well be crucial to the continuing role of the sacred in a secular society.' (p. 258).

Roof's analysis leads to the view that a new vision that has 'a vital balance of spirituality and social action' (p. 260), creating new community's through a 'far quieter rhetoric — that of the soul' has emerged. Additional support for these surveys is in the best-seller lists in which the traditional self-help literature now has as a best seller, a book on spiritual practices that calls for 'the care of the soul' (Moore, 1992). At the same time, phenomenological psychologists, like Eugene Gendlin, also see narcissism's value in self and social transformation. As Gendlin asks: 'Has *experience* now become a possible source of social criticism?' (1987, p. 251).

Social Theory and Education

In each of the two preceding paradigmatic waves of change in social theory and education, I have tried to show that the academic changes lagged and altered, but were deeply bound up with a set of wider cultural changes. Both radical theory and poststructural analyses were part of a broader cultural movement (Wexler, 1976; 1987). So too, I think, with new-age culture and its differentiated, but still deeply related, representation in social theory and education.

I have not described here in any detail the full flowering of new-age culture as the emergent mass culture. Rather, I have indicated a general theory of cultural change and tried to show that there is some evidence for a move toward a culture with a different set of assumptions than what has prevailed, at least since the Renaissance; less rationalist, scientific, materialist and mechanical, and instead, more spiritual, ideational, vitalist and transcendental.

In addition, I have argued that the sociological canon, particularly Durkheim and Weber, who have functioned to legitimate positivist sociology's methodologism and scientism, were already 'seekers' of a new age, in whose theories are represented core elements of new-age culture or social cosmology. Reinforcing that tendency, I included in social theory socially oriented psychoanalytic theorists and existential philosophers who, by training, professional affiliation and inclination, are social theorists as well. This Romantic stream, reread classical sociology, and new-age cultural tendencies combine to provide the outlines of a new-age social theory.

As a beginning, here I have focused on a commonly held interest in 'energy', which is defined across a wide spectrum, from environmental electrical field, to bio-energy, to holy sparks, as Buber calls the dynamic of truly interactive pedagogy. In each case, energy reaches back to some universal life-principle and forward to both social processes and the external formation and internal process of individual lives. How these different interpretations and dynamics congeal and work is, of course, a primary theoretical issue for any new-age sociology or social cosmology, and its practical social ethic, or practice, in therapy, education, and in everyday life generally.

While the religious dimension is also quite variable, it is crucial to each of these theories. At the very causally least, religion, as in Durkheim, is the primal channel of social energy that has its source in collective life itself. More forcefully, in Weber for example, religion is not only the major template for culture and society — intended or unintended — but the dynamic principle of history, as charisma. Social goals are intermediaries of religious aspirations for salvation, and in a secular age, socioculturally revolutionary and practically redemptive paths are recontextualizations of religion. The problem of the old order, rationalization, is Puritan Protestantism gone awry, and its solution is an inner-worldly mysticism gone interpersonal. In any case, hope for a new age is a hope for prophecy and the path for the renewal of culture is spiritual.

Religiosity, most obviously with Buber, but also with Brown, Fromm and Reich, works through 'experience', where special 'states', either of mystical union with God or interactions with other human beings that are graceful, devoted, and loving are enacted. Religion provides definitions of ideal, de-alienated and unrepressed states of individual and social being. More than that, religious traditions offer paths or 'ways' to actualize the ideal state; religiosity creates 'the right way', the Tao, of living. Fromm, for example, derives a fully elaborated pathway to overcome alienation by beginning with first principles of the old testament which entail: life affirmation against idolatry; the concept of a new human/natural harmony in a 'messianic time'; and then the possibility of what he calls 'experienced values'. From religious first principles, a path of right living is detailed under the rubric of 'loving', but which in fact is a behavioural regimen for surpassing alienation.

Weber's religious solutions are infinitely less confident. But whatever ambivalence or contradictoriness may be attributed to Weber's approach to rationalism, it is indisputable, I think, that he struggled with every 'sphere' of social existence to find a 'way out' of the iron cage of life-destroying societal, cultural and personal rationalization. Ultimately, it is only by bringing what is other-worldly and opposed to mundane or economic existence into practical conduct through prophecy that his desirable states of union and love can be realized.

'Love's body' is what Brown and Reich want, in an unrepressed embodiment that defines for them the ideal or unalienated state. Brown's body is Christian and mystical, while Reich's is reductionist to 'bions' and less the incarnation of spirit (although character armour, however physical, is a residue of interpersonal and not simply bio-chemical or 'vegetative' relations) than environmental fields of energy; which can be experimentally and transferred to human energy — not by transmutation of spirit, but by implementation of mechanism.

Energy, an ideal state beyond current alienation and repression, a culturally life-affirming and generative religiosity, and harbingers of a new historic age are the commonalities of these antecedents and beginnings. Further, there is also, certainly with Reich, but less noticeably perhaps in Weber, as well as incipiently in our other exemplary theorists, the outlines of a new language for social analysis — a language which is at once religious and spiritual, but also interpretively valuable for understanding or 'explanation'; in other words, a new social cosmology with a simultaneously analytical and practically transformative interest.

The main site of this work is, of course, not the Churches, nor social movements in their articulated stages. Rather, the cultural and social transformation occurs first evidently as the 'transformation from within', at the site of the self. Education in the new age is first and foremost necessarily self-centered. The debate about narcissism (Gendlin, 1987) is not a theoretical or even moral dispute. Rather it is about two sides of a social dynamic and its consequences. On one side, there is the contemporary emphasis on 'the body', in social practice and increasingly, I think, in social theory. Any transformatively interested education for a new age will be about the body. Indeed education, as Foucault and others (in Australia, Jennifer Gore and her colleagues) have shown, has always been about the body — disciplining and binding into the social order.

New-age body education is about our first principle, 'energy', and the recovery and stimulation of life energy that has, like Weber's 'mechanical petrification', become inert. This education is about wakening the body — the energy streamings, as Reich would have had it — from their bounded death in life. Of course, the new-age therapeutic apparatus is importantly about this project. From a social psychological vantage point, such a new 'triumph of the therapeutic' is a response to the need for effective agency of human beings, which has been so far repressed interpersonally, culturally and macrosocially, that only at the bio-feedback level can the alienated self re-experience itself.

Body education is already a simultaneous sign of defeat, but also of a stirring of a counter-force, 'energy'. But the dialectic of body education for the awakening and release of bio-energies is that it is energy regeneration for residual self-effectivity that has merely the consequence of producing more individual energy for incorporation and use by the petrified and petrifying social apparatus. Incorporation occurs not only into the apparatus, but also into unthinking cults of the new age. What begins as a stirring of bio-energy for self-social effectivity — which, of course, in actuality goes beyond the minimal, biological level — becomes re-assimilated into cultural programmes as diverse as twelve-step methods, evangelical, fundamentalist religion, and mass amalgamated reductions of psychoanalysis which use the apparatus to manipulate, electronically rather than either mechanically or interpersonally, the 'unconscious'.

What Weber understood, for his own day, was that while such activity may be enjoyable, the *transformative* possibility — which he called 'revolution-ary' — is only realized when the release of energies (to now use our terms) is poured into the work of intellectualization. Without intellectualization, 'experience', however altered, remains enjoyment, working in the unintended service of incorporation into the uncritical prevailing social apparatus and its new age counterposed cultures. My point is that a social-theory-based educa-tion in a new age recognizes the need for the re-intellectualization of released energies. It so becomes necessarily an education of the mind, and not only for the body. What the new-age cultural shift can offer, however, is the opening of alternative cultural resources for learning and thinking. By that, I don't mean simply multiculturalism, which aborts a more global awareness in favour of liberal accommodation.

The work of re-intellectualization — education for the mind — of disci-plined thought with wider cultural resources, points to the other side of narcis-sism, to why a self-centered education opens a third way, an alternative 'way out', beyond the current polarity between consumption and production as the bases for educational thought and practice. Consumption, as Horkheimer and Adorno so trenchantly warned us, leads to the 'amalgamation of thought with advertising'. Production, as we now increasingly see, reduces thought to per-formance. To me, against Lyotard, performativity is not an opening to polyin-ventiveness. In reality, the overwhelming tendency in educational reform is the dynamic that Harvey (1989) has described in the regime of postindustrial flexible accumulation. Educational reform is strongly corporatist and techno-cratic, redefining both the curriculum and the student/subject as aspects of performance/skills criteria. The issue is less appropriate curriculum content, and more that the relation between subject or self and knowledge is itself collapsed, so that there is no distance between the performance/skill and the performer. Postindustrial definitions of education are centralizing (despite the rhetoric of 'flexibility') and naturalize the self's disappearance into the performance.

On the other side of performance education stands the false opposition of postmodernism, which, despite its self-presentation of anti-narrativity, is the metanarrative of consumption. It heralds decentralization and diffusion as a cultural strategy of self-destruction. Ultimately, postmodernism fuses itself, however ironically, to the consumer culture it tries to periodically escape. In that way, it fulfills Horkheimer and Adorno's warning about the incorporation of thinking into the logic of advertising — which is the lowbrow analogue to highbrow postmodern anti-representational forms of representation. Even the irony, as a form of critique and way of maintaining distance against a crushing mass cultural apparatus, surrenders to the protest of ornamentalism, substituting marginal formalisms for self-affirming thinking that stops the tearful laughter of irony long enough for mindful creation.

Recollection of the body for an energy, life awakening in new-age education can only resist feeding the electronic apparatus which now regulates the unconscious imagically by re-intellectualization — life of the mind. Given the medium of religiosity, both in the contemporary cultural transformation and in the emergence of a social theory with practical implications for education, re-minding will occur in the thrall of states of being such as moved (in American culture) William James, Whitman and Emerson. Re-intellectualization motivated by experienced values through religious states of being unavoidably recalls the language of spirit and soul.

New-age culture is not merely about a twelve-step sort of interest in mass-produced programmed 'recovery', but about a deeper recovery of the soul, a 'return' or 'turning' in Buber and Fromm's language. The recovery of the soul becomes then the transcendental polarity to the self-centered educative recollection of the body and its life energy. Fromm's theory of becoming can be read as a way of bringing the soul to life, although he still used secular, behavioural language in his struggle for 'de-alienation'. New-age culture spawns parallel methodologies, such as Thomas Moore's (1993) popular '*Care of the Soul*', which openly use the language of soul and sacred to describe the connection between transcendental being and cultural practices effecting individual lives. This entails going beyond humanism to recover being as soul basis and medium for mind and being of which body is the vessel. In a far cry from 'critical pedagogy', cultivation of the soul in a new age will call out to a teaching for transcendence; going beyond the critical social analysis that was western humanism's Enlightenment heir, beyond the 'Romantic reaction', and its vitalist history, to a new age in both social practice and social theory. I am tempted to conclude with Weber that, 'No one knows who will live in this cage in the future . . .' but, I think we already do.

Note

1 This chapter is part of a paper, the first part of which was presented as a plenary speech to the Westermarch Society in Joensuu, Finland on March 26–27, 1993. Title of the paper: 'From Sociology to Individual Practice and Cultural Renewal'.

References

ALEXANDER, J.C. (1988) 'Introduction', in ALEXANDER, J. (Ed) *Durkheimian Sociology: Cultural Studies*, Cambridge, Cambridge University Press.

BELLAH, R. (1973) (Ed) *Emile Durkheim On Morality and Society*, Chicago, The University of Chicago Press.

BENJAMIN, J. (1989) *The Bonds of Love*, New York and Canada, Random House Inc.

BOTTOMORE, T. and RUBEL, M. (Eds) (1956) *Karl Marx: Selected Writings in Sociology and Social Philosophy*, New York, Toronot, London, McGraw-Hill Book Company.

BROWN, N.O. (1959) *Life Against Death: The Psychoanalytic Meaning of History*, Middletown, Wesleyan University Press.

BRUBAKER, R. (1984) *The Limits of Rationality: An Essay on the Social and Moral Thought of Max Weber*, London, George Allen and Unwin.

BUBER, M. (1948) *Israel and the World: Essays in a Time of Crisis*, New York, Schocken Books.

BUBER, M. (1967) *On Judaism*, New York, Schocken Books.

BUBER, M. (1992) *On Intersubjectivity and Cultural Creativity*, Chicago, University of Chicago Press, translated by Eisenstadt.

BURWICK, F. and DOUGLASS, P. (1992) (Eds) *The Crisis in Modernism: Bergson and the Vitalist Controversy*, Cambridge, Cambridge University Press.

DURKHEIM, E. (1960) 'Preface to L'Année Sociologique', 1 and 2, in WOLFF, K. (Ed) *Essays on Sociology & Philosophy*, New York, Harper and Row.

DURKHEIM, E. (1961) *The Elementary Forms of the Religious Life*, New York, Collier Books.

FROMM, E. (1956) *The Art of Loving*, New York, Harper and Row.

FROMM, E. (1964) 'Forward', in Karl Marx, *Selected Writings in Sociology and Social Philosophy*, New York, McGraw-Hill Book Company.

FROMM, E. (1966) *You Shall Be as Gods: A Radical Interpretation of the Old Testament and Its Traditions*, Greenwich, Fawcett Publications, Inc.

GERTH, H.H. and MILLS, C.W. (1946) (Eds) *From Max Weber: Essays in Sociology*, New York, Oxford University Press, pp. 253–64; pp. 323–59.

GENDLIN, E.T. (1987) 'A philosophical critique of the concept of Narcissism: The significance of the awareness movement', in LEVIN, D.M (Ed) *Pathologies of the Modern Self: Postmodern Studies on Narcissism, Schizophrenia, and Depression*, New York, New York University Press.

GOVER, N. (1984) 'The Educational Conception Implied in the Psychological, Humanistic and Social Theories of Erich Fromm', Unpublished Ph.D. dissertation, Jerusalem, Hebrew University.

HARVEY, D. (1989) *The Condition of Postmodernity: An Inquiry into the Onins on Social Change*, Oxford, New York, Blackwell.

MANN, W.E. and HOFFMAN, E. (1980) *Wilhelm Reich: The Man Who Dreamed of Tomorrow*, Northamptonshire, The Aquarian Press.

MARCUSE, H. (1955) *Eros and Civilization: A Philosophical Inquiry into Freud*, New York, Random House.

McDERMOTT, R.A. (1993) 'Esoteric Philosophy', in SOLOMON, R. and HIGGINS, K. (Eds) *From Africa to Zen: An Invitation to World Philosophy*, Boston, Rowman and Littlefield Inc.

MOORE, T. (1983) *Care of the Soul*, New York, Harper Collins.

REICH, W. (1949) *Character Analysis*, New York, Farrar, Straus and Giroux.

REICH, W. (1961) *The Function of the Orgasm*, New York, Farrar, Straus and Giroux.

REICH, W. (1971) *The Mass Psychology of Fascism*, New York, Farrar, Straus and Giroux.

REICH, W. (1972) *Sex-Pol*, New York, Vintage.

REICH, W. (1980) *Genitality in the Theory and Therapy of the Neuroses*, New York, Farrar, Straus and Giroux.

ROOF, W.C. (1993) *A Generation of Seekers: The Spiritual Journeys of the Baby Boom Generation*, New York, Harper Collins.

SCHOLEM, G. (1946) *Major Trends in Jewish Mysticism*, New York, Schocken Books.

SOROKIN, P. (1957) *Social & Cultural Dynamics: A Study of Change in Major Systems of Art, Truth, Ethics, Law and Social Relationships*, Boston, Porter Sargent.

STEINSALTZ, A. (1992) *In the Beginning: Discourses on Chasidic Thought*, New Jersey, Jason Aronson, Inc.

WEBER, M. (1958) *The Protestant Ethic and the Spirit of Capitalism*, New York, Charles Scribner's Sons.

WEBER, M. (1968) *Economy and Society*, New York, Bedminster Press.

WEXLER, P. (1976) *Sociology of Education: Beyond Equality*, Indianapolis, Bobs-Merrill Co.

WEXLER, P. (1987) *Social Analysis of Education: After the New Sociology*, London, New York, Routledge and Kegan Paul.

WEXLER, P. (1993) 'Bernstein: A Jewish Misreading', in SADOVNIK, A. (Ed) *Basil Bernstein: Consensus and Controversy*, Ablex Publishing Co.

WHIMSTER, S. and LASH, S. (1987) (Eds) *Max Weber, Rationality and Modernity*, London, Allen.

Part 2

Pedagogy

5   Getting Our Hands Dirty: Provisional Politics in Postmodern Conditions

Allan Luke

Let me try to get the genre and standpoint of this piece right, or as right as it can be prior to the writing itself. This isn't a critique, rejoinder, but an essay and personal narrative. I recently read Michael Apple's 'What Post-modernists Forget: Cultural Capital and Official Knowledge' (1993b). There Apple discusses the political economy of knowledge and corporate control of education in the United States. He describes the intrusion of technocratic rationality in university teaching, and identifies the commodification of school knowledge in the case of the US public school broadcast venture, 'Channel One'. Along the way, Apple defends a non-essentialist neo-Marxian analyses of education and class. He is extremely critical of what he refers to as 'postmodernism' on the grounds that contemporary French social theory has distracted many educators and researchers from questions of the political and economic control over what counts as 'official knowledge' in late capitalist social structure, and from issues of the material effects of that control.

I found this piece and Apple's recent *Official Knowledge* (1993a) provocative jumping off points for talking about the possibilities of a constructive politics of educational policy and curriculum that draws from poststructuralist, postcolonial, feminist as well as neo-Marxian positions. For me Apple's work reframed many of the questions raised in this volume and discussants at the conference about what should count as policy intervention in what I understand to be the 'postmodern' conditions of global, corporate economic consolidation and diversification, unprecedented global immigration and shifting national and regional boundaries, hybrid social and cultural identities, and emergent, heterogeneous social formations and movements (articles by Fitzclarence, Funnell, Singh, Wexler, in this volume all take up reponses to these issues).

Here I want to use it to narratively reconstruct some political, theoretical and practical decisions I've made in the past eighteen months, working within the Australian version of 'economic rationalism' that Apple, I and others writing from critical approaches to educational theory have been so consistently critical of over the last decade. So this is, among other things, a personal and polemical description of the quandaries of political and curriculum intervention in education in the 1990s.

In so doing, I want to try to shift focus to what work in poststructuralism, feminism and postcolonialism *enables* as part of a materialist analysis, rather than what it forgets. My argument is that there is a whole dimension of intervention in the public work of curriculum building and policy making that is profoundly polysemic and heteroglossic, where matters of 'what counts' and 'in whose interests' official knowledge and cultural capital work are far from unambiguous and clear cut — an argument that was taken up in discussions with Jane Kenway, Robert Young and John Knight in relation to these chapters. I do not for an instance deny the significance of the political economy of educational knowledge and practice — but I believe that the material consequences and significance of particular forms of educational practice, as discourse, are ambiguous, even in terms of the sociological reproduction of cultural capital that Apple foregrounds (Luke, in press/1994). Whether, when and how educational interventions can have ameliorative and/or token, inclusive and/or discriminatory effects — whether, when and how they are conducive to systemic changes in the distribution of wealth, cultural capital and symbolic power and/or contributory to existing patterns of distribution is profoundly contingent on what I would call *local sociologies* — the representational *and* material politics, economics and cultural histories of locality that Foucault and colleagues have demonstrated are always at play (see Gore, this volume). As a result, I here want to argue for a local, pragmatic politics, a politics that does not dismiss political economy, but recognizes that the material conditions and effects of educational intervention are mediated through the texts of policy and curriculum, which in turn have different — often simultaneously 'open' and 'closed' (Luke, 1989) — uses, interpretations and possibilities in different sites.

In other words, while I agree with Apple that the key focus for a critical sociology of education and for curriculum theory should be on the distribution of symbolic and material resources and wealth, it is not always easy to anticipate the material consequences of the discourses of policy and curriculum — either in terms of the differential distribution of social, cultural and economic capital, or in terms of the local building of cultural resources and social identities. That is, in postmodern conditions, our capacity to 'read off' broader, generalizable effects of particular texts and practices is difficult, particularly in local and national contexts of emergent social formations and alliances, new forms of social and demographic identity, and new forms for the exploitation of the environment and the exploitation of capital. I here want to look closely at some of the contradictory and potentially self-annulling decisions facing educationists committed to an agenda of enfranchisement and critique.

Admittedly, our situation in Australia is different from the US that Apple describes: despite the steady movement towards state economic rationalism, the actual involvement of many in the educational Left with schools, state and federal curriculum and in-service initiatives remains quite significant. Many of us have been involved in curriculum development and implementation in the so-called 'equity' areas over the last decade, including: English as a second language and migrant education, gender equity and girls' schooling, Aboriginal and Torres Strait Islander education, literacy education for 'at risk' working-class children, and various spin-offs and variations from the Commonwealth Disadvantaged Schools Program. Admittedly, these programmes have been couched in ameliorative, often 'welfarist' terms, and it is not coincidental that the discourses and institutions for managing migrant, Aboriginal and working-class 'deficit' emerged in Australian education in the 1970s, when the first generation of postwar children, postwar migrants, 'officially recognized' Aborigines and Islanders reached previously élite secondary and tertiary education (Green, Hodgens and Luke, 1994). We live in relationship to a differently inflected political economy, where governmental power is used to service different constituencies, and where the actual conversion and distribution of capital is different than in the US and UK. As the recent volume of comparative policy analyses by Lingard, Knight and Porter (1993) showed, there are some similar themes and movements, but the historical and political context has encouraged some forms of discursive action and reconstructive political work that have not been available to our US, UK, Canadian and New Zealand counterparts.

In the contexts of, for example, the US, UK, Canada and India, the principal viable 'alternative' route to educational reform has required the rallying around, for example, progressivist educational practices. The institutionalization of the Left in this country has meant that, for instance, there have been vigorous debates and differences among different Left and feminist groups around, say, progressivist versus explicit pedagogies in literacy or, to take another example, between 'inclusive' curriculum and separate schooling approaches to young women's advanced science education. So the enfranchisement of 'equity' and 'social justice' issues and clienteles within the discourses of Labour educational policy has led to the participation of many feminists, Leftists and 'radical' educators in curriculum development and policy formation. This, in turn, has muddied the demarcations of critique and complicity available in those national and regional contexts where a visible, vocal Right runs education — to the point where some would say that 'we have met the enemy and it is us.'

I have worked with and alongside of Michael Apple for the past decade. His project of political analysis of curriculum and policy has had a shaping influence on those of us working to critique and rebuild political economies of school knowledge My own work focused first on critical sociologies of text knowledge. Over the last five years, I have moved towards the use of discourse analyses to examine the classroom and textbook construction of knowledge and identity, and to explore the possibilities for critical literacy curriculum intervention in Australia and elsewhere.

As a qualification to the ideology critique that Apple so powerfully introduced in the late 1970s and early 1980s, I have argued that there a danger of 'reading off' of knowledge effects and consequences in analyses of pedagogic texts and their economic sources. Work in discourse analysis, audience

ethnographies and cultural studies has suggested that there is no easy or necessary co-equivalence between: political economy: the conditions of institutional production of the text; text: the codes and semiosis of the text; and
audience/readership: the institutional conditions of interpretation of the text.
I don't doubt, as Apple argues, that there is a powerful relationship between
say, the economic basis of 'Channel One', the discourses and registers it
makes available to students, and what students and other viewers take away
from 'readings'. But the politics of representation and interpretation are complex and local, and classrooms and living rooms are the very sites where
contestation and the kind of 'play' that Bakhtinians make great stock of are
most visibly at work.

At the same time, I think that Apple's continued insistence on a political
economy of educational knowledge is crucial. There is a powerful need for
locally developed and state-developed curriculum materials that are not dominated by corporate profit motives, and there is a continuing need for a critical,
discourse analytic literacy that takes apart the 'carnival' of corporate commer-
cials in 'Channel One', just as surely as it takes apart the messages of the
evening news, sitcoms, or problematicises the textbook language of Anglo
'invasion' of Aboriginal Australia, or the new-Orientalism of, say, Oliver
Stone's 'Heaven and Earth' (see Singh, 1994). The concern with the pedagogic
production of cultural capital, of values, of technical expertise and so forth is
something that, as Apple's analysis suggests, we cannot lose sight of. Particularly in the USA and Britain, the degree to which all mainstream political
forces have coalesced around an unrepentant economic rationalism is obvious.
In this economic and political context, there is indeed a possibility that in a
rush to analyse (the pleasure of) the text, textuality and discourse, we can lose
sight of the material consequences of discourse.

But my concern here is that Apple's (1993b, pp. 307–8) description of
'what Postmodernists Forget' may not fully consider 'what Post-modernists
enable'. It is probably a waste of paper to get into the minutiae over what will
count as 'postmodernism' and 'poststructuralism' here. The bookstores and
journals are packed with writings on this topic and, as far as I can make out,
the 'differences' may have as much to do with particular interpretive communities constructions of 'schools of thought' and epistemes as anything else. My
only aside is that for many of us working in education theory and curriculum
studies in Australia, the tendency has been to see Foucault as a 'poststructuralist',
offering a sustained critique of structuralism and grand narratives with a political
vision — and to view Lyotard and Baudrillard and others as 'postmodernists',
tending towards an explicitly depoliticized standpoint. There are, of course,
extremely significant cross-overs to work in postcolonialism and feminism
but for my present purposes, and in the context of this book's other, more
theoretical chapters, an exposition of these distinctions is probably not crucial.
My more immediate concern is how they are articulated and used in everyday
pedagogic work.

What matters to me is that much of this work has not just been 'faddish' but has enabled particular analyses (and self-analyses) that have pushed us in different and often uncharted political directions. Like many of my generation, my own work in curriculum had its basis in the neo-Marxian perspective of my own New Left education in the late 1960s and early 1970s. This particular worldview sustained a sense of political direction, solidarity and purpose. But what it failed to do is to provide us with a distinctive language and politics to describe our own status as the 'subaltern': as people of colour and gender working at the margins of schools, universities and other public institutions. That is, for all of its power in explicating social structure and inequity, neo-Marxian discourse needs to be pushed towards language for talking about other kinds of identity and other kinds of solidarity and coalition — those of culture and colour, gender and sexual preference. It was only through working with feminist partners, with other people of colour, that I developed a language for talking about myself as an Asian-American-Australian writer, a language that is still quiet as I write.

This must be a language of hybridity, not of essence, as Parlo Singh points out in her contribution to this volume. And I am impatient with those 'grand theorists' — Marxist, Frankfurtian and others — who assume that these concerns of hybridity are somehow theoretical and empirical aberrations that will somehow 'go away' as surely as Bart Simpson will fade into syndication, as a reversion to the need for whole and centred, unified essential identities. Hybridity is not something I or many others opted for, it is not a vogue, not added extras to the package: we are and can be of necessity many standpoints and perspectives. This is not a matter for analytic proof or falsification. This is how many of us have survived and flourished.

Like many migrant parents, my father would remind us that we had to be both American and Chinese. No big deal, eh? But he also told us that 'when the White Boss tells you what to do, you tell them whatever they want to hear. Then you go and do what you think needs to be done.' Is this hypocrisy? Weakness and selling out? Inconsistency and deception? A big lie? In 'foundational' or 'essentialist' approaches to identity, authenticity and truth it might appear to be. But in this instance, I think it reflects the political experience of many Asians who grew up and survived in the antagonistic culture and employment market of the interwar years. This is about knowing where and when to 'pick your spots', to use one of my father's favourite baseball metaphors — about strategically deciding how and where to deploy which identity in relation to material power.

This strategic hybridity of the subaltern is not any less ontologically 'real', if that's the vocabulary you want to use, than the centred identity of the European male, the pious Christian, or the bourgeois entrepreneur.[1] As Stuart Hall (1993) recently observed, we are watching the coming apart of the fiction that the nation state is synonymous with singular, ethnic and cultural identity. Equally suspect is the model that the psychologically and ontologically real individual is synonymous with the singular, essential identity of a grand narrative. If this bothered me particularly, I'd be in psychotherapy, which historically has been a western technology for stabilization of the body into a grand narrative of wholeness and essence — but hybridity is neither deficit nor something to be fixed. With the reorganization of space, time and mobility in postcolonial nations — hybridity is as much a non-negotiable social fact as singularity purported to be.

This is far more than a 'faddish' accomplishment: the degree to which postmodernism and poststructuralism, feminisms and postcolonialisms have shifted the spotlight from 'top–down' analyses, from a focus on the means of production, from the centre to ways of thinking, talking and theorizing about and from margins has been crucial for me and many others. Far from distracting us from what Apple rightly describes as the 'power of conservative social movements', it has given us reconstructed ways of attacking them, of evading them, of dealing with them, particularly in light of their manifestations in and through mass media — in ways that, I would add, aren't descendants of the struggles of European, male workers against capitalism and tyranny in 1848, but are more closely related to urban struggles of people of difference trying to build hybrid lives within and at the fringes of fast capitalism. Hybrid targets are harder to hit.

I too am wary of what Apple takes to be the downside to poststructuralism: it is easy to lose the plot, to forget the political and get sucked up into celebratory cliches of the endless 'play of difference' and evershifting 'standpoints', a new self-indulgent textuality and political relativism that assumes that everything is discourse and that all discourse is normative and has coequal material effects. Some discourses count more than others. Some discourses are tied up with death and destruction and desecration. And some things, Marx or Marcuse, Spivak or Hooks would agree, aren't the figments of discourse: they starve, disfigure and kill people. But at the same time I'm not sure that poststructuralist or postcolonial theories of sociality and identity can be written off as a faddish preoccupation with French theory. For those of us working in a domain of practice with visible material consequences and knowledge effects, it may be of use to take such 'theoretical positions' on their word — not as truth claims *per se*, but rather in terms of the kinds of pragmatic political strategies and local interventions that they enable.

Let me explain by reference to work that I've recently been involved in: the development of competency-based literacy and numeracy education for adult, migrant and Aboriginal students. The 'competency movement' is part of the Australian Government's efforts to build a corporate, multinational capitalist agenda while at the same time arguing for social justice and equity. This has involved a perilous balancing act between funding those social programmes that traditionally have been significant to the Labour party's electoral constituencies (women, migrants, Aborigines and Islanders, the urban working class), while at the same time pushing technocratic goals not dissimilar of those of most other OECD nations (e.g., balanced budgeting, increased economic productivity and technological expansion) (Pusey, 1992). In the early 1980s this was marked by the deregulation of the Australian economy to make its traditional (colonial) markets for commodities more open, and by increased spending in areas for social programmes and infrastructure (e.g., to develop programmes for gender-equity in the workplace, childcare, Medicare and Aboriginal/Islander health). In curriculum the 1980s marked the proliferation of quality Australian curriculum in social education, gender equity, English as a second language, language and literacy, and so forth: the expansion of government-sponsored work on disadvantaged schools, all with, at the least, lip-service to issues of inclusiveness and equity.

Over the past decade, then, Labour has walked a tightrope between apparently conflicting and contradictory agendas. Particularly under Paul Keating's tenure as Prime Minister, the shift has been towards an overtly economic rationalist agenda — with stresses on 'quality assurance', accountability and so forth in educational institutions. This has involved the use of performance indicators, increased competency-based testing and so forth, all with the idea, similar to what Apple describes in the US, of getting more 'bang for the buck'. As several Australian educational researchers have shown, it has entailed increased commodification, and increased emphasis on measurement, and contracting working conditions for teachers and university academics (Lingard, Knight and Porter, 1993). However, by US and UK benchmarks, the moves towards standardized curricula and testing have been far from draconian. Despite Labour losing electoral control over state governments, there is relatively little mass standardized testing. While growing, the overall private corporate influence on Australian education is far less extensive than in the US and UK — particularly given the federal government's increasing input into curriculum development and the professional development of state school and adult-education teachers. And finally, while it has not changed the principally monocultural character of school knowledge, the debate over ameliorative multicultural policy and curriculum development in Australian education is resilient (Castles, Kalantzis, Cope and Morrissey, 1992) — without having incurred the visible backlashes of US-style official language laws and monocultural policy. This said, many of these gains appeared to be coming undone in relation to a competency movement that marked a return to the monocultural, male worker/subject.

In this local political context, let me describe an instance of intervention that highlights the difference between Michael Apple's position and historical location and mine. I'll use a story-form that parallels Apple's (1993b, p. 301) introduction, where he describes a university-staff meeting:

Everyone stared at the educational bureaucrat with amazement. Was she suggesting that competency scales were the only way to go in adult education? That we needed a single competency scale for all adult learners in adult education in Australia? How 'negotiable' was this central move to tie funding of technical and workplace training to competency scales? Surely, this is an example of stuff 'coming down from on high', of a centralized, technocratic agenda that would be used against educators and students. After all, any student of education would know that competency-based education, and its fellow travellers — criterion-referenced testing and mastery learning — has a long history going back to Ralph Turlington and Florida, and that competency standards would be used against minorities, working-class and women workers, to stream them through social services, training and unemployment systems. Further, the numbers would be used to run systems checks on educational and social infrastructures.

This was my first reaction and remains the reaction of many neo-Marxian policy analyses. In their long-awaited expansion of adult and workplace education, spurred by a recession and record unemployment, all that the government had in store for us was the avalanche of numbers, a social control and regulation device to be used against the underclass. But is this the case?

My decision to participate in the actual writing of competency scales came about through a number of factors. One of the typical rationalizations for participation in such schemes can be 'if we don't do it, the Right will'. This is dangerous business and the next thing you know, you're subcontracted to build a 'culture-fair IQ test', an 'emancipatory basal-reading series' or something oxymoronic like that. For me the turning point came in a meeting when a representative of a textile-workers union explained that her union was in favour of the competency scales. She argued that if they could be built in a culturally/gender sensitive and appropriate way, they could become powerful tools for migrant women workers and others who were involved in government training programmes. This foregrounded two issues for me: the degree to which these systems might be turned to advantage for accrediting workers' participation in government and employer-sponsored training and upgrading programmes, and, as importantly, the degree to which, as they stood, competency scales ignored altogether the identifiable cultural, linguistic, life-experience resources that women and men brought to work and training situations.

Here are the contextual issues: the Labour government had required that all employers with payrolls above 1m$ devote 1.5 per cent of their payroll annually to training schemes. Partly in response to training needs and unemployment, there has been a major expansion in technical, workplace and tertiary training in Australia — a human capital model writ large, if belatedly. At any rate, this has meant that increasing numbers of migrants and underemployed workers are involved in workplace training. For example, in the food industry, government-mandated workplace training may be the only access to educational facilities for many workers. This union official told me that if her members didn't have a competency framework — then they would go into 'enterprise' (local) bargaining with employers with no way of demanding recognition, pay rewards or career paths based on their training. Without competency frameworks, then, there was less chance of specifying how their training might fit the employers' needs and job requirements, what types of programmes the workers and unions perceived as necessary, and, perhaps most importantly, there was no way of getting recognition or a raise when, for instance, someone finished an ESL upgrading course.

So what I learned from trade unionists, adult educators and volunteer workers in colleges, and technical-college students was that the competency movement is a double-edged process. It is potentially a dangerous form of rationalizing work and work-related educational outcomes. It can offer employers, government agencies and educators abusable grids of specification for examining, mapping and streaming students into different sectors of the economy and, not incidentally, the polity. Particularly where these grids tend to be culture and gender-blind, they tended to push workers into performances and skills defined in terms of measurable against an imaginary benchmark of the skilled, mostly male, culturally mainstream worker. But at the same time it also is a way of forcing employers, educators and curriculum designers to take seriously the training and educational needs of workers and the unemployed.

What we set out to do, then, was to write an 'the uncompetence agenda' — that is, to both ameliorate and change the effects and consequences of conventional competency agendas. With collaborators Bill Cope, Mary Kalantzis, Bob Morgan, Rob McCormack, Nicky Solomon and Nancy Veel — all critical educators with a long history of social and educational activism and teaching, we tried to generate a competency framework that would 'change the subject' of competence. What follows is my account of that work (already the subject of heated debate among this team).

I viewed my own part in this intervention in terms of two poststructuralist positions: from Foucault, that discourses of educational policy have the power to produce the objects of what they speak; and from Lyotard, that educational policy and curriculum was basically a narrative format about educational development. If these two insights held, then our job was to form what Mouffe (1993) calls a provisional or 'contingent' alliance with the economic rationalists, and try to write the competent subject differently. That rewriting, we agreed, would be to construct a vision of the competent subject that would include critical literacy and social analyses, bilingualism and biculturalism, and would aim towards collaborative, non-exploitative workplaces. The effect that we set out to achieve was to move educators' and employers' attention to workers' cultural and gender resources, and to prescriptively shift their attention towards broader repertoires of effective social activity, as opposed to narrow definitions of psychological and behavioural skill.

I do not have the time here to detail *The National Framework of Adult English Language, Literacy and Numeracy Competence* (Cope *et al.*, 1994). But I here describe its broad design principles. We set out to:

1 Redefine competency to competence, to shift emphasis from psychological/technocratic models of skills in people's heads to culturally acquired and used 'repertoires' of social activities. These repertoires,

we argued, were necessarily local and needed to be taught and assessed in relation to the specific demands of workplace, community and educational settings.

2 Change the human subject of competence. Most competency frameworks, like psychological models of skill development, are stories about idealized white male subjects, and markers of 'difference' are taken as deficits or extraneous factors. Our model held that curriculum and assessment had to recognize explicitly that gender, cultural and linguistically different knowledge that workers and students brought to programmes as productive and valuable, rather than as 'deficits' and hindrances. In fact, we tried to set up the framework's logic of development in ways where the monolingual, monocultural male manager might be pressed to take some intercultural and bilingual training.

3 Shift the developmental movement in the curriculum framework away from the achievement of entrepreneurial, competitive autonomy. All competency frameworks and curriculum cycles are narratives about the development of a particular version of the ideal human subject/ worker/citizen. As Apple (1993b, p. 305) points out, the economic rationalist position builds educational interventions that have a movement towards 'an entrepreneurial or efficiently acquisitive class type': that type becomes the educational ideal of the framework (and of other populist versions of twenty-first century success like de Bono's 'lateral thinker'). We replaced this with a Vygotskian model that described development of competence as the movement from assisted to independent to collaborative competence. The latter, intercultural and gender collaboration, we argued, was key to 'productive diversity'.

4 Build a complex, multilevelled and multifaceted model of competence that defied single-digit assessment of individuals. Our aim was to define competence as it spread out across domains of communication: e.g., task, technology, identity, group, organization, civic/ political. These domains, we argued would help retain a curriculum balance in workplace and adult programmes and avoid, for instance, reductive skills models, or equally, 'consciousness raising' models that neglected explicit functional skill needs. By definition, this richer model demanded of educators more complex, multicultural and multilingual descriptive assessment, rather than 'single-shot' testing.

Needless to say, we've been criticized strongly by both the academic and educational Left and Right. Not surprisingly, several Left educators told me that we were selling out to a technocratic, economic rationalist agenda, simply giving human capital education a kinder, gentler face. Alternately, one 'poststructuralist' academic suggested that we were engaged in multiculturalist ideological social engineering.

Was this a sell out? Was it an exercise in simple reformism? We have since just completed adding a national competence to the Government's other national 'Mayer' framework: 'cultural understanding' stresses biculturalism, and cultural reflexivity in the national agenda (Cope *et al.*, 1994). Both frameworks have been adopted by the Government and are currently in national implementation.

Do these frameworks serve the interests of corporate and governmental capital? No doubt: they wouldn't have been adopted by Government and employers if they hadn't. But I think that the range of responses and construals of our activity, across the political and educational spectrum, begin to suggest the polysemy of these kinds of policy enterprises, and the ambiguity of their actual material consequences. Our attempt was to shift these interests, to bring into play other kinds of identities, cultures, life trajectories that were marginalized in conventional competency frameworks and silenced in workplace training and adult education. In effect they attempt to take a 'market-oriented' discourse on competency and *recommodify* it as a much more explicitly culturally-oriented discourse. By chance, while we were working on the document there was a federal election during which Keating and Labour were reelected. The election looked like a walk-in for the right wing Liberal Party, and in the run up we heard through the civil-service grapevine that the Liberals viewed competency-based education as a Left-wing, union agenda. We were also quietly advised that if the Liberals won, at least the term 'collaboration' would have to go.

The jury is still out on this. We were subcontracted text workers on this document. As it has become government policy, our names have come off subsequent drafts, 'applications' and versions. In these, the framework has taken on different forms, parts have been watered down beyond our control, downplaying issues of gender equity and multiculturalism. So we have no doubts that the process of commodification and political incorporation is well under way.

But I think we can claim that this work shifted the competency agenda in the country away from simple technocratic scales and psychometric means. It has generated debate and controversy. Most importantly, the framework has placed 'difference' and issues of access and equity back on the table, both at the level of policy and local adult-education curriculum practice. It has opened gaps in curriculum practice for local educators to constructively recognize and deal with issues of difference. We are now working on two applications: one for Aboriginal teacher education and another for Aboriginal and Torres Strait Islander access to technical colleges. Other curriculum writers are working on English as a second language, adult basic education and industry applications. One of the payoffs we had was from an Aboriginal educator in the Northern Territory who said that this was the first curriculum framework that explicitly located and recognized the community-based knowledges and practices of his students.

Is this a story with a happy ending? We're not sure. I can only speak for myself on this, but I'll put it simply: if I had stuck with a simple political economy analysis, I wouldn't have taken on the job. We could have stayed in the safe haven of 'critique' and taken apart Labour's economic rationalist agenda from the sidelines, as many have. We felt that there was more at issue here, that what needed to be done was an ameliorative intervention on behalf of those whose lives would be most directly affected by this agenda, the unemployed, youth, women entering the workforce, the underemployed and marginal. Yet, as we all know, good intentions are no test of the material consequences of policy and curriculum. As I've been advised by those who worked on the first generation of competency-based reforms in UK education, we'll have to wait and see.

What are the lessons here for a contemporary educational politics? We realized that our doctrinal opposition to economic rationalism would get us nowhere. There were already signs of where the Government's agenda and educational expertise were leading it: towards evaluation-driven, streaming models that stressed assessment rather than curriculum and programming. It was interesting, then, that the contracting body accepted a tender offered by a gender-balanced, culturally diverse team of researchers with expertise principally in critical social literacy, rather than competing tenders from psychometricians and more conventional curriculum developers. At the same time we recognized that there are *discursive variants of economic rationalism*: ranging from the hard core technicism of the Thatcher and Reagan agendas, to the 'social justice' technicism of the Australian Labour Party. As I have noted here, for better and worse in Australia equity, multiculturalism, gender and class remain part of available government discourses (e.g., even the Government's quality assurance programmes in higher education strongly emphasize 'equity performance indicators'). And their presence on the table in policy and curriculum enables particular kinds of intervention not possible under other North American and British variants of economic rationalism.

We can take these as signs of contradiction, of the enemy insidiously at work. We can paint these variants as monochrome, with universally corrupt local consequences. Or we can read them as signs of an entry point, what Yeatman (1993) calls 'gaps' and 'openings' for pedagogical and political intervention. What postmodern politics allowed us to do was to set aside issues of truth for the moment, and to form a provisional political coalition with government and others with the express purpose of 'changing the subject' of competency. Our aim was to shift a national agenda and this involved identifying a 'nodal point' (Mouffe, 1993) in the public discourses, and stepping in to reword it, to change the narrative structure of public policy, and to write the competent human subject differently. The issue here is not whether educational knowledge and competence is 'commodified'. In the contemporary nation state, most knowledge is commodified — that is, run for the profit motive of either the governmental economy or the corporate economy. And what we were doing was indeed a task of state commodification. But our aim was to 'reframe' or 'repunctuate' particular commodifications, so that they could be picked up and used in the local sites of technical colleges, training institutions and workplaces in ways that would enfranchise and educate.[2] At the same time, we tried to textually anticipate local misreadings of our curricular text and cut off possible abuses.

Let me loop back around to Apple's argument. I recognize the degree to which our efforts could be construed as 'designer curriculum', confluent with the grand designs of capital, with what Apple refers to as the 'dominance of technical/administrative knowledge and the industrial project'. There is, arguably, a sense in which anything we do within state educational systems — including universities — services that project, even simply as humanist legitimations of the serious work of the expansion and exploitation of capital. But we must, as Apple has insisted, draw the line about our intervention somewhere. My fear is that the assumption that power/capital is forever 'coming down from high' may destine us and our work to 'critique' and, in instance, keep us from getting our hands dirty. There is a haven in that critique. Just as there is haven in yet more deconstructive readings of every text under the sun. This is understandable in the US and UK, where critical action, where the socially critical work of feminists, people of colour and others has been boxed out of mainstream government systems at all levels. But in some Australian, New Zealand and other contexts, we have been faced with a different situation: we have been invited into the kitchen, invited in to get our hands dirty.

At times it has been paradoxical, almost humorous if the stakes weren't so high: as ironic as if Xerox asked Paulo Freire to write a basal-reading series, or where ranking Australian femocrats have taken leadership of equity units consisting of predominantly white males (which has happened), or if the South African Defence Forces recognized Nelson Mandala as their commander in chief (which they just have done). At other times, it has enabled significant intervention. Even the most angry critics of Labour's embrace of human capital and economic rationalism would have to admit that it has created a very different set of policy priorities and practices in education than human-capital agendas in the UK and US. The schooling of girls and women, commitment to critical citizenship, multiculturalism and multilingualism, issues of Aboriginal conciliation, and critical social literacy remain key nodal points in the agenda of Australian public education. They continue to turn up in both expected and unexpected forms — from 'equity performance indicators' in university 'quality audits' to targeted national priority areas for the Australian Research Council, from 'performance benchmarks' for public housing and health to guidelines for national curriculum. They may be grubby, they may be repressively tolerated, and they may be embedded within economic rationalist discourses — but they remain there as points for coalition and intervention.

I have here tried to present but one example where my colleagues and I drew the line differently. If I had followed a strict political economy argument, I would never have taken up the task. For me at least, it was in part a pragmatic politics in postmodern conditions that enabled us to position and identify ourselves as 'outsiders' to the discourses we were to reconstruct; it enabled us to see our task as principally one of rewriting texts and identities; it focused us on the need to anticipate and use the diverse and idiosyncratic local uses and 'readings' of our curriculum documents in community adult-education programmes and on shop floors; and it enabled us to rationalize and maintain (to this day) loose, practical coalitions with government and other agencies that we might have some fundamental disagreements with.

If modernist politics is conceived of as some kind of engagement with truth and the State, alternately heroic and tragic — provisional politics is about making it up as we go along, about shifting levels and subjects, about local effects of centralized edicts and policies, about pragmatic and contingent decisions, about getting our hands dirty, all the while committed to taking up issues of hybridity and marginality, economic exclusion and political disen-franchisement, but without clearcut, unambiguous normative benchmarks.[3]

You may interpret this as a rationalization of my own academic, educational and career decisions. No doubt it is. But I suspect that there are countless others involved in similar pragmatic decisions in staffrooms, classrooms, government, union and corporate offices each day — engaged in telling the boss what *he* wants to hear and then trying to do what's politically significant for particular voiceless and marginalized constituencies. For many, it isn't a matter of 'forgetting' our political economy, or even 'a willing suspension of disbelief'. It is a matter of seeing politics and political work differently, in terms of a materialist politics of discourse rather than raw analytic truths, in terms of provisional coalitions to meet the pragmatic needs of particular marginal groups, rather than essential alliances and solidarities. This needn't require that we forget about cultural capital and official knowledge. In fact, it may be one of the most viable ways of actually changing how they are shaped and distributed.

Notes

1 See Ladwig's discussion of 'nomadic intellectuals' in this volume.
2 Tony Wilden's (1982) commentary on levels and framings sets the grounds for a pragmatic materialist politics of strategy and tactics. Wilden argues that it is, quite simply, losing political tactics to respond habitually on the same level to particular adversarial communications and forms of domination. The strategic move, he argues, is to shift levels of intervention and to 'reframe' or 'repunctuate' messages at other levels or contexts of communication.
3 Thanks to Bill Cope, Mary Kalantzis, Jim Ladwig, Carmen Luke, Rob McCormack, Martin Nakata, Michael Garbutcheon Singh and Parlo Singh for debate, if not always agreement, on the issues here.

References

APPLE, M.W. (1993a) *Official Knowledge*, London, Routledge.
APPLE, M.W. (1993b) 'What Post-modernists forget: Cultural capital and official knowl-edge', *Curriculum Studies* 1, 3, pp. 301–16.

CASTLES, S., KALANTZIS, M., COPE, W. and MORRISSEY, M. (1992) *Mistaken Identity: Multiculturalism and the Demise of Nationalism in Australia*, 3rd ed, Sydney, Pluto Press.

COPE, W., KALANTZIS, M., LO BIANCO, J., LUKE, A. and SINGH, M.G. (1994) *Cultural Understanding: The Eighth Key Competency*, Brisbane, Queensland Department of Education.

COPE, W., KALANTZIS, M., LUKE, A., McCORMACK, R., MORGAN, R., SOLOMON, N. and VEEL, N. (1993) *National Framework for Adult English Language, Literacy and Numeracy*, Melbourne/Canberra: Australian Council for Training Curriculum and the Department of Employment, Education and Training.

GREEN, W., HODGENS, J. and LUKE, A. (1994) *Debating Literacy: A Documentary History of Literacy Crises in Australia, 1945–1990*, Sydney, Australian Literacy Federation.

HALL, S. (1993) 'Culture, community, nation', *Cultural Studies* 7, 3, pp. 349–65.

LINGARD, R., KNIGHT, J. and PORTER, P. (1993) *Schooling Reform in Hard Times*, London, Falmer Press.

LUKE, A. (1989) 'Open and closed texts: The semantic/ideological analysis of textbook narratives', *Journal of Pragmatics*, 13, pp. 53–80.

LUKE, A. (in press/1994) 'Genres of power? Literacy education and the production of capital', in HASAN, R. and WILLIAMS, G. (Eds) *Literacy in Society*, London, Longmans.

MOUFFE, C. (1993) *The Return of the Political*, London, Verso.

PUSEY, M. (1992) *Economic Rationalism in Canberra*, Melbourne, Cambridge University Press.

SINGH, P. (1994) 'Generating literacies of difference from the "Belly of the Beast"', *Australian Journal of Language and Literacy*, 16, 2.

WILDEN, A. (1982) *System and Structure: Essays in Communication and Exchange*, 2nd ed., London, Tavistock.

YEATMAN, A. (1990) *Bureaucrats, Technocrats, Femocrats*, Sydney, Allen and Unwin.

YEATMAN, A. (1993) *Postmodern Revisionings of the Political*, London, Routledge.

6 Foucault's Poststructuralism and Observational Education Research: A Study of Power Relations[1]

Jennifer M. Gore

> . . . And in school it was power, and power alone that mattered.
> D.H. Lawrence, *The Rainbow*

While I would not go as far as Lawrence in characterizing the importance of power in schooling, this chapter is premised on the view that power matters. Specifically, I am interested in the functioning of power in the pedagogical activities of teachers and students. The pervasiveness of power is not in question here. In literature, in film and television, in newspapers and other popular cultural forms, in the stories people tell, schooling is frequently associated with power. Moreover, educational researchers have addressed power from a wide range of theoretical and methodological perspectives. Briefly, I categorize these perspectives as:

- technical — seeking techniques to ensure a 'correct' balance between teacher and student power;
- organizational — seeking to understand the functioning of power at the level of the bureaucratic institution;
- ideological — seeking to reveal, through ideology critique, the capitalist, patriarchal, racist practices and effects of schooling and to provide visions of alternative pedagogies aimed at transforming classroom and societal power relations; and
- empowering — seeking to shift the balance of power in educational systems and institutions.

It is not within the scope of this chapter to provide a review of these various approaches. However, I want to suggest that the perspective taken in my own study of power and pedagogy builds on, but also implies a vigorous critique of, each of these earlier approaches.

My approach to power and pedagogy involves a systematic multisite study of the micro-level functioning of power relations. This approach potentially offers a more complex understanding of classrooms than earlier approaches and, subsequently, provides a more delineated mapping of possible sites of intervention in schooling policy and practice. In framing this study, some of the theoretical insights of Michel Foucault on power relations are central. In what follows, I provide an overview of the study in which I am engaged, details of aspects of the methodology, and a reflexive comment on the use of Foucauldian theory for this kind of observational education research.

Foucault and Power Relations

For the purposes of my study, Foucault's linking of what he calls 'modern disciplinary power' or 'bio-power' with modern institutions is particularly salient. Unlike the sovereign power of earlier periods, Foucault (1980) elaborates the invisibility and pervasiveness of power in modern society: 'The eighteenth century invented, so to speak, a synaptic regime of power, a regime of its exercise *within* the social body rather than *from* above it' (p. 39). The key features of this form of power are:

- power is productive and not solely repressive;
- power circulates rather than being possessed;
- power exists in action;
- power functions at the level of the body; and
- often, power operates through technologies of self.

This conception of power suggests a very different level of analysis than is evident in other approaches to power and pedagogy. As Foucault (1980) said:

> In thinking of the mechanisms of power, I am thinking rather of its capillary form of existence, the point where power reaches into the very grain of individuals, touches their bodies and inserts itself into their action and attitudes, their discourses, learning processes and everyday lives. (Foucault, 1980, p. 39)

According to Foucault, 'disciplinary power' emerged with the advent of modern institutions. Mass schooling, as one such institution, can be seen to operate in ways that demand individuals' participation in their own subjection (Jones and Williamson, 1979; Walkerdine, 1986; Meredyth and Tyler, 1993), that demand self-disciplining for both students and teachers (King, 1990). Foucault illustrates this argument with Bentham's Panopticon, an architectural structure designed such that inmates, unable to detect surveillance, regulate themselves. At the same time, the supervisors in the Panopticon are subject to surveillance by their superiors. Donnelly (1992) criticizes Foucault for generalizing the notion of panopticism to the functioning of all modern institutions, and emptying it of specific context. I believe Foucault was more cautious than Donnelly suggests. Nevertheless, it is true that, with only a brief genealogical analysis of some schooling documents, Foucault (1977) declares: 'a relation of surveillance, defined and regulated, is inscribed at the heart of the practice of teaching, not as an additional or adjacent part, but as a mechanism that is inherent to it and which increases its efficiency' (p. 176). In my study, specific practices (like surveillance) which construct pedagogical relations in various sites are the primary point of inquiry. As such, I aim to put Foucault's generalized (1984) claims about disciplinary power 'to the test of reality, of contemporary reality' (p. 46), within the specific context of pedagogical practice.

In Foucault's account of disciplinary power, his departure from many earlier analyses of power and schooling crystallizes. He explicitly characterizes a relation of surveillance as productive for pedagogy, a view which is in stark contrast with traditional conceptions of power which equate power with horror 'so that the less horror there is the less power there must be, and the more power there is the more horror there must be' (Cocks, 1989, p. 5). Such traditional approaches tend to focus on those individuals and groups which hold power. Replacing a concern with the subjects of power, my study mirrors Foucault's concern with the *mechanisms* of schooling. Put another way, rather than begin with questions of who holds power or even who exercises power, I begin with the question, 'What specific practices actualize relations of power in pedagogy?'

In short, then, the aim of this study is to employ the theoretical lens provided by Foucault's account of power in investigating the functioning of power in various pedagogical sites. Some commentators have criticized Foucault's pervasive conception of power, worried that if power is everywhere it cannot be identified or pinpointed. Of particular concern to such critics have been the political implications of Foucault's conception of power. My own project would be futile if I did not believe that power or, more accurately, power relations could be identified. If power relations operate at the level of the body, and exist in action, then they should be observable in the micro-level practices of pedagogical events. As Foucault (1977) said of the body, 'power relations have an immediate hold upon it; they invest it, mark it, train it, torture it, force it to carry out tasks, to perform ceremonies, to emit signs' (p. 24). Not only is this empirical study conceived on the possibility of observing power relations but it is premised on actual observation. Moreover, as I intend to show in a preliminary way, this study demonstrates that the circulation of power, its capillary nature, does not deny the existence of patterns and structures in the functioning of power, and so does not evade politics.

Outline of the Study

The central task of this study is a mapping of practices of power in pedagogy. To my knowledge, few other researchers have begun to systematically examine the minute practices of classrooms, examining the bodily effects of power in pedagogy.[2] Of fundamental importance to my approach is demonstrating, rather than only asserting, disciplinary power. To the extent that mapping practices of power might reveal 'spaces of freedom', illuminating that which causes us to be what we are in educational institutions, I take this is a worthwhile task. For such a task, the choice of sites for investigation would not matter providing the study is not limited to a single site, that is, providing there is some variation.

However, given other interests which underlie this study, sites were selected for particular theoretical purposes. First, this study builds on earlier work in which I explored critical and feminist pedagogy discourses as regimes of truth (Gore, 1993). Although these discourses claim alternative pedagogies characterized, in part, by more democratic relations between teachers and students than found in more traditional classrooms, my analysis of literature in these areas showed that whatever was unique about critical pedagogy or feminist pedagogy did not appear to lie in different instructional practices. Second, given Foucault's thesis on the institutionalization of modern disciplinary power, I have also speculated that it is this institutionalization within education which gives pedagogy a consistent character, despite claims to alternative pedagogies.

Hence, the study is designed to include both 'radical' and 'mainstream' sites, in order to further examine my view that whatever is different about radical pedagogy discourses does not lie in the enactment of pedagogy. The study is also designed to include non-institutionalized sites — sites where pedagogy is not enacted within a school or university (or related institution) — in order to test the 'hypothesis' (understood in its broad sense) that the institutionalization of pedagogy accounts for its specific character and for continuities across sites. This design enables the following additional research questions to be addressed: Do power relations function differently in radical and mainstream classrooms? Do power relations function differently in institutionalized and non-institutionalized sites? If there are differences along these dimensions, different patterns in the functioning of power should be observable (since power exists in action). A finding of no differences would be consistent with the alternative thesis that such practices of power are constitutive of pedagogy as a modernist enterprise.

The specific sites located for the study were:

- Physical Education classes (PE), where the explicit focus includes direct concern for, and manipulation of, bodies (*Mainstream* institutionalized);
- Teacher Education (TE) where the explicit course agenda includes critically discussing dilemmas and tensions underlying the institutional practices of schooling (*Radical* institutionalized);
- a Women's Discussion Group (WG), where no explicit political agenda is apparent (*Mainstream non*-institutionalized);

- a Feminist Reading Group (FEM), in which feminists meet specifically to address feminist texts (broadly defined) and issues (*Radical non-institutionalized*).

Approximately six months were spent in each site, with my research assistants and I collecting data at most meetings of the particular group during that time period. The following figure summarizes these sites according to the theoretically relevant dimensions outlined above:

	Mainstream	Radical
Institutionalized	PE	TE
Non-institutionalized	WG	FEM

Figure 6.1: Research sites

While claims to generalizability are necessarily limited with the selection of single sites in each cell of this matrix, and (in most cases) single groups within each site, intentionally sampling for theoretically relevant diversity through a multisite design should increase the broad descriptive validity of findings (Firestone, 1993; Maxwell, 1993).

Despite Foucault's essay on the study of power ('The Subject and Power', 1983), he did not specify in practical detail how researchers might go about examining power relations. The methodology for this study, therefore, had to be invented. As one step toward that endeavour, a careful reading of Foucault's writing on the subject of power relations (especially *Discipline and Punish*, 1977) was completed as a basis for developing a coding system which would facilitate data collection and analysis. A number of specific practices involved in the functioning of power relations — namely, surveillance, normalization, exclusion, distribution, classification, individualization, totalization, and regulation — were identified as associated with Foucault's account of modern disciplinary power. Additionally, Foucault emphasized the functioning of time and space in actualizing power relations, the linking of power relations with knowledge, and the exercise of power in relation to oneself. Coding categories were developed to characterize each of these moments in the pedagogical sites under observation. Pilot data were used to refine working definitions of these practices and develop a coding scheme (see Figure 6.2). My research assistants and I spent approximately six months achieving fairly high levels of inter-rater agreement in order to be able to use the data in quasi-quantitative ways.

As with all categorizations, this coding scheme imposes an epistemological break with the events observed. Such a break is consistent with the theoretical concerns of the project and an integral part of much scientific endeavour. I should emphasize that the study is not an ethnography in which the aim is

- Surveillance: Supervising, closely observing, watching, threatening to watch, avoiding being watched
- Normalization: Invoking, requiring, setting or conforming to a standard, defining the normal
- Exclusion: Tracing the limits that will define difference, boundary, zone, defining the pathological
- Distribution: Dividing into parts, arranging, ranking bodies in space
- Classification: Differentiating individuals and/or groups from one another
- Individualization: Giving individual character to, specifying an individual
- Totalization: Giving collective character to, specifying a collectivity/total, will to conform
- Regulation: Controlling by rule, subject to restrictions; adapt to requirements; act of invoking a rule, including sanction, reward, punishment
- Space: Setting up enclosures, partitioning, creating functional sites
- Time: Establishing duration, requiring repetition, etc.
- Knowledge: Controlling, regulating, invoking knowledge
- Self(/r/t/s): Techniques/practices directed at the self by researcher, teacher or student

Figure 6.2: Primary coding categories

to give the accounts of participants in the various sites. Rather, like Foucault's own studies, this project seeks to illuminate the *mechanisms* of schooling and mechanisms of disciplining, enumerating and cataloguing its practices, trying to represent the complexity and contingency of schooling.

Given the complexity of the coding categories, and the level of interpretation required in applying these constructs to specific classroom events, it was clear that reliable observational scales would be impractical. Hence, in fairly typical qualitative mode, I decided to begin data preparation with detailed descriptions of classroom events. Such detailed descriptions were also desirable in order to enable other analyses of the data. These detailed descriptions were completed, wherever and whenever possible, by two observers noting not only what was said but also what various participants did. When two observers were present, one focused on the main classroom activity (e.g., primary speakers and activities) while the other focused on secondary events (e.g., students not involved in primary discussions). In each site, an audiorecorder was also used to provide an additional source of data. The relatively small size of the women's group and feminist group made two observers too intrusive, so data collection was restricted to one observer and audiorecording. Given the multiplicity and complexity of classroom events, no claims are made to have comprehensively recorded any session even with these measures. Indeed, the theoretical concerns of the project neither depend on *full* accounts nor deem such accounts possible. Instead, as Bourdieu *et al.* (1991) say, I 'renounce the impossible ambition of saying everything about everything, in the right order' (p. 10). The aim of data collection in this project was to construct detailed accounts of 'visible' and 'articulable' (Deleuze, 1988) events in each site, where the visible refers to what is seen, with both form (e.g., 'school') and substance (e.g., 'students'), and the articulable refers to what is said, with its own form (e.g., 'education') and substance (e.g., 'ignorance'). Semi-structured interviews were also conducted to address a number of issues beyond those informed by the observational processes.

Field notes, session transcripts and interview transcripts were coded using the categories outlined above and entered using *Ethnograph* computer software. The following example illustrates this coding process.

An Illustration

The following extract from a Year 11 physical education class combines my field notes and the lesson transcript.[3] I begin this illustration by demonstrating the coding process, using the primary set of categories developed for the study, and then broaden the focus to the dimensions of disciplinary power Foucault outlines and to patterns evident.

The teacher is writing notes on the board which the students are to copy in their books. As usual most of the students are copying the notes and chatting about various other things.

1 Teacher says 'Right-o. This is about to go guys' (gesturing to the writing she has done on one half of the board).
space, time, totalization

2 The students make noises of protest. 'No.' 'No.' 'No, it's not.'
exclusion

3 The teacher replies 'If you can't stop talking and do your work, why should I wait?'
normalization, totalization, time

4 She gestures to another section of the board which has some writing from another teacher and says 'I'm not sure if he wants this left.'

5 Natalie says 'Oh, who cares?'

6 Teacher replies 'I do.'
normalization, self/t, individualization, space, exclusion

7 As the teacher keeps writing, Nat says to her: 'Hang about.'

8 Annaliese adds 'Just hang ten, baby.'

9 Zac follows with 'Just mellow out, Miss [and, in a soothing voice] let the blood flow to your fingers.'
individualization, normalization, time

10 The teacher keeps writing and announces 'As soon as I get to the bottom of here [gesturing to the side of the board she's writing on], this comes off' (the other side).
regulation, time

11 A student says 'Hey, Miss, what do ya think about Michael Jackson, eh?' (Jackson has just been accused of child abuse)
12 The teacher converses with the students about this for a few minutes, taking time away from her writing.
13 The discussion shifts to Brooke Shields and her pictures in *Inside Sport* magazine.
    individualization, knowledge

14 As they keep talking, the teacher rubs off the first section of the board.
15 Some of the students scream 'Aaaahhh!' 'Aaaaahhhh!' 'Mi-isss!'. These screams are followed immediately by laughter.
16 The teacher says 'I told you.'
    exclusion, normalization

17 Madeleine says 'Miss, we can't exactly write if you stand in front.'
    exclusion, distribution, space, totalization

18 She replies 'I was over here.' There is quite a lot of noise in the room so she repeats more loudly 'I was over here. You had full vision.' Even so, she stands much farther to the side as she continues writing.
    self/t

19 Madeleine announces 'I'm not writing.' She turns around to Ted and does not write for the rest of the period.
    individualization, exclusion, self/s

20 Jerry, drawing on the material they've recently learned in this class, says 'She's a fast twitch person.'
21 Some chuckles are heard. I can't see the teacher's face, as her back is to me.
    classification, knowledge, individualization

22 Zac asks her 'Have you been to see the school counsellor, yet?'
23 The teacher says, perhaps jokingly, that she will make an appointment tomorrow.
    individualization, exclusion, time

24 Jerry says 'Miss, can you stop for a sec?' She says 'No.' He adds 'Helen wants you.'
    time, individualization

25 Helen, who is sitting beside Jerry, says 'Oh, Jerry, you lying bugger!'
    exclusion

26 Zac continues the struggle over the quantity of notes the students have to copy 'I can't see the blackboard' (but he makes a face suggesting that he is making this up).
    space, individualization

27 Tom asks 'When are you going to start getting us out of class, Jenny?'

This was in reference to the interviews I was planning with the students. I said I wasn't sure yet and turned my attention to the teacher, trying to avoid being drawn into conversation.
individualization, time, totalization, space, self/r

28 A few minutes later, a girl says 'Miss, slow down, the bell's going to go soon.'
29 She continues writing.
time, individualization, normalization, exclusion

30 Then Jerry finds success 'Miss, what's the third word in the fourth line?'
31 The teacher turns, steps back from the board and replies 'gaseous'.
32 'No', says Jerry, 'the one under'.
33 The teacher tries again 'gases'.
34 Jerry says 'No', again.
35 The teacher reads the whole sentence 'Gases diffuse along concentration gradients also called pressure gradients.'
36 Jerry is laughing. It appears he wasn't after word clarification at all, but trying to achieve the slowing of the teacher.
knowledge, individualization

37 She returns to writing.
38 A student announces 'She's suffering from stress.'
classification, individualization

39 A few moments later, Remus says 'The bell's going, Miss, so go easy, eh?'
time, normalization, individualization

40 She finishes the section.
41 When the bell goes a couple of minutes later, most students leave the room immediately, although a couple remain to finish the notes.

42 Tom, trying to finish, says in an exasperated tone to Nat, now standing at the front of the room, 'Can you move please!'
space, individualization, exclusion, self/s

This extract, selected at random from the mass of data collected, employs most of the specific categories within the coding system at least once. In itself, the use of these codes in this brief example highlights the extent to which the categories have proven useful and relevant for analysing pedagogical data. The process of coding reproduced here also demonstrates the co-incidence of various specific practices of power, and the rapidity with which 'exercises of power' occur, thus highlighting Foucault's view that power relations, actions upon other actions, are simultaneously local, unstable, and diffuse, not emanating from a central point but at each moment moving from one point to another in a field of forces (Deleuze, 1988).

More specifically, of the codes used, individualization (fourteen times) occurred most often. In comparison to explicit regulation (1) we see that, in this episode, power relations were enacted through the more subtle techniques to exclusion (9) and normalization (6). Time (9) and space (6) were more often the explicit focus of the classroom action than was knowledge (3). These comparisons point to potentially interesting claims about schooling that will be verified by analysis of the entire data set for each site rather than specific episodes like this one.

Hence, the coded data sets are undergoing analysis for the prevalence of particular practices of power (the proportion of surveillance, classification, etc., in each site), the direction of exercises of power (teacher to student, student to student, student to teacher), the substance of the exclusion, normalization, and so on, (what was the object of the normalization? How was it carried out? what reactions were discernible? etc.) and other patterns. Such patterns emerging from these analyses will be the focus of a later chapter.

Evidence of Disciplinary Power

With reference to the illustration above, and in relation to the particular dimensions of disciplinary power outlined at the beginning of this chapter, there is certainly evidence of power relations functioning in the ways Foucault suggests. Lesson events show evidence of the circulation of power relations among the students (24, 25, 42), between the teacher and students (1–3, 5–9, 14–18, 22–24, 26, 28–29, 30–36, 39–40), and between teachers (4–6).

Power relations, in this account, are both productive and repressive. For example, they produce laughter (15, 21 36). With Jerry's reference to fast twitch muscle fibres (20), there is also (even!) evidence of knowledge produced in earlier lessons. In a sense, he uses against the teacher the very knowledge she has 'given' him. Furthermore, the informality and familiarity evident in this passage show the classroom to be other than a repressive 'prison-like' institution — e.g., in the suggestions that the teacher 'mellow out' and deal with her stress (7–9, 22–23, 38) and in the tangential discussions (11–13).

Power relations, in this example, clearly operate upon the bodies of teachers and students — e.g., the position of the teacher (17–18, 19), and later Natalie (42), attempting to stop or slow the teacher's writing on the board (15, 17, 24, 26, 28, 30–36, 39), Madeleine's putting down of her pen with her decision to stop copying the notes from the board (19).

Some of these practices of power can be seen as technologies of self — e.g., the teacher's concern not to upset another teacher by erasing his work (4–6), the teacher standing to the side to maximize student visibility of her notes (18), Madeleine's announced decision to cease writing (19), Jerry's clever use of student norms to engage the teacher (30–36), the teacher interrupting her writing to address Jerry's question (31–35), Tom's decision to remain after the bell to complete his notes (42), my own avoidance of contributing to disrupting the lesson (27).

Interestingly, the greatest success the students have in their endeavour to slow the teacher comes when a student provokes the teacher to more fully execute her task *qua* teacher — that is, to assist with his learning by clarifying her writing on the board (30–36). When students complained that they couldn't see or that the bell would go, the teacher was largely unresponsive, but when a student indicated a concern with completing the task itself, the teacher was incited to shift her own focus. The other fairly obvious ploys to *get out of* work did not have the same 'power' as did an apparent attempt to *do* the work. From this example, it seems that perceptions of what teachers and students do, or are supposed to do, influence power relations in the classroom. Put another way, it will be interesting to analyse the data for ways in which discourses on schooling and on teachers and students support power relations.

Patterns in the Circulation of Power

Power circulates in this classroom but the exercise of power is certainly not equal for all participants. The main action arises from the teacher's attempts to have the students complete a task she has set. The exercises of power by students are primarily reactive to this task. According to Deleuze (1988),

> To incite, provoke and produce (or any term drawn from analogous lists) constitute active affects, while to be incited or provoked, to be induced to produce, to have a 'useful' effect, constitute reactive affects. The latter are not simply the 'repercussion' or 'passive side' of the former but are rather 'the irreducible encounter' between the two, especially if we believe that the force affected has a certain capacity for resistance. At the same time, each force has the power to affect (others) and to be affected (by others again), such that each force implies power relations: and every field of forces distributes forces according to these relations and their variations. (Deleuze, 1988, p. 71)

Most exercises of power in the illustration occur between teacher and students, rather than, for instance, between particular students, although there are instances of such power relations.

These patterns in the data (of teacher as more active and students more reactive, and of most exercises of power being between teachers and students) are suggestive of the structured circulation of power relations and point to more political analyses than some scholars have thought possible with a Foucauldian approach. That is, as these data illustrate, Foucault's notions of power as circulating, existing in action, and not necessarily repressive, do not violate traditional understandings of power vested in the position of the teacher. As illustrated, exercises of power by the teacher in this example *were* of a different order than exercises of power by the students. What this Foucauldian approach adds to current dominant understandings of power in pedagogy is the micro-level detail of how power is exercised and of specific ways in which the power relations of classrooms are not all embracing but, at least at specific moments, are escapable. By extension, this analysis should be able to pinpoint practices in the power relations of pedagogy that need not be as they are. Such patterns in the data will be explored at length in the ongoing analysis.

Other Dimensions of the Study

In order to produce more finely textured and contextualized accounts of power relations than are possible with the reduction that occurs in categorization, the data are also being examined for themes and patterns in more grounded ways, typical of qualitative studies. Categories which have emerged from this analysis are as follows:

• Explicit power:	Explicit discussions of, or references to, power–power relations and authorities (textual, institutional, embodied)
• Explicit bodies:	Explicit discussions of, or references to, bodies (including e.g., bodily functions, body types, bodily control)
• Specific regimes:	The invocation of a specific power-knowledge nexus or discourse (e.g., professionalism, fairness, separatism vs femocrat, denouncing the abuse of alcohol)
• Specific rituals:	The enacting of a specific ritual (pertaining to group or social norms) (including e.g., pouring tea/ champagne, designating responsibilities, handing out tests, using journals)
• Power techniques:	Powerful/ engaging/ interesting stories/ descriptions of power relations exercised in the various sites (accepting that so much of the data is about power, this code is used simply to highlight mechanisms/ devices/ practices of power — e.g., the look, silence — and their consequences)
• Bodies disciplined:	Powerful/ engaging/ interesting accounts that involve bodies
• Transgressions:	Disruptions, transgressions (including inversions), pleasures, (e.g., jokes)
• Identity/positioning/being:	Self or other references to particular subjectivities and ways of being (e.g., experience, epistemic privilege, credentials, self-deprecation, social-group identity)
• Teacher–student differentiation:	Specific events/ accounts/ practices which differentiate teachers and students from each other
• Teacher–student integration:	Specific events/ accounts/ practices which integrate teachers and students with each other
• Researcher:	Any interaction between researcher and teacher/s or student/s
• Power dynamics:	Invoked or enacted (e.g., if reference is made to masculinity or sexism, or if behaviour might be interpreted as enacting masculinity or sexism). Specific dynamics coded are: gender, race, ethnicity, class, sexuality, religion, language, disability, age

Figure 6.3: Secondary coding categories

With all of these treatments of the data, the scope of this project is clearly much larger than this paper can convey. Some aspects of the study which I am, or will be, pursuing include:

- continuities across sites and time;
- dominant discourses of schooling;
- the disciplining of student and teacher bodies;
- the disciplining of male and female bodies, (and others by social group);
- the specific nature of bodily disciplining;
- points of possible intervention in pedagogy;
- a theory of pedagogy (through the examination of practices which may be constitutive of pedagogy); and
- a critique of Foucault's analysis of power.

Conclusion

In this chapter, I have provided an overview of my study on power relations in pedagogy, outlining key theoretical and methodological considerations and providing one small example of methodological technique. Focusing on that aspect of the methodology involving the first coding system, I have demonstrated one way in which Foucault's analysis of power relations can be used to examine and support so-called empirical research in education. To the extent that the coding system adds to the methodological tools available to researchers using poststructural theories to investigate power relations, I trust this chapter makes a contribution. Should others find the ideas and techniques reported here to be useful or even stimulating, I shall be pleased. Certainly, I offer this, at this embryonic stage of the overall research endeavour, in the hope of stimulating dialogue with others who share related theoretical or methodological interests.

As I have argued about pedagogical practices (Gore, 1993), I would also argue that specific research techniques are in themselves neither liberatory nor oppressive, structural nor poststructural, modern nor postmodern. While I am employing conventional *techniques* in this study, the poststructuralism of the *methodology* should be judged by the theoretical questions posed, the analyses conducted, and the reports written. What may look here like a possible 'taming' of Foucault, is only a temporary moment in what I hope will be a creative and exciting application of his work to the context of schooling. For many scholars, Foucault's work has enabled or prompted a great deal of theorizing in making sense of his often fragmented, sometimes inconsistent work and in relating his work to other major theoretical and political positions. The vast intellectual labour which has gone into such processes is indicative, I argue, of the fact that Foucault's work is in need of some taming if it is to be applied to contemporary social and institutional practice. Thus, my own approach, signalled in the part of the research agenda outlined here, is to begin my own theorizing, in the specific context in which I work, by employing Foucauldian theory in a reconsideration or 're-assembling' of what we are today (in our institutionally located work) in education.

Notes

1 I am grateful to the Australian Research Council for the funding which has supported this project.
2 Reid, J. *et al.*, are working on a project on the construction of the schoolgirl but, to my knowledge, their work is yet to be published.
3 Each small episode is numbered to facilitate reference to particular incidents in the ensuing discussion. Pseudonyms, selected by the students, are used throughout.

References

BOURDIEU, P., CHAMBOREDON, J.-C., and PASSERON, J.-C. (1991) *The Craft of Sociology: Epistemological Preliminaries*, Berlin, New York, De Gruyter.

COCKS, J. (1989) *The Oppositional Imagination: Feminism, Critique and Political Theory*, London and New York, Routledge.

DELEUZE, G. (1988) *Foucault*, Minneapolis, University of Minnesota Press.

DONNELLY, M. (1992) 'On Foucault's uses of the notion of "Biopower"', in ARMSTRONG T.J. (Tr.) *Michel Foucault Philosopher*, New York, Harvester Wheatsheaf, pp. 199–203.

FIRESTONE, W.A. (1993) 'Alternative arguments for generalizing from data as applied to qualitative research', *Educational Researcher*, 22, 4, pp. 16–23.

FOUCAULT, M. (1977) *Discipline and Punish: The Birth of the Prison*, New York, Pantheon Books.

FOUCAULT, M. (1980) 'Prison Talk', in GORDON, C. (Ed) *Power/Knowledge: Selected Interviews and Other Writings 1972–1977*, New York, Pantheon Books, pp. 37–54.

FOUCAULT, M. (1983) 'The subject and power', in DREYFUS, H.L. and RABINOW, P. (Eds) *Michel Foucault: Beyond Structuralism and Hermeneutics*, 2nd. ed. Chicago, University of Chicago Press, pp. 208–26.

FOUCAULT, M. (1984) 'What is enlightenment?', in RABINOW, P. (Ed) *The Foucault Reader*, New York, Pantheon Books, pp. 32–50.

GORE, J.M. (1993) *The Struggle for Pedagogies: Critical and Feminist Discourses as Regimes of Truth*, New York and London, Routledge.

JONES, K. and WILLIAMSON, K. (1979) 'The birth of the schoolroom: A study of the transformation in the discursive conditions of English popular education in the first-half of the nineteenth century,' *Ideology and Consciousness*, 5, 19, pp. 59–110.

KING, M.B. (1990) 'Disciplining Teachers,' Paper presented at the Annual Meeting of the American Educational Research Association, Boston, Massachusetts.

LAWRENCE, D.H. (1915) *The Rainbow*, London, Heinemann.

MAXWELL, J.A. (1993) 'Understanding and validity in qualitative research', *Harvard Educational Review*, 62, 3, pp. 279–300.

MEREDYTH, D. and TYLER, D. (Eds) (1993) *Child and Citizen: Genealogies of Schooling and Subjectivity*, Griffith University, Institute of Cultural and Policy Studies.

WALKERDINE, V. (1986) 'Progressive pedagogy and political struggle', *Screen*, 27, 5, pp. 54–60.

7 Keeping an Untidy House: A Disjointed Paper About Academic Space, Work and Bodies

Wendy Morgan and Erica McWilliam

Pre-positions and Pro-positions

Erica: For my European grandmother's generation, untidiness ranked with tardiness or sloth as qualities most unbecoming a woman. To be a middle-class woman was to aspire to being a lady, and to be a lady was to tidy away the unsightly and unsavoury, the embarrassingly biological, the socially unpardonable. From bodily functions to living spaces, women worked like euphemisms, covering over multitudes of unmentionables with damasks of decency.

While first-wave feminists railed against the housekeeper/concubine syndrome, it is ironical that an obsession with tidiness was maintained metaphorically in the feminist writing of the 1970s and 1980s. This is evident in the way in which the collective feminist 'we' works in feminist texts to tidy the body of liberationist thought so that any rude ideological bits are not allowed to protrude. Whatever solidarity or sense of unity was intended by the feminist 'we', however timely it proved to be historically, and however much the intention was to move away from the traditional locations of women's work, the insistence on 'we' has left a problematic legacy of housekeeping duties for women in academe. These duties must be taken up alongside the necessary work of feminist advocacy. The urgency of adopting 'pro-positions' about social justice has not diminished, despite the more subtle shifts in the language of backlash politics that can make social injustice issues less apparent.

Wendy: From your talk of 'pro-positions' I want to move to 'pre-positions'. From my grandmother I learned the precedents about precedence — about who cedes pride of place to another, through doors or at table. No unladylike jostling, please. You and I from our academic fathers have more recently learned to concern ourselves about other priorities: in writing a jointly authored paper, for instance, about whose patronym will precede *et al.*, in the title and will therefore be an item in another form of housekeeping: checking the larder shelves of citation lists. In these days when tenure becomes less tenable for so many (women) academics — they have no holding space for a breather — this textual practice has material effects. (Readers may imagine for themselves the unprecedented manner in which you, Erica, and I decided on the order of our names which authorize this chapter.)

But claiming the space to draw breath and speak for oneself, or for our two selves, or for 'us' more generally — I, me, you, we, Erica, Wendy, us — these are ways you and I identify ourselves as distinct from, and also related to, one another. Like any terms, these pro-nominals are signifiers that give us positions within a world constituted by a language through its systematic organization of differences. Those categories could create a 'prison-house' of language — to appropriate for a different use Jameson's term (1974). But since words as signifiers are stand-ins, metaphors, they can work as definitive, categorical terms only by denying the untidy slopping over of meanings. We (who?) need those terms to think with; and we need to be suspicious of any single or unified identity they appear to box us into.

Perhaps being 'in the dog box' for so long has taken its intellectual toll. Certainly an obsession with where women are located in academic spaces continues to dog feminist texts. As authors, you and I are persisting with this theme, insisting on its fertility for feminist work but resisting its neatness and its potential for the conflation of differences. It's time to 'come clean' about the importance of *un*tidiness. But beyond untidiness, 'keeping a(n untidy) house' has much to recommend it as a metaphor for contemporary feminist writing because of what it suggests about being transgressive, about the importance of 'negotiating enabling violations' (Spivak, 1989) in orthodox academic spaces.

Allen (1992, p. 71) has drawn attention to the contradictions apparent in the metaphorical constructions of feminist theorizing — homelessness, exile and exclusion outside academe *and* imprisonment, alienation or muteness within it. She mentions the metaphor of the 'sleepout syndrome', particularly pertinent to Australia, where the colonial verandah was closed in as a sleep-out, to accommodate the spatial demands of a postwar household. I would want to exploit this sort of metaphorical positioning of feminist theorizing because it is both connected with, and marginal to, 'mainstream' scholastic space. Though outside the security of the residence proper, the verandah can nevertheless provide much-needed relief from the heat of the kitchen. Being 'verandahed' can mean staying fresh and cool, although it does risk being exposed to the elements. Quite rightly, the academic house has become increasingly overcrowded. Impertinently, irreverently, new bodies have moved in to occupy what were once spaces reserved for the Old White Boy's Club. With the press of disparate groups each jostling for semiotic space, the imperative should be more than a tacit acknowledgment of untidiness as appropriate to scholarship. I want to encourage it, to leave bits of feminist theoretical bric-à-brac scattered throughout the halls of academe, to give academics cause to watch where they put their theoretical feet, and, when it seems apposite, to indulge myself in the free-play possibilities of cool outside spaces.

An intriguing metaphor — though I'd query how free your play can be. You'd concede, I think, that we'd want to deconstruct the simple binarisms of freedom and constraint, play and work, in and out, hot and cool, centre and margins, as if these were always fixed. Those locations of meaning were different for me in chilly New Zealand. My foremothers sent their men outside into the workshop or shed, domains they could keep as untidy as they liked. And the women, inside, maintained an (impossibly) clear demarcation between the public terrain of the 'living' room (where no one could possibly live, it was so tidy, so plumply plush) or the 'front' room (confronting the street, an affront to comfort) and the kitchen. But we moved between those different disconnecting centres, which offered differently disconnected subject positions. So we in the academy move around in different spaces within and across whose boundaries we play. That's not your uncircumscribed free-play; though we may use our movement among those discursive positions to carry out the housework of a 'labour of re-inscription' (Kirby, 1993, p. 26).

You and I, as feminist teachers and writers, do not choose to carry out that 'labour of re-inscription' in ways that conflate what should remain differentiated in our separate pre-positioning of ourselves and our pro-positioning about others. I am a feminist, a teacher and an educational researcher. And that, I argue, is still a triple whammy in academe. As a teacher, I am aware that teaching continues to be low status as a topic of theorizing. It is the scholastic kiss of death to use the term 'teaching' in the title of any symposium or conference, signalling as it still does a meeting of 'pragmatists' as distinct from theorists. For critical theorists, talking 'pedagogically' has provided a way of not talking about teaching in any technical sense whatsoever. Technique has become the unspeakable. Moreover, as a feminist teacher, I am aware of the particular challenges to disciplinary projects that continue to characterize feminist work, and the potential for that work, in turn, to be 'ghettoized' as a subdiscipline. Thus as a feminist-teacher I am doubly sensitive to the issue of spatial location. I stand in danger (still!) of being relegated to Women's Studies and the token Gender Equity Lecture (an 'equity lecture' being an interesting example of an oxymoron).

As a researcher in education, I work in a low-status discipline, which has an unenviable record of ensuring that few 'non-academics' are direct and tangible beneficiaries of its research culture (Tripp, 1990). Further, it is a culture which is dominated by positivism, manifested in tedious and predictable doctoral theses and desperate, hopeful imitations of scientific 'method'. The strong anti-intellectual tradition among primary and high-school teachers is testimony to how this does not pay off for other educational professionals.

But you labour on, variously, in the house of academe. Like any, this metaphor of an untidy house contains — enables and constrains — our thinking. If it stands in for both our academic working activities and our work, our writing, the latter is also necessarily constituted by metaphors, as is all language.

You and I know how much we each think and write via the associative, suggestive play of metaphors. (Just look at the metaphors in our writing on these pages so far.) If we're each constructing a house of distinctive metaphors for our meanings, it may be difficult to inhabit the other's compatibly or use a home-improvement kit to reconstruct them into a semi-detached bungalow. Those metaphors we think with think us, in a way: we are figures of speech. And need therefore to scrutinize the rhetorical ploys in our own and others' tropes, their 'turns'. So we shall, in what follows, as we discuss our use of space for playing out our critique in the real (Foucault, 1981) in our lecture rooms.

Lecture-room Jesturing

a mask which points to itself (Barthes, 1972, p. 98)

Contexts and Concepts

Postmodern Pedagogies

There are a number of quite contradictory demands being made of me as a tertiary lecturer and feminist in postmodern times. These demands are distilled, at least to some extent, in the oxymoron 'postmodern lecture'. Linguistic juxtapositions have, of course, been with academics for some time. 'Student teacher' is a perennial in teacher education. The notion of giving an 'equity lecture' has dogged feminists and others for a briefer if more challenging period. Patti Lather (1989) has fingered another with which many may be familiar — the concept of 'advocacy research'. Like the pernicious 'fun run', these linguistic collisions can put a severe strain on the body of our work.

University campuses now speak more contradictions: 'greater access' and 'limited parking', 'quality teaching' and 'fast track credentialling', 'better scholarship' and 'bigger numbers'. Adding the 'postmodern lecture' to this list is almost guaranteed to bring on a dose of PMT (Post Modernist Tension) in many academics, especially those critical pedagogues who were used to an unreconstructed (uncooked?) Apple a day. I have certainly written about the frustrations of attempting to stay abreast of 'post haste' vocabularies myself (McWilliam, 1993). And I know that Foucault is still the 'f' word for many foundationalists. The accusation being increasingly made is that there has been an unnecessary and dangerous pressure on academics to be *nouveau* smart' (Storr, 1987, cited in Lather, 1989, p. 8) and that this is directly attributable to New French Theory. Whitson (1991, p. 73) draws attention to the pervasiveness of the metaphor 'babies being thrown out with bathwater' in the anti-postmodernist literature. That the baby might be *soluble* is dismissed as a slippery postmodern concept by those who seek greater certainty from their neonates.

The point Ulmer (1985b) makes is a crucial one here — that the need to rethink pedagogical practices is not the result of a particular attitude to Derrida, deconstructionism or any other figure, concept or method identified with New French Theory. Rather, as he asserts, it is the challenge made to educational discourse by revolutions in the arts (the break with Renaissance traditions of representational realism) and the development of film and television (Ulmer, 1985b, p. 38). New French Theory cannot fairly be accused of being a linguistic imperialist in a struggle for hegemony over educational discourse. Instead, such theory is a manifestation of the way texts have been 'reconstructed' as multichannelled, not monolithic, heterogeneous not homogeneous. Maxine Greene makes the point that new sign systems are appearing all around us and it is through these that human beings (young people in particular) are making new sense of their worlds. She states:

> Young people, perhaps especially, live on the surfaces, organise their lives by means of surfaces — choice, speed, chance — and the image systems that help them make sense . . . fast moving young people often wear masks, living among simulations that substitute things for other things. (Greene, 1993, p. 209)

This new cultural field and its different textuality means that students and teachers 'increasingly inhabit different conceptual worlds and participate in different information and social networks' (Green, 1993, p. 208). The challenge for educators/scholars, according to Bill Green, is to respond more appropriately to the image format as a 'new vulgate', i.e., to develop new genres that will serve the electronic era as well as the lecture/essay did in the era of the printing press.

If, as Bill Green argues (1993), postmodernity demands the *transmutation* of pedagogy in a new era of 'disorganized schooling', what might it mean for conventional pedagogical practices in the university lecture hall? What more is to be done than provide 'whizz-bang' technological resources which allow delivery to be more functional and more dazzling in terms of what it can display? Is there any other way to conceptualize the challenges of reconstructing the lecture as a postmodern event?

Pedagogically speaking, the postmodern lecture is an oxymoron because it is premised on delivery of information-as-*expertise* from the knowing one to the unknowing many. The conventional lecture is made highly problematic by a world of electronic textuality and epistemological uncertainty, in which 'authority' can be dispersed and made invisible. The problems this poses for pedagogy are, of course, not necessarily ameliorated by online education or other more 'flexible' delivery modes. It is the notion of 'delivering the goods' itself that is still being side-stepped and will remain the Achilles heel of tertiary teaching. The fact that so many lecterns (like so many alternative learning 'packages') are fixed, bolted to their foundations, on guard against decentring, says a great deal about the grounding of tertiary pedagogy in modernist assumptions about the nature of knowledge. Lyotard argued over a decade ago that the age of the professor is ending because:

a professor is no more competent than memory bank networks in *transmitting* established knowledge, no more competent than inter-disciplinary teams in imagining new moves or new games [my emphasis]. (Lyotard, 1979, p. 53)

Elizabeth Grosz insists that feminist work must always be, at least in some sense, a *reactive* project (Grosz, 1990, p. 59). Yet this does not necessarily mean abandonment of traditional spaces. Spivak (in Kirby, 1993) argues, rather, for the project of 'negotiat(ing) enabling violations' of modes, forms, spaces and events. In the light of this, it is important to explore more fully what postmodern pedagogical possibilities exist when, rather than abandoning large group onsite teaching, feminists generate 'new moves' and 'new games' to decentre lecturer authority over knowledge production.

Postepistemology: The House of Theory and the Rock of Faith

The textshop, then, functions best as general education, being to the sciences what the carnival once was to the Church. (Ulmer, 1985b, p. 61)

In a Master of Education foundational course in which I represent aspects of poststructuralist theory and postmodern feminisms, I argue that knowledge, constructed in texts and discourses, can never be true in all times and places, revealed (as opposed to produced), certain, stable, and beyond politics. I turn these theories as deconstructive critiques on the grand narratives of various contemporary theories of education and educational politics. In so doing, I face a conundrum, summed up in the stricture of Zavarzadeh (1992, p. 29) that 'poststructuralist pedagogy removes the "walls" (the traces of the political) by offering textuality as a panhistorical truth, which is considered to be beyond ideology'. Here are two problems. First, how may the teacher avoid transmitting the idea that all (textualized) knowledge is uncertain except the truth that knowledge is uncertain? Second, how may readers go beyond the license of a carnivalesque 'free play' of textuality to say with Luther, 'Here I stand' (politically), while still conceding that meanings are unstable?

The first problem offers a binary opposition poststructuralism may deconstruct. It's not a matter of trying to separate the true from the false (thereby establishing a new true) but rather of destabilizing assumptions about the validity of a text's meaning — as if it could transcend interpretation, or as if 'proper' interpretation could establish the correct meaning. Instead, we inquire into *how* meanings are produced. That entails examining texts in contexts, including those that offer school-teaching methodological fixes and theory-driven interpretive practices.

University lectures are also contextualized texts; and university courses require students to produce texts within those contexts. What strategies may enable us to keep meaning in suspension? The example Erica and I describe below (it is only one of a number of strategically used 'corrective moments' in our lectures) sets multiple meanings in play for students by juxtaposing text to text in lecture-theatre theatrics, in such a way that students' attention is directed to the framing discourse of the lecture text.

Such metaknowledge of discourses (Gee, 1990, pp. 146–8) is a necessary, if insufficient, condition of students becoming alert to the politics of meaning: to the circumstances and discourses which put in play or seem to stop the play of meaning; and to the circumstances and discourses which might enable different groups to produce different readings.[1] And so my second problem may in part be answered.

Since poststructuralist textuality deals in the provisional, the undecidable, the playful, and since authoritative disciplinary knowledge is now paradoxical — beyond belief —, our pedagogy cannot properly take the form of transmission via explication and a disciplinary codification. It must unsettle the master-teacher's authority and the student's discipleship. For, as Lusted (1986) puts it:

> If knowledge needs to be conceived as produced in exchange, so too must all agents in its active production be conceived as producers, the divisions between theorising, writing, teaching and learning be dissolved. (Lusted, 1986, p. 5)

Reiteration of knowledge is of course strictly speaking impossible. But even a poststructuralist teacher's attempt at summarizing theory may lead to a classroom discourse which is apparently imitative, whether the teacher mirrors other masters or the apprentices mimic the teacher.[2] If the pedagogy remains unchanged, a demonstration of textual deconstruction may resemble traditional lit-crit analysis; a 'resistant reading' may become a fixed position for articulating new orthodoxies; and a theorized teaching turn into a teaching of theory as certainties that govern knowledge. And should we try to avoid this by resorting to 'inquiry learning', we may set up a different limitation, of students not going beyond what they may come to know 'naturally', unaided, as if they could be the originary source of their knowledge.

Who can teach us how to evade these risks? There is a growing body of academic writing about postmodern pedagogy; but even in volumes devoted to the topic there are almost no specific, detailed accounts of how teachers have translated poststructuralist theories into a concordant classroom practice (so Cahalan and Downing, 1991, p. 294).[3] The most notable — or notorious — exception is Ulmer (1985a, 1985b), although his 'lec(ri)tures' focus on his own theatrical enactments rather than on how and what and why this will enable his students to learn. Reader-response teachers such as Scholes (1985) and a range of feminists (e.g., Luke and Gore, 1992) have attended more closely to the conditions of learning, doubtless because of their commitment to negotiating the processes and positions of coming to knowledge. But we need still further examples of how professing poststructuralist teachers and students enact their theories.

Theories that are themselves in disarray. Since theory can no longer have as its telos a logically impeccable body of certainty, it must dissolve into theorizing. (The Greek root of our word is a verb, *theoreo*, 'look'; it does not tell you what you will see by looking.) Theorizing is always historically and culturally situated, always rhetorical and performative, always produced in the exchanges between participants, whether in classrooms or elsewhere. Consequently, I have come to think of the proper business of a poststructuralist pedagogy as ' doing theorizing', in such a way as to interrogate any monologic authority (of text or teacher) and to foreground the play of multiple, contingent meanings. 'Doing theorizing' is to display the traces of the shifts, the struggles, resistances and desires of those who are coming to 'see'. It differs from the teaching or learning of theory as institutionalized, codified knowledge which has (apparently) erased all such traces.

It may be argued that we all 'do theorizing' all the time, anyway. No doubt; but I am interested in a project of theorizing that is deliberately, explicitly metacognitive in focusing on the conditions of our cognition. I do not see it as an anti-intellectual do-it-yourself kit for building a house of cards — for there are already rehearsed arguments students need to engage with, if they are to get beyond a personalist faith in the sufficiency of their own opinion. Nor do I naively expect that my students will become philosopher-kings, colonizing hitherto untractable wildernesses. Doing theorizing does mean students are not simply consuming theories produced at centres of industry elsewhere; it does mean coming to ask the questions that follow when an explanation previously taken for granted becomes itself in need of explanation. And it does mean teachers having to give up determining all the questions and all the responses.

That may be our agenda. Shall we attempt to insist that our students 'do theorizing' as our project of enlightenment? We grumble that our students desire only a credential, another 'article' they can bank on for the future; that they want fifty-seven handy hints for packaging the short story (or whatever); and that they reject as idle machinery the theories we wheel into the lecture room. Such hostility, according to Eagleton (1983, p. viii) 'usually means an opposition to other people's theories and an oblivion to one's own' — including, perhaps, to one's emotional investments in certain ideologies. Now if ideologies work at the level of such investments, rather than at the purely rational level, then a poststructuralist project of critique as 'doing theorizing' will not get to the heart of the matter. Unless we can find ways also to work with as well as work on the affective.

I believe that one way to work at this level is through some new kinds of embodiment or dispositions of the bodies of students and teachers. The example which follows (selected from a range of our experiments with pedagogical processes) shows the teachers enacting theories — moving from telling to showing — in such a way as to prompt students to do theorizing about what is being performed before them. (This is a very different theatricality from Ulmer's.) Such a classroom practice is deictic rather than exclusively didactic.

Rites of Exchange: The Problems of Space and Speaking Positions —
A Role-play for Two Feminist Lecturers

1   *authoritative speaking position:*
Erica (from back of lecture theatre): Is this where you want me?
Wendy (centre front): Well, you're certainly coming across loud and clear, and you're certainly subverting my position here in the centre front, but I'm concerned that this places the group between us: our voices cut across them or even go over their heads. And of course, however we interact, I am still the teacher up front.

2   *competing centres*
Erica (takes up position at the far left front): How about if we move to the margins and leave the centre empty? That's another way of using space to question the central position for speaking authoritatively.
Wendy (from far right): Yeah, well you're certainly far left of me, at least where I'm taking up my stand, but from where they're sitting you're extreme right. Do you want that? And that's another difficulty: we look as if we're standing fixed in those positions and there's no room to move. You may move from the centre to the margins, but then we each look as if we're setting up new competing centres. That doesn't feel right.

3   *dialogic mode*
Erica (arranges two chairs and both sit facing one another): At least we're not shouting across an empty centre here, but we're engaging in a dialogue, in a more collegial way.
Wendy That's certainly more comfortable. Bit like a knitting circle though? We're certainly engaging with one another in matey manner, but while we're in this tight little huddle we might be in a footy scrum. *We* know what we're saying, but we're still excluding them, not inviting them into our conversation. We're just a cosy little coterie.

4   *the united front* (both together, side by side, facing audience):
Erica Well, together then, united we stand etc . . .
Wendy Brothers in arms? A united front? A solid phalanx? Bit militaristic perhaps? A pretty formidable confrontation? How could they get a word in edgewise?

5   *towards a postmodern reflexivity* (both turn backs to audience and towards video, which Erica activates . . . and watch and listen to themselves on screen talking about how this doubling up, this duplicity, feels more comfortable. It means there's scope for self-critique, when they watch themselves representing themselves (whoever those selves are). . . . And then the TV figures turn to watch themselves on TV conducting a similar dialogue, which ends with the point that of course, they're still — always — within a frame.)
Erica . . . Does that mean *we've been* framed?

Wendy (picks up mask, puts it before face, turns to audience and repeats): . . . Does that mean *you've been* framed?

The idea of being 'seriously playful' is one that has great value for postmodern pedagogues. As witness to this pedagogical event, the students/audience enjoyed the 'performance' enough to begin to participate in it. Spontaneous comments about margins, centres, ('Who's left?' 'What's left?' 'What's left out?' and so on) were signs that students participated in our doing from their position of (responding) audience, rather than simply 'consuming our content'. Of course, they also love the sight of lecturers being 'irreverent' about their own knowledge and practices.

This playfulness, however, does not demand an end to conventional teaching practices. As Ulmer (1985b, p. 53) points out, it is neither necessary nor desirable to shift to a postmodernized pedagogy that abandons the lecture. Parody works better 'alongside' conventional practices. As lecturers we did not feel compelled to generate an hour long dramatic performance. Rather, we provided 'corrective moments' that allowed particular sorts of engagement with ideas, depending on the sort of theorizing being undertaken. These included a visit to the psychoanalyst/feminist, a husband–wife conversation with a feminist lecturer keeping them under surveillance, and so on. The lecture as piece of a pedagogical work, then, actively interrupted its own feminist narrative, working within–against its own logic (Lather, 1991) in order to construct a more duplicitous one.

This means, then, that lecture halls as spaces in which physical bodies come together can still be appropriate venues for postmodern pedagogy. The postmodern challenge to pedagogical practices is not simply the challenge of providing simply 'alternative mode' delivery services to off-campus bodies. While new technologies can and will provide a range of options for transmission well beyond what is offered in conventional tertiary teaching, there are other and more demanding ways of understanding the postmodern challenge to pedagogy. Every mode must be milked of what it can offer, including the large-group teaching onsite situation. There are some undeniable pluses in bringing students and lecturers together to share jointly a space and a process, though of course, status, knowledge and functions are never *equally* shared. The types of spaces that have now become available for sharing, through online, vis-à-vis technology, simply add to the possibilities (and the headaches for the feminist lecturer as critical instructional designer).

As Ulmer (1985b, p. 58) has argued, the goal is one of simulating the experience, the pleasure, of creativity. What we share with Ulmer is the goal of allowing students to bypass initiation as a modernist/specialist to confront the provisional, permeable character of all knowledge (p. 62). What we feel we have added to the examples cited by Ulmer is the momentary decentring of lecturer authority (our authority and control is none the less for that) through a creative use of the lecturing team and the lecturing space as well as the lecture-as-text. Role-play or dramatic performance is not a pedagogical 'product' here but a postmodern performance or event generated by and generating new processes and forms of engagement with educational ideas.

Within a poststructuralist pedagogy, such role-playing has several valuable functions. It is a metaphor, which simultaneously is and is not what it represents. Unlike a lecturer's exposition, it does not pretend to say what it means, as if its referentiality were unproblematic. Instead, it ruptures the lecturer's customary monologue and the students' silence. It is dialogic, dialectical: it sets text alongside text and articulates different meanings which are negotiated among speakers. And so too the students must negotiate meanings as they move in speculation between the concrete vivid particulars of an enacted narrative and the concepts they infer. Such movements between immersion and distance are characteristic of Brechtian theatre, but here it is the dramatic performance instead which is unsettling, estranging, even while the audience become involved in it.

The lecture begins before it announces its beginning. Rehearsal is thus (also) performance. And so we rupture the genre of the lecture, whose 'staging' usually entails the sequential exposition of concepts in a given time and space.[4] Students' surprise at this redefinition can problematize what they have taken for granted. And so the lecture becomes available as a text too, like any other institutional practice. This movement between dramatic and expository modes in the one lecture is likely to foster students' metadiscursive awareness.

Role-playing is also an act of embodiment. The body is too often still ignored in academic education, despite theorists' recent re-emphasis on the body as a text inscribed with social discourses. In our example, we lecturers are no longer the authorities who show only one side of themselves in facing the lectured body.[5] Erica and I deconstruct the fixity of that position and thus estrange ourselves from the institutionalized knowledge-and-power usually enacted at the podium. And in other cases, when teachers or students role-play they take up subject positions elsewhere, inhabit those dispositions bodily. (This is very different from a Stanislavski method of empathetic absorption in another. In any case, postmodern condition as characterized by mediated images and vicarious representations of desire make it impossible for us to be autonomous, self-present, unified individuals.) If through such acts students and teachers come to think about the productive contexts of those embodied acts, this too approaches 'doing theorizing'.

Last, and crucial, is pleasure: the actors' and audience's enjoyment of their participation in a playful (sub)version of academic work. Like the populace at large, many students would resist new ways of thinking that unsettle the foundations of their knowledge and identity. Laughter may relax their suspicion and hostility, making them more open to uncertainty. Of course, laughter can also be a restorative, insofar as any parody may serve conservative interests, confirming the everyday norm in the very act of temporarily and ostensibly overturning it. However, if in the shifts back and forth between opposites each undermines the claim of each to truth, then there can be no unproblematic reassertion of a tidy order of knowledge as the rule at the end of the day or the lecture. Such pedagogic play, then, is strategically useful insofar as it encourages theorizing about the instability of knowledge and truth. And the instability of identity. For as Erica and I play ourselves (not *are* ourselves) we shift from the role of lecturer to that of actor, and our students are thereby reconstituted as audience and so embody another subject position . . . Partly and temporarily, of course, and always within the structures and practices of a tertiary institution, within and against which such acts of transgression signify, to retheorize learning.

Keeping an Untidy House

Theorizing about Education Discourses

In keeping with our example, a number of students have felt licensed by our playful subversiveness to transgress the genre of academic analytical exposition in their own writing. (They are required to analyse an educational policy document from the reading positions offered by three theoretical discourses.) They have used a range of other genres and metaphors and texts, from *Alice in Wonderland* to tabloid newspaper to the letter-to-mother, in order to interrogate the self-sufficient meaning offered by the document. This kind of textual appropriation may well give rise to an implicit theorizing, as the students move between analytical and metaphorical thinking and must thereby develop a metadiscursive awareness.

Useful though this poststructuralist pedagogy is, there is still scope for development. The role-playing, for instance, could have been further utilized. The students here were spectators and consumers who did not participate in the dialogue except through occasional interjections. They watched a duologue between their lecturers 'doing theorizing' in a particular way; their own consequent theorizing may have been underdeveloped. Indeed, both lecturers and students need to reflect consciously on their theorizing, in an explicitly constructed inquiry into the discursive production of theoretical and educational knowledge and the part teacher and student play in this. Such points about the cultural constructedness of knowledge were mentioned in the lecture. But in as much as the significance of those role-plays was mostly implicit, students who are most competent in the interpretation of literary narratives will have the advantage. In future we need to be more explicit about the textuality of lecture/performance in order to help the students develop a metatextual awareness.

But even if it were so developed, would such poststructuralist pedagogy still be merely an instance of what Zavarzadeh (1992, p. 39) calls a 'pedagogy of evasion . . . [which] focuses on the relation of the subject to the discourses of knowledge and quietly brackets the subject's relations to social practices'? Whether or not the latter charge sticks, we should not therefore underplay the subject's relation to 'the discourses of knowledge', since this is implicated in social practices, and the activities of lecture rooms are also social practices. In such spaces we may play our part in dismantling the architecture of educational regimes of truth.

Postmodern Pedagogies as 'Quality Teaching'?

If the challenge of generating postmodern pedagogical moments brings feminist academics up against all manner of paradoxes in daily work, all this work must happen in the context of paradoxical developments in the larger context of a reconstructed 'corporatist' higher education culture. Karmel (1991) has identified four such paradoxes for Australian universities:

- demands for responsiveness to national priorities versus deregulation of markets;
- direction of size and shape of a unified national system from the top versus dismantling of command economies;
- largeness as the criterion for membership of a unified national system versus a shift to smaller units in big business conglomerates;
- advocacy of firmer direction of universities by chief executives versus a shift to flatter organizations, industrial democracy and risk management.

This 'regime of truth' has real effects on academics, not the least of which are the ways in which versions of what constitutes 'good teaching' can be articulated. The issue of 'quality teaching' in higher education is certainly on the agenda, given its importance as a means by which the 'clever/capable' country is to be constructed. While 'quality teaching' must jostle for space against the demands of the 'competitive grant culture' and the 'consultancy culture', both of which have changed forever the nature of academic work practices and styles of management, it is not simply that these changes have challenged tertiary pedagogy. The concept of 'quality' is already framed through a policy discourse of performance indicators and the like which disallows the reporting and evaluation of postmodern pedagogical events as demonstrated 'quality teaching'. Certainly there is no indication that Wendy and I did 'more for less' in terms of resources. There was no smart 'packaging' of materials, and indeed, we actually wasted resources by requiring two lecturers when we could surely have 'got the information/message across' with just one lecturer. Opting for a second becomes prodigal, not provocative.

The response from university administrations to the challenges of 'more quality' still seems to be based in a sort of childlike faith that 'beyond 2000' technologies can be co-opted to meet any and every 'postmodern' learning need. We are seeing a fundamental reworking of pedagogy through the means by which education is being 'delivered' to students-as-clients. The current buzzwords are 'flexible' and/or 'open' mode, and the result has been a flurry of activity which makes *in*-servicing decidedly *out*-moded. University teaching is packing up and leaving home, and the vehicles are online, satellite and CD-ROM facilities, audio-conferencing, electronic mail, computer-text conferencing, open-learning centres and the like. New 'smart' lecture theatres, looking very much like large cinemas (with all that this speaks about where the *action* is), have begun to replace older, smaller classrooms. Yet on campus, the lecture/ tutorial format, and the actual approaches used within it, have limped on, with pedagogical practice (one lecturer as centred authority — mass students as passive recipients) hardly missing a beat (or should that read 'dull thud').

Demanding more 'quality' from university courses, substituting electronic texts for conventional ones, moving learning 'off-campus', putting an end to the conventional lecture, none of these in isolation will respond to the demands of changing contexts and cultures in postmodern times. Instead, content and process must cease to be understood as a binary system in knowledge production. When this is actually manifested in teaching and learning situations as a wide range of diverse and engaging teaching and learning events, academe will be appropriately 'untidy' enough to be keeping its pedagogical house in order.

Notes

1 Schilb (1992, pp. 59–60) offers a similar suggestion: 'As feminist criticism and pedagogy have repeatedly suggested, textual study can eventually lead students to analyse how "political antagonisms" influence the very acts of reading, writing, and thinking, but a class will probably not reach this point if it is encouraged simply to appreciate how textual meanings abound rather than to ponder how social circumstances might cause its members to interpret a work differently.'

2 For Ulmer (1985a, p. 174) the central problem for poststructuralist education is 'how to deconstruct the function of imitation in the pedagogical effect'.

3 The following is merely a selection from the available literature of writing I have found variously useful: Aronowitz and Giroux (1991); Berlin (1993); Cahalan and Downing (1991); Johnson (1985); Kampol (1992); Leitch (1985); Luke and Gore (1992); Nelson (1986); Scholes (1985); Schilb (1992); Shumway (1992); Ulmer (1985a, 1985b); Zavarzadeh (1992).

4 'Lecture as text, rather than as work, hence textshop rather than workshop — operates by means of a *dramatic*, rather than epistemological, orientation to knowledge' (Ulmer, 1985b, p. 39). I dispute this opposition: the performative is itself an approach to the epistemological, even if more implicitly; but the former is in my 'textshop' a condition of coming to know, in a complementary if different way.

5 'The excentricity of the teaching body, in the traditional topology, permits at once the synoptic surveillance covering with its glance the field of taught bodies . . . and the withdrawal of the body which only offers itself to sight from one side.' Jaques Derrida, *Politiques*, p. 87 (cited in Ulmer, 1985a, p. 174).

References

ALLEN, J. (1992) 'Feminist Critiques of Western Knowledges: Spatial Anxieties in a Provisional Phase?', in RUTHVEN, K.K. (Ed) *Beyond the Disciplines: The New*

Humanities, Papers from the Australian Academy of the Humanities Symposium, 1991, Canberra, Highland Press.

ARONOWITZ, S. and GIROUX, H. (1991) *Postmodern Education: Politics, Culture and Social Criticism*, Minneapolis, University of Minnesota Press.

BARTHES, R. (1972) *Critical Essays*, HOWARD, R. (Tr.), Evanston, Northwestern University Press.

BERLIN, J. (1993) 'Literacy, pedagogy, and English studies: Postmodern connections', in LANKSHEAR, C. and McLAREN, P. (Eds) *Critical Literacy: Politics, Praxis, and the Postmodern*, Albany, SUNY Press, pp. 247–69.

CAHALAN, J. and DOWNING, D. (Eds) (1991) *Practicing Theory in Introductory College Literature Courses*, Urbana, Illinois, National Council of Teachers of English.

EAGLETON, T. (1983) *Literary Theory: An Introduction*, Oxford, Basil Blackwell.

FOUCAULT, M. (1981) 'Questions of method: An interview with Michel Foucault', *Ideology and Consciousness*, 8, pp. 3–14.

GEE, J. (1990) *Social Linguistics and Literacies: Ideology in Discourses*, Basingstoke, Falmer Press.

GREEN, B. (Ed) (1993) *The Insistence of the Letter: Literacy Studies and Curriculum Theorising*, London, Falmer Press.

GREENE, M. (1993) 'Reflections on Postmodernism and Education: Review Essay', *Educational Policy*, 7, 2, pp. 206–11.

GROSZ, E. (1990) 'Contemporary theories of power and subjectivity', in GUNEW, S. (Ed) *Femininst Knowledge: Critique and Construct*, London, Routledge, pp. 59–120.

JAMESON, F. (1974) *The Prison-house of Language: A Critical Account of Structuralism, and Russian Formalism*, Princeton, NJ, Princeton University Press.

JOHNSON, B. (1985) 'Teaching Deconstructively', in Atkins, G.D. and JOHNSON, M. (Eds) *Writing and Reading Differently: Deconstruction and the Teaching of Composition and Literature*, Kansas, University of Kansas Press, pp. 140–8.

KANPOL, B. (1992) *Towards a Theory and Practice of Teacher Cultural Politics: Continuing the Postmodern Debate*, Norwood, NJ, Ablex.

KARMEL, P. (1991) 'The Greening of Tertiary Education', Paper presented at the AITEA Conference, Darwin, 7–11 August.

KIRBY, V. (1993) 'Feminisms, reading, postmodernisms: rethinking complicity', in GUNEW, S. and YEATMAN, A. (Eds) *Feminism and the Politics of Difference*, Sydney, Allen and Unwin, pp. 20–34.

LATHER, P. (1989) 'Deconstructing/deconstructive Inquiry: Issues in Feminist Research Methodologies', Paper presented at the New Zealand Women's Studies Association Conference, Christchurch.

LATHER, P. (1991) *Feminist Research in Education: Within/Against*, Geelong, Deakin University Press.

LATHER, P. (1993) 'Fertile obsession: Validity after poststructuralism', *Sociological Quarterly* (forthcoming).

LEITCH, V. (1985) 'Deconstruction and pedagogy', in ATKINS, G.D. and JOHNSON, M. (Eds) *Writing and Reading Differently: Deconstruction and the Teaching of Composition and Literature*, Kansas, University of Kansas Press, pp. 16–26.

LUKE, C. and GORE, J. (1992) *Feminisms and Critical Pedagogy*, London, Routledge.

LUSTED, D. (1986) 'Why pedagogy?', *Screen*, 27, pp. 2–14.

LYOTARD, J. (1979) *The Postmodern Condition: A Report on Knowledge*, Manchester, Manchester University Press.

McWilliam, E. (1993) 'Post haste: Plodding research and galloping theory', *British Journal of Sociology of Education*, 14, 1, pp. 199–205.

Morgan, W. (1993) 'Feminism/Postmodernism', Lecture Notes for EDN601 (Major Issues in Education), Faculty of Education, Queensland University of Technology (unpublished).

Nelson, C. (Ed) (1986) *Theory in the Classroom*, Urbana and Chicago, University of Illinois Press.

Schilb, J. (1992) 'Poststructuralism, politics, and the subject of pedagogy', in Kecht, M. (Ed) *Pedagogy is Politics: Literary Theory and Critical Teaching*, Urbana, IL, University of Illinois Press, pp. 48–69.

Scholes, R. (1985) *Textual Power: Literary Theory and the Teaching of English*, New Haven, Yale University Press.

Shumway, D. (1992) 'Integrating theory in the curriculum as theorising — a postdisciplinary practice', in Kecht, M. (Ed) *Pedagogy is Politics: Literary Theory and Critical Teaching*, Urbana, IL, University of Illinois Press, pp. 93–110.

Spender, D. (1989) *Man Made Language*, London, Routledge and Kegan Paul.

Spivak, G. (1989) 'Feminism and deconstruction, again: Negotiating with unacknowledged masculinism', in Brennan, T. (Ed) *Between Feminism and Psychoanalysis*, London, Routledge, pp. 206–23.

Tripp, D. (1990) 'The Ideology of Educational Research', *Discourse*, 10, 2, pp. 51–74.

Ulmer, G. (1985a) *Applied Grammatology: Post(e)-Pedagogy from Jaques Derrida to Joseph Beuys*, Baltimore, Johns Hopkins University Press.

Ulmer, G. (1985b) 'Textshop for Post(e)pedagogy', in Atkins, G.D. and Johnson, M.L. (Eds) *Writing and Reading Differently*, Kansas, University of Kansas Press, pp. 38–64.

Whitson, J. (1991) 'Poststructuralist pedagogy as counter-hegemonic praxis' (Can We Find the Baby in the Bathwater), *Education and Society*, 9, 1, pp. 73–86.

Zavarzadeh, M. (1992) 'Theory as resistance', in Kecht, M. (Ed) *Pedagogy is Politics: Literary Theory and Critical Teaching*, Urbana, ILL, University of Illinois Press, pp. 25–47.

Part 3

Identity

8   Stories In and Out of Class: Knowledge, Identity and Schooling

Lindsay Fitzclarence, Bill Green and Chris Bigum

Introduction

Stable societies are always faced with the challenge of successfully integrating the upcoming generation within the frameworks maintained by former generations. In simple terms, this depends to a large extent on the stories which are told by one generation to the next. With the emergence of a comprehensive industrial society, mass education has become directly implicated in the process of intergenerational story telling. Within liberal democracies, such as Australia, the dominant story told within schools implies that children will have the opportunity to move from home, to school, and then on to full adult life. Certainly within the period of the postwar long boom, the stories involved the idea that employment followed the period of education.[1]

During the 1980s new stories were advanced by policy makers and politicians. They argued that if Australia was to be a fully fledged nation in the new association of nations, it must be prepared to undergo fundamental economic and social restructuring. In more specific terms, the story translated to the following observation:

> The Federal Government is promoting its vision of economic restructuring as a panacea against the 'banana republic' syndrome. Business, industry and academe are to become more competitive and creative. New technologies are needed and a workforce skilled to use them. (Slattery, 1989a, p. 13)

Slattery was responding to a number of significant policy developments of the time, developments which implied that there was a need for a unified national struggle for Australia to become a competitive nation in the bigger, combative, context of international market-based relations. During the late 1980s, the Government announced plans to integrate the different parts of tertiary education into a unified sector, outlined plans for a national school curriculum, and did away with the youth dole scheme in order to increase school retention rates in the post-compulsory phase.[2] Each of these developments was an aspect of what was called micro-economic reform. This aspect of an overall economic reform strategy was designed to work in conjunction with macrolevel reforms, such as deregulating the banking system and linking Australia to the international telecommunications grid. Collectively, the reforms were designed to make Australia a competitive economy in the emerging high tech, deregulated, international market-place.

In the colloquial terms of mass-media journalism, the developments of the 1980s were designed to make Australia the 'clever country'. In the more coded language of political and educational theory, this term was shorthand for altering the course of public education, away from a particular if somewhat skewed realization of the mental–manual distinction towards a more value-added emphasis on mental, or intellectual, forms of training. The Labour politician and social commentator Barry Jones (1990) describes this trend in the following way:

> What we have been experiencing in Australia in the 1980s is not an industrial society in decline and in need of temporary support of tariffs, quotas and bounties to restore it, but a new type of society with different economic bases. Knowledge and skills have replaced raw materials and muscle-power or the imperative to work harder. (Jones, 1990)

Jones' reading that a new society is replacing an older one is more than descriptive. His assessment of the nature of recent social change has been used to give form to many aspects of policy reform, including education. For example, the movement towards a new education system, which is consistent with Jones' assessment, can be seen in the following pronouncement from a meeting of ministers of education in 1989:

> Schools should develop students' literacy; numeracy and other mathematical skills; skills of analysis and problem solving; understanding of the role of science in society; knowledge of Australia's history and geography; and capacity for moral judgement. (Slattery, 1989b, p. 1)

Alongside these blueprints for change, there is another set of stories. For example, there is a popular view that Australia as an example of an egalitarian society will effect change that is equitable in terms of costs and gains, and from which in the long-run everyone will benefit. Hence politicians have reworked stories about the weak and vulnerable being cared for by the strong and secure. For example, in 1988 when the Prime Minister of the time, Bob Hawke, pronounced that '. . . by 1990 no child need live in poverty' (Edgar *et al.*, 1989, p. xviii), there tended to be a tacit support for both the intent of the statement and the processes which were being lauded.

It has been left to organizations such as the Brotherhood of Saint Laurence, the Human Rights Commission and the Australian Catholic Bishops Conference to highlight that, despite the claims such as those made by Bob Hawke, now, in 1994, income and wealth difference is as extreme as ever, and there is emerging evidence of a significant underclass developing *despite* the restructuring developments of the last decade. This pattern of inequity is translated into life inside schools. Thus research by Connell, White and Johnston (1991, p. 23) highlights that '. . . class inequalities in education (measured by a range of outcomes from school progression to test results to secondary retention to tertiary entry) persist on a massive scale in contemporary Australian education'.

Critical Voices and the Politics of Difference

How are the developments associated with education's place inside the restructuring process to be critically interpreted? An answer to this question is imperative if there is to be any hope of a new form of educational practice and theory. The starting place for considering an answer is with the major theoretical developments which have previously attempted to throw new light on the dark side of education — that side which has not adequately been represented in the dominant stories of either the economic reformers or their conservative counterparts.

The reforms of the last decade can be seen as responses to significant forms of social change dating back to the late 1960s and early 1970s. At the most general level, this shift can be seen as the dawn of a postcolonial era in which nation states were repositioned with regard to one another. In very simple terms, this implied that apples grown in Tasmania were no longer afforded an automatic market in Britain.

The cultural shifts of the last two decades opened the way to a new line of analysis about the structure of education within society more generally. During the 1970s a range of critical scholars of education presented accounts that demonstrated the ways in which education contributed to the ongoing reproduction of social class divisions. Jean Ely's (1978) work is an example of the thinking of the time:

> Australian educational history can be compared, in some ways, to a never-ending relay race. It has been run, and is still being contested, between members of various socio-economic strata of the community. The 'haves' race on the inside tracks, handing on the baton under auspicious circumstances from generation to generation. The upwardly mobile often begin at, but hope desperately not to finish on, the outer tracks. Many stay willingly and sometimes unwillingly, on the outer lanes. Some contestants have fallen out altogether. Generations of outer runners in the relay race have been sustained by educational opportunities offered to them. The extent of these opportunities has depended largely upon prevailing economic conditions. Economic prosperity generally makes the race easier for the outer runners, while depression lessens its chances. (Ely, 1978, p. 1)

Such work eroded the dominant status of those who had pedalled the line that education is an open pathway to the good life for all students. By the start of the 1980s, educational theorists who continued to perpetuate the myths surrounding the egalitarian outcomes of social democracy rarely went unchallenged. However, the 1980s also produced new lines of critical analysis. Scholars using poststructuralist approaches 'discovered' multiple ways in which schools make a difference to students' life chances. The universal aspects of class analysis were progressively replaced by a theory of difference and specificity. Accordingly, Gunew (1993, p. 17) asserts that 'the issue of cultural difference has become an inevitable qualifier of any questions to do with gender or class'. While such developments have helped produce new understandings about social complexity, they have also acted in some versions at least to deflect attention from certain other enduring inequities. In particular, the new theoretical developments have not been all that useful in critically appraising the structural reforms associated with the high-tech pathway which has been followed by policy makers and politicians with regard to the dominant economic reform process.

One reason for the major support of this political reform package is that many of the voices which might once been heard to call out in protest or warning, are simply not heard anymore. Within academic circles, one reason for such silence is that the politics of 'difference', associated with the poststructuralist turn, has gone hand-in-hand with the political and economic restructuring of social life in Australia in the last ten years. The bipartisan accord, linking unions and government and many different interest groups, has required what Gramsci once called organic intellectuals. Wexler (1992) neatly sums up this issue when he observes:

> The culture of the emergent symbolic economy — an economy of electronic networks and numerically controlled machine production, an economy of robotics — does not yet have an ethic that creates institutional commitment. [Moreover, as he continues] University intellectuals are not by and large working on such an ethic and on recreating the moral bases of institutions and public life. They are themselves caught in the dynamics of a decline of public life, as it is acted out in the university. (Wexler, 1992, p. 156)

Many proponents of a social theory of difference have, in various ways, been incorporated into the restructuring process by acting as advocates for particular interest groups. The attempt to develop a perspective of the bigger picture of cultural change, with all its complexity and contradiction, has accordingly not been a primary purpose of many contemporary theorists. Johnson (1993) describes this tension as a seeming paradox:

> [A]t a time when social divisions are becoming more pronounced and economic inequality is increasing both locally and globally, the

language of class and empowerment seems to be dropping out of the lexicon of social analysis. (Johnson, 1993, p. 62)

Johnson is right to name the paradox in the way he does. Along with writers such as Rizvi (1993), he offers an articulate account of the political nature of educational work and reminds us of the injustices which continue to be effected within existing educational arrangements. However, much work of this kind still tends to be more concerned with generating understanding about 'ways poverty *articulates* with other categories of social difference such as gender, ethnicity and disability' (Rizvi, 1993, p. 45). While undeniably important, such a view makes the cultural plurality of contemporary society the focus of analysis and critique. This approach, given that that is its primary focus, fails to register the full impact of cultural changes associated with the information revolutions that are being experienced worldwide. In what follows, we turn to consider these issues more directly.

Social Change and Schooling

It is an assumption of this chapter that an adequate critical theory of contemporary schooling needs to be set within an adequate theory of social change more generally. That is, there is a need for a perspective on the enormity of the cultural changes associated with the increasing significance of an information-based culture. Specifically, and strategically, there is a need for a critical understanding of the forces which are behind the drive to produce the so-called 'clever country'. Clearly Australia is no longer an outpost of the British Empire, or a nation which 'rides on the sheep's back'. Both national identity and the structure of the national economy have been subject to marked change over the last two or three decades. A developed understanding of such change is a *sine qua non* for a form of education which contributes to genuine social justice. To this end, the following section of the chapter outlines some details of a research project designed to explore issues related to the impact of the information revolution and the 'emergent symbolic economy' (Wexler, 1992), in the day-to-day processes of schooling.

In 1990 the Australian Research Council funded a two-year research project titled *Schooling the Future*.[3] This project was designed to explore the question: 'Are schools now dealing with a student who is quite different from students of previous eras?' A subordinate question was: 'Have schools and educational authorities developed curriculum rationales on what are essentially inadequate and even obsolete assumptions about the nature of students?' (see Green, 1993; Green and Bigum, 1993). In formulating these questions, the research team was influenced by the emerging concerns about the relationship between education, media culture and the workforce. In particular, the research was responding to a range of policy documents focused on the issue of increasing retention rates. While the research team acknowledged the very real demands associated with the retention phenomenon, we challenged what seems the founding idea in much of these initiatives that changes in retention patterns were simply an episodic phenomenon created by the contradictions of an economic recession. Instead, we were influenced by an increasing volume of literature exploring the idea of a cultural transformation which has generated complex new forms of social relationships as a result of the changes produced by new forms of information exchange. In particular, we were concerned with the impact of the emerging information technologies and their associated cultural fields, seeing these as having altered the time/space dimensions of social exchange. Some of the major themes which captured our attention include the speed of information exchange, the proliferation of information vectors, the decoupling of economic activity and employment in association with the emergence of new forms of 'work', the emergence of a global economy, and the digital collapse of computing, broadcasting and publishing.

Our hypothesis was that the changes noted here have altered the conditions of everyday life for all of us, but particularly for the younger generation. Identity formation was increasingly linked to postmodern commodity culture (Langman, 1991). Hence, as one commentator has observed: 'Today's children learn to consume — choosing their clothes, their drinks, their toys for Christmas — long before they learn to work' (Brett, 1993). Our explorations led us to conclude that identity formation influenced by media culture is a key feature of life for young people in particular. More specifically, identity, consumer culture and learning have come together in complex new ways (Kenway *et al.*, 1994). As such, mainstream education has been drawn into new forms of social arrangements (Tinning and Fitzclarence, 1992). The ascendant role of the media is therefore at the centre of our claim about the emergence of a different student. A short anecdote clarifies this issue.

Joyce Gray, the daughter of itinerant farm workers, was born in 1924. She started school at the height of the 'Great Depression' of the 1930s and finally left school in 1939 to take a job in the State Electricity Commission of Victoria. During her school years she helped her parents milk cows, a tedious job prior to the advent of milking machines. She remembers how around this time test cricket was being played between Australia and England. She records

> Very few families had a wireless set on which to follow the live proceedings, but a family named Mowat who lived on a farm about a mile from the school did have a set. As the Australian team batted and compiled each 100 runs they rang a big bell similar to the old school bells to broadcast the score so to speak. The clanging sound was heard over quite a distance. (Gray, 1983, p. 15)

In reflecting on the meaning of this story, it is our sense that children of the 1990s, the so-called 'Nintendo generation', are linked to the wider world, and therefore experience their relationships with others, in ways which are fundamentally different from those experienced by the working-class population of former times.[4] The research team was eager to explore the ways in which contemporary students developed different forms of relationships and through them came to a sense of self-understanding of who they were in space and time. We were united in our scepticism about essentialist certainties that had, and continued to, characterized many forms of education theory and practice. That is, we were very sceptical about educational ideas that perpetuated the belief that all students would move neatly through the education system and onto a secure place in the adult world beyond. In this sense, we accepted a position neatly expressed by John Hinkson (1991, p. 5) when he declared, '. . . in postmodern circumstances multiple realities are not "mere" philosophical concerns or concerns of mind. They are expressions of the very texture of our life settings.'

We settled on a study designed to explore what it is like to be a student working through the first phases of the Victorian Certificate of Education (VCE), the curriculum-development programme intended to address the changing demands of post-compulsory education (Collins, 1992). The study has been conducted in the main in two secondary schools via interviews and contextual data collection.[5] At the same time, we studied media representation of the VCE, and of schools and young people more generally, via an archive of several hundred newspaper reports. We have also conducted two case-studies of what we came to recognize as significant cultural events for many contemporary students: the 'Rock Eistedfodd'[6] (Fitzclarence *et al.*, 1993b) and the 'Deb Ball'.[7] Methodologically, we developed an emergent cycle of investigation and analysis, based on the relationship between critical ethnography and cultural studies.

Constructing the Student Subject

In what follows, we seek to present an account of post-compulsory schooling, student experience and media culture, drawing specifically from the archive developed out of the work of the project so far. This is necessarily selective here, but all the same it should allow a picture to emerge of the complexity of curriculum and identity formation in what for us are distinctively postmodern conditions.

Particularly striking was the nature and significance of the transactions between education and the media. By this we refer to media representations of education and schooling reform, as well as of young people generally, in and out of class and school contexts. Time and time again, both in our interview data and as reported in the print media, students referred to the pressure of working in what was then the new context of the Victorian Certificate of Education, and to feelings of stress and anxiety. Significantly, this was often exacerbated by media coverage itself, particularly in its increasingly tight coupling with educational policy and practice. At the start of the 1992 school year (the second year of the introduction of the full VCE), the major print outlets became involved in a vigorous debate about the new VCE. The *Herald Sun* and *The Age* are the two major newspapers covered in the study.

The following is a sample of February headlines in both of these papers.

Herald Sun VCE Joy but Future Uncertain/Boiling Point/Chaos Threat to Schools/Students Brave Bleak Forecast/Youth Jobless at 40.5 per cent *The Age* Student Intake Slashed/VCE Again — It's Unbearable/Suicide/ Do You Feel Part of a Lost Generation?

How are students' experiences being constructed at this point? Uncertainty about future prospects is a metatheme here, a theme which has the power to bring into question the perceived value not just of the VCE but of schooling more generally. The following is a reaction to this media representation as experienced by a Year 12 student:

Q OK you've pulled a newspaper out of the letter box and you've had a hard day and it says 'High percentage of students can't get in to tertiary education', and you felt what?
A Like giving up, thinking what am I doing, I mean, this is not going to take me anywhere this VCE, not going to get it, just thought all the negative things I suppose that you could think.

Q What did you do after that?
A Well I didn't feel like doing any homework much, I don't know, I didn't really do anything . . . I think I just listened to music thinking about you know, what's going to happen and uni's finished and why am I doing it kind of thing?

Q And what happened then? How did you resolve that?
A Oh it just took a few days then I thought, Well if I give up now, then I haven't tried it and I could get in' kind of thing. Yes, I might as well keep going, I've got as much chance as everyone else. Mm, I've done so far, I might as well finish the year, because even if I leave now there's still nothing.

Q So this is just a sort of graphic story as part of what I was talking about before. Hard day, bad news, and so you've thought about it, did you talk with anybody about it? Did you walk inside and say.
A Yes I said something to Mum, I can't remember what I said, something about 'There's no use going to school', you know, because you know all these people can't get into unis or something. I told them my feelings.

Q And what did she say?
A She agreed, but I don't know, I can't remember.

These are the reflections of a focused student in a secure school–family environment. Despite this security, she was clearly tipped sideways by the media messages. Fortunately, possibly because of it, she managed to get back on the rails. The issues she described were repeated many times over in interviews with other students, and the need for an adequate support system across the board cannot simply be assumed.

A second period of media focus is taken from the end of first semester 1992.

> *Herald Sun* VCE Maths Crisis/Pope Admits VCE Mistakes/Uni Hits VCE Burnout/When All the Study Goes for Naught/Fight for a Future/More Turmoil Hits VCE/Stress Crisis Rocks Schools
> *The Age* Study Break Plan to Ease VCE Rush/Concern for Health of Class of '92/VCE: Still More Changes Needed/VCE Alternative Gains Support

At the mid-year point, the media attention on education issues had reached saturation point. Every day carried VCE updates, including a number of editorials focused specifically on the issues surrounding the fate and fortunes of the new certificate. Few students or teachers managed to remain untouched by this overexposure. The following comments illustrate this point:

Q What do you see is the greatest influence on those kids? Is it family, or is it peer?
A Oh the media, I think it's the media, television, entertainment, films that have been put out, the sort of you often hear of talking about soap operas and the films they've seen and pop culture, magazines, music, that's probably the biggest influence on their lives.

Q In getting down to students themselves, have you seen any changes in their just general attitudes or expectations of school?
A Yes I'd say that in the last couple of years, and probably the media is more responsible for this than kids' attitudes, that they're constantly told that there's no future for them, there's no jobs so even though they're going to stay at school until Year 12 or even go on and do a tertiary course, they're ultimately going to end up unemployed or, you know, on the scrap heap or whatever, and so that does affect their attitude.

Students consistently reported that they saw themselves as victims of unjust policy changes. This point of view was generated and maintained by the mass media, and became part of the restricted code of students' own analyses of their experience. One front-page newspaper article, headlined 'Students' 'Victims of Education Experiment', featured an attack on the curriculum reforms associated with the new certificate by a conservative educator 'whose classroom has become the unlikely battleground in an ideological war over Victoria's controversial Victorian Certificate of Education'. He was reported thus:

> Mr Donnelly's concern now is for the potential victims of the fighting, the teenagers whose futures have been caught up in what has become the greatest experiment — bold or foolish depending on your point of view — in education in Victorian history.
>
> 'It is a tragedy to think of a lost generation of students. I really don't want to think of that', says Mr Donnelly. (*The Weekend Australian*, March 23–24, 1991, p. 1)

This became a recurring theme. It was given an extra twist by students themselves playing around with the notion of the 'VCE' as standing for 'Victims of Cruel Experiment', which was then picked up in interviews, both unsolicited and explicitly, as follows:

> **Q** Do you think you're a victim of a cruel experiment like most of the guys do here?
> **A** Oh a little bit, a little bit. It's kind of, we're the first ones to do the new VCE . . . The teachers don't know what they're doing . . . which doesn't make it easier.

Stress remained a major and ongoing concern. Asked to comment on the demands of the VCE, students responded as followed:

> I think sometimes they are too stressful . . . Last term we were given three days off . . . I think a lot of students needed the days off because they just couldn't hack it. We got a notice saying that Year 11s were having three days off due to stress reasons.
>
> I know a lot of people came up to me and said that they couldn't cope with the work and that they were leaving. A lot of kids were having really big fights with their parents which they'd never had fights before.
>
> The teachers weren't prepared for Year 11, they didn't know it was going to be this hard. It doesn't seem true . . . Like, your parents go: 'Oh, don't be stupid, you can't have real stress when you're this age'. But you can, believe me.

Indeed, anxiety, stress and even despair are common features of the lives of many students we studied. It was very much associated with the complexity and sheer pace of change, seemingly something with regard to which no one in schools has much agency or influence over. This is something teachers were keenly aware of:

I find here that we're disenfranchising a lot of kids because they don't understand and they don't understand even their rights as kids, so unless teachers are able to take time, and I don't think staff understand it either.

In one week here earlier in the year, I had to help five homeless kids, five kids in their Year 12 year who had been kicked out of home in the space of a week. And they all come in here for assistance because I have contacts with all the local agencies and Austudy stuff and rental assistance and stuff like that.

We have a fair amount of social dislocation in the school as well . . . Particularly amongst the 11s and 12s, not so much the juniors, homelessness, hassles with families, hassles with parents, not being able to really cope all that well with their peers. We have a few children who are out of their homes and they're homeless and our welfare coordinator has had to do a fair bit of work with some of those kids to try and keep them at school.

The welfare role of teachers and the school becomes more and more significant, and inextricable from curriculum work itself. Yet for many teachers, the pace and scope of change now constitutes the major feature of life as a curriculum worker.

Q What would you consider to be the major changes to education and your teaching.
A It's certainly become more hectic . . . well, since the advent of the Blackburn Report, education has been horrific, one year has never been the same as the previous.[8]

These reports highlight the role of the media and information technologies in and about schools. Despite all the political rationales associated with micro-economic reform of education, and the consistent pronouncements about the Government's social-justice platform, the data indicates a major breakdown in the legitimacy of the role of education for many students who were part of the study. Students reported that they attended school without a clear sense of the traditional reasons for being there, or indeed any commitment to schooling. As one student put it: 'I left half way through last year because I didn't like school . . . I was working in Adelaide then left to come home . . . I was searching for a job for 6 months . . . It was boring staying at home.' Another observed that 'It's OK. It's better than being jobless or unemployed.' The following blunt assessment was in response to being asked for 'a reflection on VCE 1991': 'It pretty [much] shits me, I don't really belong here. I'm here because I can't get a job . . . it's really no use, me being here.'

A powerful image of schools generated implicitly by students and more or less explicitly by teachers and various commentators, was as 'holding pens' or 'parking bays'. This image can be considered against more general patterns of change in retention rates; whereas the proportion of students continuing on to Year 12 was 35 per cent in the late 1970s, this had risen to more than 70 per cent by 1993 (and close to 80 per cent in Victoria), with policy anticipation that by the year 2000 the figure will be up towards 95 per cent. This trend needs to be seen in the context of what is increasingly recognized as continuing patterns of structural unemployment. The following is a teacher's view of the 'holding pen' theme:

> We've got a lot of kids in Year 11 and 12 who just would not have been here going back two to three years ago. Traditionally we were a tech school, very strong trade teaching area and kids went off to [factories, industry]. Now a lot of those kids at the moment are coming into school, they don't want to be here, there's not much hope for them in the very near future with apprenticeships and the sort of skills that they were trying to get and they're going through the motions of coming to school, some of them accept the challenge, but many of them are just treading water.

Set against these themes, a contrasting idea emerged. Some comments suggested that schools were seen to offer secure havens, and sites for social life. For many students, the opportunities to participate in 'extra curricula' activities and in so doing to form and maintain relationships with peers was the major reason for attending school. That some students declare that the opportunity to take part in the 'Deb Ball' is their prime reason for staying at school — or the Rock Eisteddfod, or other school-cultural events — is a telling comment on grand claims about education's role in producing 'the clever country':

> **Q** What are the good things about school?
> **A** Just the fact that you're learning and being with other people, helping other people sometimes with their work, getting involved in school activities and stuff.

> **A** The only reason I stay here is to do my Deb in October.

In some instances, there is recognition of the need for self-discipline and the advantages of structure, by learning through experience to cope with complexity:

> **Q** Is there anything you would like to add?
> **A** Only that when the VCE first came out I really hated it. I thought it was stupid and they were confusing everyone — sort of like a 'why me?' kind of situation. But now I think it's better cos it's making us more

organized and we've got to do things thoroughly. We can't just do things slap-dash.

Among other things, this is good training for life and work in the information age.

Time in school also provides the opportunity to 'network', to establish circuits of communication and information which have as much to do with making connections and forming relationships as with curriculum matters. For many students, the networks are maintained and developed via telephone communications after hours. As one teacher observed: 'A lot of that stuff is networking among themselves where they are sharing information with each other and asking each other stuff about what's going on here, what's going on there.' It's clear, then, that the networking system serves to sustain and enrich social interaction, actively combining presence and absence.

However, a dominant and recurring theme is one of profound alienation, linked to which is the notion of 'the great divide'. The social divisions between students appears to be increasing. On one side are those students with the support networks designed to help integrate them into institutions beyond school. On the other side are the students without the cultural supports needed to help make sense of current changes.

Q How are they coping?

A They're not, largely they aren't, we've got two different groups of kids. We've got the kids who really want to go well and like every other school in the state and all the stuff you read, they are completely stressed out and they're stressed out because I think last year was an exceptional year, a lot of kids missed out, a lot of kids did VCE and then missed out on placements.

But what we saw the minute the press came out and said '14,000 kids missed out on their placements', everybody here has now panicked and they've panicked and they've gone home and they're doing an extra twenty hours a week study and so what's happened is all of our best kids here have dropped subjects, have dropped out, and most of them have been under medical supervision at some stage. Because they read in the papers about what's happening, see the sorts of scores they're going to need to achieve and completely stress out over it.

Then we've got the middle group of kids who, yes, they would have done Year 12 anyway, have now realized that they'll never get into university and have almost given up, they don't really know why they're here.

Then you've got your 'bottom of the rung' kids who are only here because the job market is really, well, doesn't exist.

Uncertainty about the purposes of education, reflected in the themes of 'alienation' and 'the great divide', can be considered against employment trends.

Unemployment figures reflect a steady rise since the 1960s. The structural unemployment reflected in these figures is particularly focused on the youth sector. It should be noted that the figures are controversial and seen by some commentators to obscure the full extent of unemployment and therefore changes in overall work patterns. Gregory (1992) charts general unemployment figures for the last thirty years in the following way; from less than 2 per cent in the 1960s, through 3.5 per cent in the 1970s and 7 per cent in the 1980s, to 11 per cent in 1993. This pattern of unemployment has impacted dramatically on the youth sector, and accordingly 71,600 full-time teenage students registered as unemployed in March 1993 (Heriot, 1992, p. 55). Viewed historically, patterns of youth employment have also changed (Heriot, 1992, p. 127), increasing the pressure on many students as they struggle to combine part-time jobs with school work, at the same time as they contemplate a future of possible unemployment for young people generally.

Asked about whether he had noted any changes in students' general attitudes or expectations of school, one teacher commented:

> Yes I'd say that in the last couple of years, and probably the media is more responsible for this than kids' attitudes, that they're constantly told that there's no future for them, there's no jobs so even though they're going to stay at school until Year 12 or even go on and do a tertiary course they're ultimately going to end up unemployed or, you know, on the scrap heap or whatever and so that does effect their attitude. Kids in general haven't changed, kids adapt to their environment so I think that basically kids are the same, there's no difference there, you know the economic background that they come from, or the area that they live that determines this sort of outlook on life. But the general outlook of kids in the last couple of years has been, you know, a bit despondent, they don't seem to . . . they don't enjoy their schooling because it means nothing to them, or they have this concept that it's going to mean nothing to them.

One thing that seems undeniable is that education and schooling are negatively experienced by many students. Although there seems to be a general consensus on this across the student population, it is more focused and intense in the post-compulsory phase. The reasons are perhaps obvious: much more is at stake, and at risk. As one student in our study put it: 'Year 12 is only one year in comparison to the rest of your life, but it determines your future [. . .].' Among the findings in a recent report by the Australian Youth Federation, significantly enough entitled 'The Lost Generation', was that 'there was contempt and anger at Australia's secondary schools, with schooling seen as an unhappy and unproductive experience' (*The Age*, Monday, November 8, 1993, p. 2). In another article, perhaps ironically entitled 'The Best Years of Their Lives . . .', 16-year-old Simon is quoted thus: 'I think a lot of us have been unprepared and had a whole lot of information thrown at us and not known what to do with it. A lot of kids shut down through overload. Basically, it's easy to make mistakes' (*The Sunday Age*, September 29, 1991 [*Agenda*, pp. 1–2]). Something that emerged with particular force, in fact, was the intense scrutiny that young people as a social group were subjected to in the media, with considerable concern expressed about their welfare. For example, from the same article:

> Like cars and films and kitchen appliances, every generation of chil-
> dren is more advanced than the one it succeeds. The teenagers of the
> 1990s have more than any other generation of the twentieth century:
> certainly more material things, more money, more choices and more
> freedom. But do they have more pressures, more problems and less
> real satisfaction? Do kids still have fun?

What public statements such as this indicate is complex: a combination of nostalgia and anxiety on the part of the established generations, increasingly sensitive to the loss of security and certainty and the prospect of significant breakdowns in the traditional forms of authority. Do kids still have fun? Are these the best years of their lives? On the evidence it would appear unlikely, at least with regard to the official experience of schooling. This is succinctly captured in the following, from 18-year-old Rachel:

> You are 17 or 18 — this is the time of your life for having fun. You
> should be able to relax. Next year when I'm free I will be able to read
> what I want, to sit and relax, talk to others, go to Melbourne when
> I want and talk about things I'm interested in. Everyday, walking in
> the gate, I'm switched into school mode — it's a bit like being schizo-
> phrenic.

Part of what is at issue here is an opposition or disjunction between the realms of work and play, between pleasure and the boredom and alienation that marks so much of students' academic life in school — between isolation and abstraction on the one hand, and community and immediacy on the other. Here there is a need to take into account Wexler's (1992, p. 128) observation of 'how much in fact all of school life, for the students, centres around the daily project of establishing a social identity'. The point to emphasize is that this may be at odds with the official project of the school, geared as that is to the abstract competitive academic curriculum, in all its seriousness and hyper-rationalism. Whatever else it is, schooling is clearly not about 'fun'. Even such an ostensibly student- and learning-referenced reform programme such as the Victorian Certificate of Education, with its emphasis on 'process' and 'project', is fraught with complexity and contradiction, as became clearly evident in the debates and struggles surrounding its implementation.

Lindsay Fitzclarence, Bill Green and Chris Bigum

New Formations of Class and Identity

Elsewhere we have suggested that what is at fundamental issue in the current relationship between media culture and student experience, with specific reference here to the post-compulsory phase of schooling, is the formation of a distinctive postmodern student-subject (Green and Bigum, 1993). That is, the young people who are presently the subjects of schooling are also to be understood as the exemplary subjects of postmodernism, itself understood in terms of the relationship between new technologies (and their associated cultural fields) and the consumption-commodification complex. Importantly, this notion of postmodern subjectivity must be grasped as a matter of at once being and becoming. This is because students and young people generally are clearly subjects-in-process, and also because postmodern identity formation needs to be viewed historically and with due regard to local–global dynamics (Hayles, 1990).

Linked to this is the notion of changed and changing relations between education and the media; or rather, between mass compulsory schooling and the electronic mass-popular media. Education and the media are to be seen as competing mass-communication systems, or discursive fields, each with its own projected subject. Increasingly there is a struggle underway between them for the hearts and minds and bodies of the young: the citizens and/or consumers of today and tomorrow. Each clearly has an interest in constructing and securing the future, and therefore significant investments in the present. Located somewhat uneasily in the contested space between them, understood in these terms, is the student, at once subject and object of their gaze and their attention.

This helps in understanding the construction of the school subject, as outlined previously. Schooling becomes more than ever a complex rite of passage fraught with liminal anxiety, its traditional promise of a future increasingly blighted by the uncertainties and intensities of the present. Ontological insecurity goes hand-in-hand with the (ir)reality of everyday life in the late twentieth century. As the 16-year-old cited previously put it: 'A lot of kids shut down through overload. Basically, it's easy to make mistakes.' In Mackay's (1993, p. 224) terms, this is symptomatic of 'an emerging "wait-and-see" mentality' among many young Australians today — a characteristic 'withholding of commitment' that he describes as an entirely understandable position to adopt in a time of such complexity and change. What is at issue here, then, is the formation of a particular practice and performance of the self: a way of being and becoming somebody, in the context of school and society.

Hence our concern here is with the notion of a new form of social subjectivity, in specific relation to young people's ongoing identity work in the techno-cultural spaces of postmodern consumer culture. This is not necessarily a matter of 'high-tech' media culture, as a recognition of the way that contemporary existence is thoroughly suffused with, and informed by, electronically

146

and mass-mediated practices, values and perceptions, in a new complex confusion of techno-nature and everyday life. The notion of *identity* is quite crucial here. How is identity formed in these circumstances? What are the contexts and resources for identity work? How is identity itself to be understood? And what has changed and is different about postmodern identity formation? This is an important insight for understanding life in and out of school, and the changing circumstances and subjectivity of young people today, as well as the widespread public anxiety about contemporary realizations of youth and schooling. For Philip Wexler (1992), it is a matter of recognizing and attending to the nature and quality of self-production in school, as a focus for students' meaning-making and interactional labour. As he writes of his own study of life in school:

> When I tried to encapsulate what students were doing in these high schools, their words summed it up best: becoming somebody. They were not struggling to become nobody, some high postmodernist definition of a decentered self. They wanted to be somebody, a real and presentable self, and one anchored in the verifying eyes of the friends whom they came to school to meet. (Wexler, 1992, p. 7)

Wexler's work suggests further a growing disjunction between the official project of schooling and that of many students, who as a constituency are increasingly disaffected and even alienated. The changing text and context of students' identity work becomes therefore a matter of fundamental concern.

Given this, an important theoretical issue here is the poststructuralist notion of subjectivity itself. Classically defined against and in specific reaction and relation to the humanist subject-individual, it needs now to be reassessed in order to allow for a reconceptualized sense of agency and praxis, and a critical view of the emergence of new forms of the self. The problem is doing this with due regard for the changing *material* conditions of possibility and intelligibility for postmodern identity formation. As we have suggested, what is at issue here is the new significance of media culture in identity work and educational practice, linked to which is the growing importance of *generation* as a social difference-dynamic. Does this mean that social power is now to be understood as differently configured? Quite possibly. That is surely the implication of the following comment by someone involved in youth theatre, taken from our archive: 'Kids from Lalor and Toorak live in the same worlds; they are linked by popular image culture.' Given the quite different socioeconomic character of these Melbourne suburbs, a new pattern of relationships between class and generation is suggested.[9] That is certainly something that cannot be dismissed out of hand. All the same, it would be unwise to overlook or gloss over powerful continuities in social structure and social power. In Wexler's (1992) terms:

> Against the background of a seemingly shared youth mass culture, what students struggle for in becoming somebody and how they

interactional life project during high school — the 'best
'r lives — is different depending on where their school is
' larger societal pattern of organized social differences
...es. (Wexler, 1992, p. 8)

One important dimension of 'post-poststructuralism' is therefore the return to, but also the renewal of, *class* as a significant category for social analysis, and hence new interest in the relationships between class and schooling and class and identity-formation. It is critical, however, that this is properly understood and theorized. It does not mean that the initiatives and interventions, questions and challenges of poststructuralism *per se* can now be safely put aside and forgotten; nor does it mean that those who have so far successfully avoided engaging with the poststructuralist challenge can now comfortably get back to business as usual. The game itself has changed quite radically and dramatically. The passage through poststructuralism has clearly been both traumatic and necessary, in a complex dialectic of crisis and change. In Jane Flax's (1992) felicitous formulation, it may have meant 'the end of innocence' — a problem for the Left as much as for anyone else, if not more so — but at the same time it has generated new possibilities and projects for social analysis and critical theory.

A crucial issue here is the question of new formations of class and identity. For theorists such as Frow (1993) and Rowe (1993), among others, a rapprochement between poststructuralism and Marxism is not only possible but necessary.[10] This is because of the significance of the problematic of *representation*, rethought through postmodern lenses. As Rowe (1993) writes:

The fact is that we have hardly begun to theorize the ways post-industrial economies have transformed the elementary terms of class, production, consumption, and the commodity, among many other crucial categories for any social theory. In these postmodern economies, the means of production are no longer primarily *material* but discursive. (Rowe, 1993, p. 49)

In a similar fashion, Wexler (1987) has argued that education and schooling, as well as critical theory and social analysis, must now be understood in terms of decisive transformations in culture and economy. As with commentators such as Hinkson (1991), he points to significant shifts in the relationship between education and the media, and an increasing emphasis on identity formation and new techno-cultural realizations of the symbolic order. As he writes:

The relation between mass discourse and individual formation and motivation is the emergent education relation. Where the forces of production become informational/communicational, semiotic, and the formation of the subject occurs significantly through mass discourse, then it is that relation which is the educational one. The mass communications/ individual relation now already better exemplifies the educational relation than does the school, which as we know it, with all its structural imitations of industrial and, later, corporate organization, is being surpassed, as new modes of education develop. (Wexler, 1987, p. 174)

This he sees explicitly in terms of an emergent postindustrial social order, and for him, there is a significant *structural* complicity between postindustrialism and poststructuralism. Hence:

[T]alk of a postmodern self belongs in the context of particular historical changes in macrosocial organization and microsocial, everyday institutional practices rather than as an aesthetic extrapolation from postmodern textualism. (Wexler, 1992, p. 146)

With this, we come to one of the key issues and problematics of the study. The changes which are being described here point towards the sort of issues which scholars such as Bowles and Gintis (1976) and Ely (1978) reported nearly two decades ago. More recently, work by Apple (1986) and Connell *et al.* (1982) has continued to argue the case for a critical understanding of the relationship between schooling and social structure. However, there are now clearly new issues at stake. In particular, there is the clear influence of the print and electronic media in helping to set educational and social agendas. At the same time, the media acts to produce definite forms of socially structured response to attempts to reform the upper-secondary school curriculum. Our study data suggests that the policy pronouncements about the need to produce a 'clever country' fall uneasily on many students and staff. To this end, the complex role of the stories told in the media in shaping the form of everyday life requires careful consideration. On this topic, the social theorist Stanley Aronowitz (1989) notes, with specific regard in this instance to working-class males:

Today, working-class kids may still look forward to getting working-class jobs, but forging a class identity is more difficult than ever. They confront a media complex that consistently denies their existence or displaces working-class male identity to other, upwardly mobile occupations, for example, police, football players, and other sites where conventional masculine roles are ubiquitous. (Aronowitz, 1989, p. 204)

Aronowitz is registering that what is at stake is the very question of identity formation; an identity shaped by the powerful forces of the mass media. As such, being able to describe 'who we are' and 'who we are becoming' is a *sine qua non* for an adequate form of interpretation. Becoming the 'clever country' tends to disguise more than it reveals, because it suggests a homogeneity of experience and purpose. A new critical sociology of education will need to demonstrate who wins and who loses because of the restructuring of the education system. In order to effect such work, it will be necessary to adequately describe the cultural patterns associated with the emerging division of labour. As Rowe (1993) states:

> The old categories, terms and assumptions regarding class boundaries and the general distribution of labor will have to be abandoned before new coalitions can be imagined. (Rowe, 1993, pp. 67–8)

The cultural changes alluded to in this chapter can be thought of as features of a postmodern society. The concept of postmodernity is used here to describe complex material changes in contemporary social formations, with 'the postmodern' understood in Hinkson's (1991, p. 8) terms as 'constituted in the flow of images which is now so characteristic of our social lives'. That is, the postmodern world is dominated by communication networks promoted by media and information revolutions (Hinkson, 1991, p. 8). This means that general changes in production are accompanied by pervasive changes in not only class relations but also the construction of class consciousness.

Barry Jones (1990) has described the social dimensions of the changes through use of the categories of 'information rich' and 'information poor'.[11] This categorization, however, is unsatisfactory. The use of a binary logic organized here around the concept of information does not offer a complex enough perspective of the way that information networks interlink with other social divisions and associations. What is important is to see *both* continuity and discontinuity in the distribution of cultural and economic resources:

> The new economic activity of the global money markets does not replace the older economic activity that is based on manufacturing and industry any more than manufacturing and industry replaced agrarian activity. (Williams and Bigum, 1994, p. 2)

They draw on notions of 'second nature' and 'third nature' from Wark (1993), who points to an overlay of one with the other. This second/third nature relationship is described thus:

> Second nature, which appears to us as the geography of cities and roads and harbours and wool stores, is progressively overlayed with a third nature of information flows, creating an information landscape which *almost entirely* covers the old territories [my emphasis]. (Wark, 1993, p. 163)

The point is to acknowledge both the persistence of traditional kinds of social division and the significance of new and emergent forms of the social. What this suggests is the need for a multifaceted form of interpretation, one that retains the sober analysis of the early work in the new sociology of education, which recognized significant asymmetries of power, and at the same time makes use of perspectives on complexity associated with the poststructural turn. Furthermore, new formations of class and identity in education need to be understood with specific reference to the centrality of knowledge and information in postmodern capitalist societies. The current restructuring of curriculum and schooling in Australia, consistent with the rhetoric of the 'clever country', must therefore be examined very carefully in terms of a postmodern politics of culture and identity.

Conclusion

In previous generations, many students would have left school for work in factories, shops or farms, and the skills and capacities required for such work were quite well understood. Now, however, these forms of manual labour have been replaced by machines and 'off shore' production. The farmers of Gippsland, fruit growers of the Riverland, and metal workers of Wollongong all are coming to recognize that an understanding of new technologies is central to their work in the complex new labour market-place. Accordingly, intellectual training — linked to what neo-conservatives label 'the basics' — has come to the fore in educational reform. This has meant that working-class culture has been placed at risk in order to place a higher premium on the intellectual skills championed by people like Barry Jones. At the behest of policy makers in the nation's capitals, educators have been called on to engage in a form of 'cultural cleansing' in order to help produce the new clever country.

The political reform juggernaut of the late 1980s and early 1990s has managed to incorporate most sectors of the polity. The incorporation has been effected through a bipartisan arrangement linking firstly unions and government, and then drawing in many different interest groups. This 'politics of consensus' has meant that the reform strategy has proceeded with only marginal dissent. The reforms as noted above, coupled with a period of sustained financial stringency designed to minimize inflation, have been generally seen as necessary measures to produce structural adjustments in the economy. Given the general absence of dissenting commentary, however, there is urgent need for a critical appraisal of the political and social machinations of the reforms. The following is a list of issues emerging from the reform developments which are meant as a means of contributing to such appraisal.

- In what ways do schools, and students within them, connect to the processes of the wider culture?
- Who are the winners and losers as a result of the structural changes of the last decade? Despite the use of egalitarian pronouncements, associated with the politics of consensus, do the reforms significantly disadvantage certain groups?

151

- How do the reforms account for the emergence of an increasingly large cohort of students who experience 'inadequate education, no job, no financial help, no future' (Mackay, 1989, p. 11)?
- What forms of curriculum practice appear to consolidate dominant interests, and which forms challenge the status quo in order to effect democratic transformation?
- What are the prospects for a politically progressive form of postmodern schooling, understood as both a public service and a social obligation?

Answers to such questions are not easy, or immediately forthcoming. One reason for this interpretive lacunae is the absence of a shared perspective about what constitutes an adequate form of educational theory for these new times. Clearly, however, such a (re)new(ed) politico-theoretical position is needed now, in order to generate new stories about what is worth passing on to the next generation.

Notes

1 Johnson (1993) provides an excellent overview of changing social influences associated with curriculum reforms, specifically in terms of the politics of social class.
2 For a detailed list of education developments associated with the restructuring process, see Emerging National Priorities for Australian Principals (APAPDC, 1994).
3 The Project Team included Richard Bates, Chris Bigum, Lindsay Fitzclarence, Bill Green and Rob Walker, all from the Faculty of Education, Deakin University at Geelong, with assistance from Janine Collier, Meredith O'Neill and Karen Tregenza.
4 See also Fitzclarence (1993a).
5 The schools were located in two different social class contexts; however, in the account which follows we have not made that distinction explicit in reporting on the research. That is a matter for another occasion.
6 This is a national competition whereby schools perform a dance routine set to rock music and which picks up a particular topical theme. In 1993, 500 schools and over 50,000 students competed.
7 Schools in the state of Victoria, and elsewhere to some extent, have witnessed a resurgence of interest in debutante balls in which girls are formally presented to members of the school's adult community. These events cater for students in mainly Years 10 and 11.
8 The 1984 report on the restructuring of education in Victoria which initiated changes such as the VCE.
9 It is clear, also, that there would be significant gender distinctions and differences involved in any such assessment. A more comprehensive account of contemporary 'youth', media culture and postmodern schooling would therefore need to take more explicitly into account the intersections of class, gender, ethnicity and generation, among other social difference-dynamics.

10   See also Aronowitz (1990).
11   For a similar formulation, with reference more particularly to the United Kingdom, see Murdock and Golding (1989).

References

APPLE, M.W. (1986) *Teachers and Texts: A Political Economy of Class and Gender Relations in Education*, New York and London, Routledge and Kegan Paul.

ARONOWITZ, S. (1989) 'Working-class identity and celluloid fantasies in the electronic age', in GIROUX, H. and SIMON, R. (Eds) *Popular Culture, Schooling, and Everyday Life*, Toronto, Ontario Institute for Studies in Education Press.

ARONOWITZ, S. (1990) *The Crisis in Historical Materialism: Class, Politics and Culture in Marxist Theory*, Minneapolis, University of Minnesota Press (2nd ed.).

AUSTRALIAN PRINCIPALS ASSOCIATIONS PROFESSIONAL DEVELOPMENT COUNCIL (APAPDC) (1994) *Emerging National Priorities For Australian Principals*, Millswood, South Australia, The Orphanage Teachers Centre.

BARROWCLOUGH, N. (1994) 'Postcards from the edge', *Good Weekend*, April 30, pp. 30–4.

BRETT, J. (1993) *The Age* (Saturday Extra), July 11, p. 6.

BOWLES, S. and GINTIS, H. (1976) *Schooling in Capitalist America*, New York, Basic Books.

BROWN, J. (1993a) 'Suicide rate leaps for bush teenagers', *The Australian*, September 11, p. 5.

BROWN, J. (1993b) 'Suicide, murder rate linked to unemployment', *The Australian*, May 25, p. 7.

COLLINS, C. (1992) 'Upper secondary education in Australia: Differing responses to a common challenge', *Journal of Curriculum Studies*, V 24, 3, pp. 247–60.

CONNELL, R.W., ASHENDON, D.J., KESSLER, S. and DOWSETT, G.W. (1982) *Making the Difference: Schools, Families and Social Division*, Sydney, Allen and Unwin.

CONNELL, R.W., WHITE, V.M. and JOHNSTON, K. (1991) *Running Twice as Hard: The Disadvantaged Schools Program in Australia*, Geelong, Deakin University Press.

EDGAR, D., KEANE, D. and McDONALD, P. (Eds) (1989) *Child Poverty*, Sydney, Allen and Unwin.

ELY, J. (1978) *Reality and Rhetoric: An Alternative History of Australian Education*, Chippendale, NSW, Alternative Publishing Company in association with the New South Wales Teachers' Federation.

FITZCLARENCE, L. (1993a) 'Images from Morwell, Melbourne and the moon: Curriculum as an element in the "Extended Family of Eyes"', in GREEN, B. (Ed) *Curriculum, Technology and Textual Practice*, Geelong, Deakin University Press, pp. 53–66.

FITZCLARENCE, L., BIGUM, C., GREEN, B. and KENWAY, J. (1993b) 'The Rock Eisteddfodd: Media Culture as a de facto "National Curriculum"', Paper presented at the Annual Conference of the Australian Curriculum Studies Association, Brisbane, July 1993.

FLAX, J. (1992) 'The end of innocence', in BUTLER, J. and SCOTT, J.W. (Eds) *Feminists Theorize the Political*, New York and London, Routledge, pp. 445–63.

FROW, J. (1993) 'Knowledge and class', *Cultural Studies*, 7, 2, May, pp. 240–81.

GRAY, J. (1983) 'The Early Years: 1924–1940', Unpublished manuscript.

GREEN, B. (1993) 'Aliens and Their Others', Keynote Address, The Fourth National

Conference of the Australian Guidance and Counselling Association, Adelaide, Sept, 1993.

GREEN, B. and BIGUM, C. (1993) 'Aliens in the classroom', *Australian Journal of Education*, 37, 2, August, pp. 119–41.

GREGORY, R.G. (1992) 'Aspects of Australian Labour Force Living Standards: The Disappointing Decades 1970–1990', The Copland Oration, 21st Conference of Economists, University of Melbourne, July 1992.

GUNEW, S. (1993) 'Feminism and the politics of irreducible differences: Multiculturalism/ethnicity/race', in GUNEW, S. and YEATMAN, A. (Eds) *Feminism And The Politics Of Difference*, Sydney, Allen and Unwin.

HAYLES, N.K. (1990) *Chaos Bound: Orderly Disorder in Contemporary Literature and Science*, Ithaca and London, Cornell University Press.

HERIOT, G. (1992) 'Australia 2000: Strategic Issues and an Analysis of the External Environment Through the Year 2000 with Specific Reference to the Broadcasting Industry'.

HINKSON, J. (1991) *Postmodernity: State and Education*, Geelong, Deakin University Press.

JINMAN, R. (1993) 'More suicides, fewer road deaths', *The Weekend Australian*, March 13–14, p. 3.

JOHNSON, K. (1993) 'Social class and the curriculum: Transformations old and new', in SMITH, D. (Ed) *Australian Curriculum Reform: Action and Reaction*, Belconnen, ACT, Australian Curriculum Studies Association and Social Science Press.

JONES, B. (1990) *Sleepers, Wake! Technology and the Future of Work*, Melbourne, Oxford University Press.

KENWAY, J., BIGUM, C., FITZCLARENCE, L., COLLIER, J. and TREGENZA, K. (1994) 'New education in new times', *Journal of Educational Policy* (forthcoming).

LANGMAN, L. (1991) 'Alienation and everyday life: Goffman meets Marx at the shopping mall', *International Journal of Sociology and Social Policy*, 11, 6/7/8, pp. 107–24.

MACKAY, I. (1989) 'Black hole for young drop-outs', *The Age*, March 16, p. 11.

MACKAY, H. (1993) *Reinventing Australia: The Mind and Mood of Australia in the 90s*, Pymble, NSW, Angus and Robertson.

MURDOCK, G. and GOLDING, P. (1989) 'Information poverty and political inequality: Citizenship in the age of privatized communications', *Journal of Communication*, 39, 3, Summer, pp. 180–95.

RIZVI, F. (1993) 'Broadbanding equity in Australian schools', in MACPHERSON, I. (Ed) *Curriculum in Profile: Quality or Inequality? — Curriculum '93 Conference Report*, Brisbane, Australian Curriculum Studies Association, pp. 39–45.

ROWE, J.C. (1993) 'The writing class', in POSTER, M. (Ed) *Politics, Theory, and Contemporary Culture*, New York, Columbia University Press, pp. 41–82.

SLATTERY, L. (1989a) 'Teachers join in national strategy', *The Age*, April 5, p. 13.

SLATTERY, L. (1989b) 'Goals set for nation's schools', *The Age*, April 15, p. 1.

TINNING, R. and FITZCLARENCE, L. (1992) 'Postmodern youth culture and the crisis in Australian secondary school physical education', *Quest*, 44, 3, December, pp. 287–303.

WARK, K. (1993) 'Suck on this, planet of noise! (Version 1.2)', in BENNETT, D. (Ed) *Cultural Studies: Pluralism and Theory*, Melbourne, Dept of English, University of Melbourne.

WEXLER, P. (1987) *Social Analysis of Education: After the New Sociology*, London and New York, Routledge and Kegan Paul.

WEXLER, P. (1992) *Becoming Somebody: Toward a Social Psychology of School*, Washington and London, Falmer Press.

WILLIAMS, M. and BIGUM, C. (1994) 'Networking Australian Schools: Preliminaries, Problems and Promise', to be published in proceedings of *Apitite '94*, June 28–July 2, Brisbane.

9 Corporatism, Self and Identity Within Moral Orders: Prestructuralist Reconsiderations of a Poststructuralist Paradox

Robert Funnell

Structuralist approaches are generically paradoxical. They initially promise much but fall away as the so-called positioning powers of a structure or a discourse conflict with the experienced situations of social actors as persons and the contexts of institutional life. Structuralism, in various reformulations, has directed educational research and theory. Its main power has been to explain positioning and distribution of agents within a culture, a social system, as a production of discourses and the reproduction of cognitive dispositions. Where early French structuralists such as Althusser negated the power of agents over structure, there has been an ongoing effort, beginning with Bourdieu (1977) and Giddens (1979), to recompose theory to show how subjects, selves, actors, everyday people and groups did, could, or might act back on given conditions. Poststructuralist theory in its present state represents a significant shift from early structuralism. Variance in the positioning by structures other than class are emphasized to the extent that relations of power and relative autonomy within structured conditions allow for differences in the construction of identity within them. This identity or self, is most often seen as positioned within a second order language and reliant on a voice, a new set of discourses, that will allow power and participation within first-order practices, conversations and institutional relationships. The possibilities inherent within poststructuralism relate to issues of: how the right combinations of interest groups can be assembled to influence knowledge and power over state policy; which types of social actors can be thrown into the debate; and, how these kinds of social actors can be grown within situations of rapid social change. If these questions are to be taken further, then it is necessary to return to prestructuralist problems about the relations between the self, the life world and the theoretical systems meant to bridge them. Such problems, as applied to identity, self and career within institutional settings, are exemplified in works by G.H. Mead, Vygotsky, Schutz, Burger and Luckmann, Goffman, Fromm, C. Wright Mills, Sennett and Cobb, Studs Terkel, Sartre and

Raymond Williams. They can be taken to a new level and in new directions with the knowledge and the insights into the paradoxes of structuralism. This consideration of prestructuralist problems is not a 'nostalgia for a past era' but a reflexive 'bending back' of sociology upon itself, its theories, methods and practices, so as to buttress its future position (Bourdieu and Wacquant, 1992, p. 36). It is here that the oppositions between 'being' (permanence) and 'becoming', which Harvey (1990, p. 283) sees as being central to modernism's history, should be reconceptualized.

This chapter is concerned with the convergence of two previously separate moral orders; those of private-sector corporatism and public-sector bureaucratic administration of state services and, with the problems inherent in the formation of identity and self required within the transformation from one order of codes and sets of values to the other. Employers and workers are now, as Poster (1993, p. 78) contends, 'enmeshed in codes and practices in which they constitute themselves as subjects in terms of morals or values'. Such enmeshings constitute moral orders. Moral orders, for Harrè (1983) and Foucault (1985) emphasize two elements. One element of a moral order is concerned with codes, the expected behaviours, rules and values and the mechanisms to enforce them on a large and local scale. The second element, related though independent, concerns self-formation, the projects for identity, the self-reflexive processes of subjecting oneself in a particular manner to codes, values, rules. Theories seeking to go 'post'structuralism and modernism, concentrate on 'dissolution' (Dean, 1992). They attempt to understand how a self is decentred into discourses, culture(s) and localized versions of them and to show how people are made subjects of dominant codes. In so doing, they offer truncated analyses of the psychological conditions in which people centre and orient themselves to these codes and discourses. With the prime emphasis on the positioning power of codes, structuralist-based theories and methods are rarely able to deal with questions of 'becoming' (Wexler, 1992), of the methods and techniques available for the self to take an ethical position to codes and values (Foucault, 1985) and, of the manner in which identity as a project can be taken up within moral orders pertaining to institutional conditions of change (Harrè, 1983).

The main task in this chapter is to arrive at an outline of a social psychology through which transitions towards the codes of corporatism can be situated as an aspect of the life careers of those working in restructured public institutions. This is done in three sections. The paradox of structuralist-derived theories — of being able to analyse structural positioning and distribution of agents and, of not being able to explain the social psychological processes of becoming a person — is the topic of the first section. The section concludes with a comparison of Foucault's (1985) account of the Hellenic era with present trends in corporate change as an example of how poststructuralist theory might address the formation of self within corporatism. A brief overview of the scope of the sociological field in which corporatism is situated comprises the second section. This is done through examinations of the positions of Pusey (1991), Hunter

(1992) and Lyotard (1984). In the third section a direction toward a social psychology is offered by drawing on the works of Harrè (1979/1993; 1983).

Structuralism, Poststructuralism and Beyond?

Poststructuralist approaches are tied to metaphors of a positioned identity and a decentred self. Poststructuralist, and other related forms of critique locate the tensions between the ideal in theory and the real in the here and now, but ultimately, they tend to reverse one for the other (McCarthy, 1991, p. 5). Such theories, for example, show the forms of distribution into structured positions and the discourses holding people in them. An aspect of this type of analysis however, is a tendency to conceptualize agency as a process of freeing, of potential to escape from, of refusing to participate in institutional practices and power relations. Resistance theory (e.g., Willis, 1974) provides an example of this form of analysis from within structuralist, Marxist, theory where agency was silenced by the 'calling' of Althusserian social-class structures. In such theories aspects of agency concerning the processes of becoming, of attaining a place of value within institutional respect hierarchies as a focus of identity and self-formulation and reformulation are left unanalysed. More recent analysis of the rise of corporate and economic policy in education (Ball, 1990; 1991; Codd, 1992; Lingard, Knight and Porter, 1993) continues within a range from structuralist to poststructuralist and historical portrayals of the rise of a new right and a new managerialism in schools. Such analyses concentrate on the roles of new codes of conduct and the ways in which behaviours of staff are measured and placed under surveillance. These theories are becoming so general that all reactions are covered by universal concepts within a concentrated oppositional stance to 'discourses of corporatism'. The danger is a repeat of earlier eras of structuralist-influenced theory — the intellectual critique gathers such a generalizing force that it is accepted that those experiencing change see it through the lenses of globally constructed sociological theories. The fields of experience of social actors and the political action expected of them in social theories, rarely coincide. Conceptualized structure and the experiences of a situation are built from different practices.

It is only recently, for example, that sociologists labelled most classroom conflict as 'resistance' to, and most school practices as 'reproductive' of class structures, ignoring the fact that lives within schools, families and work operate at different levels of meaning (Connell, 1987). Structuralist-derived theories of education lack a social psychology which will show not only positioning to universal-like structures and discourses, but also explain how people reorient themselves to messages coded at the level of the life world of the institutions in which they operate. Structuralist-oriented analysis is primarily about positioning by structure and discourse into which the self is decentred. Institutional life encompasses moral orders, hierarchies of respect and contempt, in which becoming someone rests on one's personal trajectory or career being at the respect end of the hierarchy. Within a moral order, some careers are available for those who resist, are given a liberating voice, who make it and, who once established in a new position, might see their life trajectory as one of a successful escape. Many more careers in the institutional hierarchy of values for identity are up for a claim by those who, in the majority, remain and seek to establish a place of worth in the order of the institutions where their identities and selves are constituted. The self may be positioned through, and decentred into, a range of discourses but it is centred in the course of establishing a moral career. Psychologically, structuralist and related theories more often than not ask too much from actors whose commitments are much more to their own position within a localized moral order than to structural emancipation.

Explaining the processes of becoming, cannot be done from theory and methods concerned with positioning without the assistance of a social psychology that allows for both processes. Structuralist theories are exhausted when determinism overtakes possibilities for liberation. Theories 'post' an earlier structuralism risk a pouring of new clay into used theoretical moulds. In what follows, I contend that an understanding of the social psychological processes of becoming and of self reformation requires a return to prestructural questions and methods. It is here that the new directions for poststructuralist approaches need to be redressed.

Foucault, Moral Orders and the Self

Some new directions for poststructuralism, that allow for notions of becoming a person of worth in a moral order, are to be found in Foucault's (1985; 1986) later position on self-constitution which he termed 'ethics'. For Poster (1993, p. 64), this third period in Foucault's theory is a return to the existential work of Sartre (1967) on the self as containing a project — an attempt to realize oneself in a particular way. A contrast is evident between Foucault's structuralist position he calls 'archaeology', to a poststructuralist one, 'geneaology', to the problems of the person in relation to the questions of the Enlightenment (Foucault, 1986) in the final volumes of *The History of Sexuality*. In this manner, 'Foucault returns to a prestructuralist problematic but from the position of a poststructuralist' (Poster, 1993, p. 76). It is from such a viewpoint that I also suggest a need for a return to prestructuralist problems as a means for a fuller analysis of the present transformations towards corporatism. This is done through a consideration of Foucault's conceptualization of morality and of his analysis of structural in the Hellenic era.

Moral Codes and Self

Foucault (1985, pp. 25–32) devotes a chapter of the second volume of *The History of Sexuality* to 'Morality and Practice of the Self'. There, he outlines

his methodological considerations for the study of the 'forms and transformations of a "morality"'. The word morality Foucault suggests, is ambiguous.
It may be seen either as a moral code, sets of values, 'rules of conduct',
prescribed in the family, education, etc., or as a morality of behaviours against
which individuals can be measured and brought into desired relations to rules
and values. A third meaning of the term refers to self-formation and the
concern in this order is with questions how does one 'conduct oneself' ethically and recognize and establish one's relation to rules, values and codes as
one is being obliged to put them into practice (1985, p. 26). Every morality
comprises two related though relativity-independent elements. One is the
codes of behaviour and the other is the forms of subjectivation or code-
oriented moralities and to moralities of self. Foucault then (1985, pp. 28–31),
suggests a continuum of relationships between these two moralities. When
the emphasis is on the code, for example, analysis should 'focus on the instances of authority to enforce that code' the requirements for learning it, how
infractions are penalized and the conditions in which the subject must submit
to them at the risk of being punished. Conditions where people are 'urged to
constitute themselves as subjects of moral conduct', analysis turns to models
providing conditions for 'self-reflection, self-knowledge, for decipherment of
the self by oneself, for transformations that one seeks to accomplish oneself
as a subject'.

A remarkable aspect of Foucault's turn in his theory at this stage of its
development, is the similarity it has, not only with Sartre's (1967) existentialism, but also with Goffman's (1961) concept of institutions and the conditions
in which identity is formed within them. In his book *Asylums*, Goffman
proposed conditions ranging from closed or total, to open institutions and of
the moral orders and the possible moral careers of those within them. Institutional conditions afford actors a career, through some risk of punishment or
personal valuation to take up roles within ritualized forms derived from codes,
rules, values, etc. Foucault's (1985, p. 29) advice on the methods for a study
of the history of these codes would probably lead to similar results to those
who followed in Goffman's approach. Two prestructuralist problems, those
about the centring of the self in the life world, and the institutional conditions
in which this occurs, are those which have to be worked upon to shape a
social psychology appropriate to a study of self and identity in conditions of
transition to the codes of corporatism. As a final point to this section, I will
suggest a starting point for such a study.

Self and Others in Periods of Transition:
Points of Departure

Foucault's analysis of the Hellenic era can be read into the present forms of
corporatism. In the third volume of *The History of Sexuality* Foucault (1986)
studies the Hellenic era as the Romans begin to change the government of the

Greek cities. Analogies can be drawn between the transitions in that period with the descriptions of present ones of corporate changes. Some similarities are raised here not to suggest that direct comparisons should be made between the ancient polis and twentieth-century corporatism but to point to methodoligical aspects lacking in the present debate. The point of interest concerns Foucault (1986, p. 71) hypothesis that altering relations between one's self and others in this era was neither the necessary 'consequence' of social changes nor an 'expression' of an ideology. The emphasis is rather on reforming one's relation between 'self and others', the responses to them and the 'new styles of existence' which follow. When meaning is forged out of the situations of those dealing with corporate change, now and in the Hellenic era, it is likely that comparing one's position with that of others is done more to stylize new ways of operating than with consideration to the nature of corporatism and the ideologies surrounding it. In following Foucault, linking ideology and social restructure directly to individuals hinders understanding the alterations to self and others taking place. To make any stronger connections, between the Hellenic era and the present, would involve a consideration of Foucault's belief in Nietzsche's (1967) notion of history as eternal recurrence which is not of issue here.

The errors, for Foucault, in previous histories of the building of Roman-like cities in Greece in the third century were that they were analysed, as decentralization in corporatism is placed today, 'in negative terms as a decline of civic life and a confiscation of power by state authorities operating from further and further away' (Foucault, 1986, pp. 80–2). The 'choice', now as 'in the Hellenic era is not one of whether to participate or to abstain'. It is one of self-orientation in a world, already bureaucraticized but with reoriented power relationships. Previous relations of power have to be accounted for and read into the new. Even before the Romans, Hellenism 'was already a world of cities', it had 'never given security', nor been 'a shelter from the storm' and had 'remained the primary form of social organisation even after the military power had passed into the hands of the great monarchies'. To make an analogy and to paraphrase Foucault: corporatism is presently viewed negatively, as operating from far away through centralized bureaucracies while the state takes power, thus forcing a decline in civic life. This is the core of critiques of the codes of human capital, of the New Right and classical economic theories of education and the bureaucracy. Personally, I share some, often strong, reaction against corporatization of public services. This is due to, as Bourdieu would argue, my position within the field: as a graduate and employee of the university system; from my personal trajectory into this field; and, due also to watching careers of talented colleagues in education either being prematurely terminated or being subjected to the restrictions of micro-economic competences. Sociologically however, corporatism has to be analysed as a new configuration of historically generated power relations between a state, its bureaucracy, the bureaucracies of big and small businesses, the media and other players who seek a position within this new game. It is the game and its moves that have changed. Old moves no longer gain the expected yardage nor assure positional advantage. There is presently no way around this fact.

Corporatism should not escape critique, but the present forms of critique too often positions the 'bad' against the 'good' leaving aside matters of how people should or must deal with what the implications change are for them. Education bureaucracies, for example, have been criticized constantly for a number of decades as being unresponsive and inconsiderate of what goes on in schools and colleges. Schools have been shown to be reproducers of inequalities. Critique which once focused on reproduction has now switched towards corporatism and it has taken on board similar conceptual weaponry. There has however, been some selective memory concerning the research information about bureaucratic and state inefficiencies and the form of critique in which it has historically been based. New economic ideologies have taken over from progressivism in the policy debates as corporate managerialism replaces older forms of bureaucracy, yet an ideology and a bureaucracy remain. Within Hellenism, scenarios of frustration and retreat could be sustained for only so long and, 'recurring choices between retreat and activity' have to be met eventually through determining a stance towards expected activities and determining which activities were now most viable (Foucault, 1986, pp. 94–5).

The new imperial government of the Greco-Roman age looked for 'assistants and allies' who could, persuade 'those subjects under your rule who you are not treating as slaves' that they will share 'advantages and authority'. In seeking complicity, the right numbers of people had to be found who were 'necessary to govern at the right time and in the right way'. What was needed was a 'managerial aristocracy' that would furnish those people necessary to 'administer the world'. Complicity was to some extent ensured because the Greek cities were organized on a 'verticality' that required power over oneself and others and a making of oneself adequate to one's status. This approximates with the accounts of the hierarchical bureaucracy that today's corporatism seeks to replace with flatter structures. The soul, self, required to govern in the new era could reside as well in a Roman knight as in a freeman's son or a slave. This may have brought about 'some withdrawal behaviours', but above all it led to 'a problemitization of political activity'. This facet both in corporatism and in the Hellenic era, suggests that the area for the basis for understanding the relations between those in the old morality of self to the new, rests in the recruitment of a new cadre of managers. With a movement from hierarchical bureaucracy to recruitment by complicity, the rules of self relations alter as well. Forms of political activity (management) became detached from status and now appear as a function to fill (not as professional laws of governing) but on ethical relationships.

With complicity to a position in the new management cadre as the prize, new problems of political activity tied to the fortunes of personal destiny emerge — of sudden and too much success and its withdrawal. This means that the exercise of power was a precarious exercise, success and failure are measured, not in terms of efficiency but, in accordance with the emerging codes. Here, the self must be prepared for the anxiety that reversals in the elaboration and administration of the code will cause. The principle of political activity — the management and administration of one's duties at all levels was a personal responsibility — duties (political and public) were assigned arbitrarily. On this basis they could be given and taken away by accident (Foucault, 1986, p. 84). Therefore:

> ...the new rules of the political game made it more difficult to define the relations between what one was, what one could do, what one was expected to accomplish. The formation of oneself as the ethical subject of one's own actions became more problematic...

The problems of identity within Hellenism, as within corporatism, are those of how to define one's identity and tie it to one's self before, during and after rapid social change. It is the defining of oneself before, during and after such change that is the core problem within corporate restructures and for those working within public-service institutions. Foucault's analysis of Hellenism, applied to corporate change, suggests a redirection for poststructuralist and postmodernist theories to a better understanding of alternations to the self as a relation between moralities of self and code-oriented moralities. Further, it cannot be assumed that people in institutional settings respond directly to either the ideologies of corporatism or, to the logics of the restructuring of the bureaucracies managing them. What is of most consequence is the altered relations between those involved and how a position must be taken to them. Foucault's notion of codes of subjectivation locates the field of relations to these codes, but is not equipped to deal with the ontological aspects of moralities of self (Poster, 1993). These, I argue, are a point of entry to a social psychological study of the transitions to corporatism which are not allowed for in present theory.

The Theoretical Field of Corporatism

There are well-known analyses of ideology and social change within corporatism in the international literature. Common themes carry across these writings that need not be repeated here. Roughly defined, and with some overlap, there are three sociological categories of critique. One situates corporate restructure as 'a crisis of the state' — after Habermas; another is the neo-Weberian analysis of the role of the Bureau which sees corporatism as the State's necessary response to present economic conditions. A third critique is of the hegemonic power of the new managerialism — discourse analysis, poststructuralist and postmodernist. For the purposes of the arguments of this chapter, three authors are said to represent each of these positions in the field of the present analysis of corporatism. The first is Pusey's (1991) work on 'economic rationalism' which draws on Habermas (1975, 1979). A second, neo-Weberian, position on the historical function of the bureaucracy is that of Hunter (1992). Aspects of Lyotard's (1984) *The Postmodern Condition* are said to depict analyses of the discourses of managerialism.

Economic Rationalism: Loss of Vocational Identity

Since the 1980s restructures of public services and state bureaucracies have been linked to the influences of new forms of human-capital theory and free-market economics favouring deregulation and a minimalist role by govern-ments (Marginson, 1993; Gleeson, 1994). Implementation of 'new right' policies derived from such theories have been attributed to politicians pushing this agenda, for example; Reaganomics in the United States, Thatcherism in Brit-ain, Rogernomics in New Zealand. In Australia, 'economic rationalism', after Pusey (1991), is referred to as a similar force behind corporate restructure of the State's public services through 'corporate managerialism'. In such a situ-ation, a market economy replaces 'democratic politics and public planning as the system of production' and education (and other public sectors) are seen as branches 'of economic policy rather than a mix of social, economic and cul-tural policy'. The State takes a deregulatory role while its ministers and senior bureaucrats take a centralist, interventionist stance in public-service reforms, restructuring their departments on lines of managerial efficiency (Marginson, 1993, p. 56). Pusey's (1991, pp. 169–70, 197–8) model, via Habermas (1975, 1979) and Offe (1975), proposes that the mechanisms for steering the State out of a crisis of capital cuts ties between civil society, culture and the foundations of identity formation outside the economic sphere. The process, for Pusey, was begun and continues in the hiring and selective promotion of government ministerial advisers trained in classical economics and corporate management. This is accentuated by a corresponding retrenchment and lowering of status of senior public servants trained in the professions to which the service is aligned. As a consequence, shared tradition is replaced by calls for 'flexibility' to change. There is a culling of 'dead wood', but also of established wisdom, a loss of corporate memory and a demoralization of staff as performance is judged more on economic efficiencies and less on professional expertise. As the steering capacity of the State tends more towards its economic system, mass loyalty towards existing moral cultures breaks down.

Pusey's and related critiques (Yeatman, 1987; Wilenski, 1987) focus on the splintering of the 'moral culture(s)' within bureaucracies and civil society as values tying professional ethics and career vocation supplanted by managerialism and 'posivitistic economists' (Pusey, 1991, pp. 182–3). The critiques of corporatism from Pusey and others often find some resonance with people delivering services such as education and health in restructured schools, colleges and hospitals (Yeatman, 1987; Lingard, O'Brien and Knight,

1993). A similar stance is taken of humanities-trained public servants having their self-positioning towards their vocations fragmented. In this form of critique, what is dislodged by the tenets of economic codes is a loyalty towards shared professional values, a form of 'good will', a cementing organic solidarity. Everyone's position has a 'use by' date in corporate restructure. For the State, as for the corporation, loyalty and previous performance are ignored. It is in short-term gains that demonstrate short-term economic efficiencies that organizational strategy is ascertained. This continues to cause confusion about the role of the public servant — teacher, nurse or bureaucrat whose values have been directed towards service and those requiring it. From within this form of critique the bureaucracy must allow professionals a space to self-position themselves to restructured institutions on the ethical values of their vocations — the dollar, the 'bean counting' mentality of restructuring tears the heart out of a profession.

It is this dissonance between codes of service and their measurement as economic efficiency that separates managers and administrators from teachers, nurses and social workers and other public-service employees. Teachers, as Shona Hearn (1992, p. 81) argues, have a disregard for the codes and values of economic policies that is shown in the manner in which the destinies and careers of people have been disregarded in the restructuring of the New Zealand schooling system. To exemplify this situation, she refers to a Maori folk poem to provide an analogy for how people within teaching institutions are experiencing the emphasis of the economic over the social aspects of schooling:

> If you pluck out the heart of the flaxbush where will the bell bird sing?
> If you ask me what is the most important thing in the world, I will tell you.
> It is the people, it is the people, (it is the people).

Without further analysis of this poem, it is apparent that the processes of implementing and an acceptance of the economic over the social amounts to Sartrean act of 'bad faith'. As teaching jobs disappear, schools are closed, class sizes rise and schools and colleges are forced to consider legislation and finding more of their own resources (Lingard, Knight and Porter; 1994). Economic rationalism is the 'other' which pushes teachers towards a denial of a self, founded on educational values, professional, ethical, and moral worth. The questions here are those about the extent to which self and group expressions of status and moral value can be sustained as a form of 'true self' in the transition from one set of codes to those of another and, in contrast whether notions of the developing self ought to be considered at all. Existing places within the field of education, and other public services, are an outcome of an earlier struggle. There, progressivists supplanted traditionalists, 'new' versions of social-science disciplines justified their positions in the literature over functionalists and empiricists and, the expanding public service rewarded policy made on these lines of thought. The field has shifted. The bureaucracies of the State and the private sector are in new forms of strategy and operation. Reconstruction of the identity of the State as corporation can be done through legislation and policy. The reconstruction of personal identity towards this new formation is more complex. It is a form of deracination, a lifting out of fertile soil for some and a planting of mutated and experimental plants into new seeding plots for others. Those entering and being dislodged in this field have to endeavour to attach and situate themselves to the new codes. This is a psychological matter that is overly sociologized. It is too easily assumed that identity corresponds with, and can be linked with, the theoretical explanation of an oncoming ideolology or with the dynamics of a social change. The logic of such explanation is explored in the following sections of this chapter.

Auditing the Critique Department: Humanist Misunderstandings of the Roles of Bureaucracy and the State

Hunter (1992), theoretically 'audits' the criticisms of Pusey (1991), Yeatman (1988) and others of economic rationalism to establish them as part of an historical tradition for intellectual critique of the bureaucracy. Pusey's contention, is that the 'new classing' of the public service is at the basis of a cultural conflict between those trained in the humanities and those trained in neo-classical economics. The latter, who have a 'trained indifference' to the great traditions of the public service, have generated a crisis of identity, not only within public-service employees, but between the integrity of the bureaucracy and the State which is 'grounded in identity, civil society, community and everyday culture(s)' (Pusey, 1991, p. 18 in Hunter).

> The different intellectual strata are thus identified as components of a 'collective subjectivity', and we return to a view of the bureaucracy as a (flawed) means for the realisation of moral personality. (Hunter, 1992, p. 17)

This form of critique, in which the Bureau become the perpetrator of 'amoral' acts through which the public good is 'surrendered', Hunter terms 'humanistic'. The basis of his audit is based on a premise that the State and the bureaucracy are not established for 'the means of realising certain ultimate principles (of self-realisation and self-determination) attributed to autonomous human subjectivity' (p. 16). Humanistic critique mistakenly establishes necessary relations between the rationalities of the State, the bureau and humanistic ideals. These are 'pictured as the realisation of the rational and moral capacities of self-determining individual subjects' (p. 21). Hunter's argument, follows Weber in that the rationalities of the private and public, of culture and organizational structure are tied to different 'status ethics'. The first set of ethics refers to the nature of the State:

Sociologically speaking, the modern state is an 'enterprise' just like a factory: This is its peculiar historical peculiarity. (Weber, 1968, p. 1394), quoted in Hunter, 1992, p. 15)

The second ethical condition refers to the relations between the State, the Bureau and to those employed by the State to do achieve the objectives of both.

. . . whatever else it may be, the existence of managerial practices and economic objectives common to public bureaucracies and private corporations, is not a sign of the disintegration of the state's moral personality. (Hunter, 1992, p. 20)

Tension arises because the objective necessity of these ethical conditions is not considered and because 'the image of a self-determining personality', inherent in such critique is inadequate for 'social and political analysis in general and for investigations of modern bureaucracies in particular'. The critiques of the new managerialism are part of an 'ethos' that humanist intellectuals attack as depersonalizing.

So, no matter how appropriate the integrated self-realising personality is as the goal of the humanist status ethic, . . . it is utterly incapable of theorising the relation between this ethic and that of the bureau. It can only tell us how this relation looks from the perspective of those inducted into humanism's status ethos . . . (Hunter, 1992, p. 29)

It is perhaps on this premise that Hunter provides three reasons for a break from humanist models to begin investigations of the ethical organization of the corporatized bureau. For Hunter (1992, pp. 20–1)

bureaucracies are the organisational home of ethical and political objectives that cannot — in principle or in practice — be reduced to the ultimate ends of humanism (self-determination, the just society).

the ultimate ends of humanism, cannot be generalised to 'humanity' — and thence to bureaucracy — because they are the goals of a specialised practice of ethical cultivation and the social strata trained in this practice.

the aura of crisis that surrounds the critique of bureaucratic reason is best seen as the instrument and effect of humanism's historical dislocation, as a status ethos, from the political reality of the bureaucratic state.

The State, for Hunter must be organized technically and rationally pursue the political, economic and social ends of security, prosperity and welfare. The current focus of the State on new managerialism and economics is a necessity and not 'the deliberate abandonment of ultimate ends in the political domain'. The techniques required in the formation of the State are of a different order to those concerned with the ends of human self-realization. The bureaucratic and corporate identity is the one which directly matches that required by the State — no matter what its purpose. Moralities related to the self and its formation have no necessary relation with decisions about the ethical nature of the tasks one is asked to perform. These are left within the spheres of private life. Bureaucratic identity and self are however more closely merged at the level of the cadre of management whose task it is to lead the transformation from one direction to the other. Thus for Hunter (p. 31) '(f)rom an historical — that is non-humanist — sociology', the Bureau differs from other forms of organization in that it requires an 'impersonal' self coupled with charismatic or gifted leadership.

From Hunter's perspective, humanist critique of the new managerialism as the amoral arm of misguided economic ideologies represents a mundane 'oppositionalism', one not geared 'to know political reality in the empirical sense'. The historical construction of the Bureau as a system of government necessarily places it 'beyond the cognitive and moral reach (of) . . . morally-based theories of society'. Hunter's points are not always palatable, but they help to form a more complete view of the restructuring within corporatized bureaucracies and as importantly, the turn against humanities-trained intellectuals in state policy-making bodies (Ball, 1991; Stevenson, 1993). His argument is that as the Bureau falls in line with the new codes of the State, it recruits a cadre of managers complicit to the purpose of implementing them, is by now evident. The form which the new bureaucracy takes relies also on the amount of confrontation required to displace the old moral codes and managerial groups and the moral position of management as they and others perceive them. This is also evident in the responses of people who are dealing with devolution of the administrative functions of the bureaucracy and new 'flexible' employment procedures in schools and colleges. Such themes are dealt with in postmodernist literature (Harvey, 1989). It is however in Lyotard's (1984) text that explanation of the self being altered by codes and discourses is most evident.

Lyotard and the Performative Self

Lyotard's (1984) well-known text on postmodernity exemplifies a French, generically structuralist, tendency to decentre the self and to disperse it across a system while placing its constitution under normative powers. Thus, while meanings become localized, self and identity are formed through the economic system and organized through performance as the central moral code within that system.

Corporatization of national governments and a push for free-market economics as the means to rationalize public services and reduce national debt are about system change. Systems, whether national economies, corporations and their divisions, public-service departments and institutions, are changed through restructuring and strategic planning. Planning, for the system and its subunits, comprises a moral order of definable codes of behaviour and values. The means for gaining such change and inculcating values mirrors what Lyotard (1979/84) in talking about technical competence in science, describes as:

> . . . the principle of optimal performance [which]; involves maximising output [the information or modifications obtained] and minimising input (the energy) expended in the process . . . (Lyotard, 1984, p. 44)

In addressing performativity, Lyotard situates it within two binary opposite value systems. For example, the 'game' of optimal performance pertains not to 'the good, the just or the beautiful, etc., but to efficiency', where moves for change are 'good' only if they do something better and expend less financial energy in so doing. Corporatization, in this sense, is about technical competence. Its proponents similarly describe change and moves toward it in terms of efficiency and productivity within systems less complex than government bureaucracies and more like the lean, decentralized super corporations (Peters and Waterman, 1982, Osborne and Gaebler, 1992). The technical competence most sought within corporations is what writers on corporate culture such as Limerick and Cunnington (1993) call 'the management of meaning'. For this to occur, the strategy and mission of the corporation must be much more a part of the language and practices at the level of production than in traditionally organized workplaces and public-sector departments.

The idealized corporate organization is the prototype of simple, low complex, efficient and productive systems and subsystems. The self-managed, corporate-competent worker is the new universal ideal (Kanter, 1985). The codes and values of managerialism have to be adhered to not only within the system and its subunits, but more crucially in the relations between management and workers. Here, Lyotard's critique of systems' models as a paradigm to describe society is apt and describes the codes and values that result from them. The following points, unless acknowledged otherwise, are taken from, and at times paraphrase, Lyotard (1979/84, pp. 46–64).

Taking the (current economic) performativity of a social system as a criteria, public services such as education, training, health, etc., are subsystems. Each subsystem is judged on its efficiency, productivity, ability to skill and reskill, so as to compete in world and local markets. To function, the subsystems must reduce complexity and, at the same time, devolve responsibility for performance to networks of workers — hence an emphasis and a tendency for chief executives and their senior staff to assess their moral worth on their thoroughness in decentralizing and devolving central operational tasks to work groups (Watkins, 1992; Funnell, 1993). Devolution however, increases the speed of information flow, and initially weakens the capacity of the central body to monitor local developments. To do this requires measures that will bring the aspirations of individuals in line with system goals. 'Administrative procedures should make individuals "want" what the system wants in order to perform well.' Some of the 'advantages' for the system which follows are that it: excludes adherence to other discourses; requires the renunciation of fables; demands clear minds and cold wills, makes the 'players' assume responsibility for their proposals and the rules for submitting them and making them acceptable. All functions of knowledge in use are turned around so that they appear to relate to the criteria of efficiency and in so doing they function as 'the apprenticeship of the imagination'. Corporatizing a system is a dismantling and remounting of the historically derived languages of work, service, professional training. It deprives those in the system of their narrative culture.

Within the framework of input–output performance as competence criteria, Lyotard argues, 'the system can count severity among its advantages'. That is, requests of hardship to meet an unmet social need for instance, are viewed, not for how they might alleviate the hardship but on how such an alleviation might increase the system's performance. Needs, whatever their form, are not system regulators, unless not addressing them might destabilize the system itself. The agenda is thus driven by those 'who identify themselves with the social system conceived as a totality in quest of its most performative unity possible'.

If all that can be asked within the organizational subsystem are questions of; 'Is it marketable? Is it efficient?', then competence and performance are assured. The bonus or the dilemma, dependent on the viewpoint, is that competence, efficiency, productivity and so on, cannot now be defined by other criteria. Lyotard's analysis suggests that those who are not favourably placed within the new structures have no voice with which to raise issues that are of importance to them. The self must be performative and it has no 'other' on which a sense of identity can be based and legitimated. Demonstrations of performativity may have little or no grounding in what was once seen as 'good performance'. Thus for example, jobs such as cleaning, security services, grounds maintenance, etc., will disappear as full-time positions and re-emerge as being done by contractors. In other cases a whole production division may be bought and sold and workers laid off irrespective of their contribution, pride in their work, loyalty and competence.

Lyotard, I think, correctly shows that the new approaches to management, work and production from an input–output systems model such as those used in science. As an ideology, competence is judged on economic measures of performativity. What is more, the measures of the 'other' in the old system are severely restricted at the level of policy development and direct decisions about strategy in the new. Appropriate as this analysis is, it need not follow that these within actual settings operate as if this is the case. At some

Codes of Behaviour

New Managerialism
(Hunter)

Economic Performativity
(Lyotard)

State and Bureau

- New Employment Procedures
- Decentralization
- Moral Cultures
  (Pusey, Foucault Vol. 2 and 3)

Institutions

- Moral Orders
- Moral Careers
  (Harrè, Goffman)

Codes of Subjectivation

Figure 9.1: Moral orders within corporate transitions

crucial point this must be reconsidered. Where this fits in the overall debate is now discussed.

The Scope of the Debate

Important as the theories discussed above are, the question unanswered is how people take responsibility for the shaping and reshaping of their lives during periods of corporate restructuring. When corporatism is viewed, using Foucault's (1985) terms, as a morality containing codes of behaviour and codes of subjectivation, then the extent to which corporate change affects self and identity can be ascertained. A contrast of these codes with analyses of the codes of corporatism at the levels of the state bureaucracy and restructured institutions allows a representation of the theoretical debate in the positions outlined this far shown in diagrammatic form in Figure 9.1.

The quadrants differentiate between codes of behaviour (e.g., sets of values, rules of conduct and how they are enforced and measured) and the forms of subjectivation and the moralities of self-formation. These were discussed in the earlier section on Foucault's analysis of the Hellenic era. The State, the Bureau and actual institutions are the fields to which theory and research are directed. Each quadrant indicates an aspect of the field of corporate change within bureaucracies and highlights the 'feel for the game' carried within the literature on corporate change related to that quadrant. Debate about codes of behaviour, those relating to the State and the Bureau are placed in the two quadrants above the horizontal axis of the diagram. Here, Hunter's position, of no necessary relations between the State, the Bureau and individual development can be substantiated, but only at this level. In this quadrant also, lies the theory about the roles of the State and its relations to policy.

Analyses of how codes are measured and enforced in institutions such as Lyotard's depiction of the discourses of performativity fit within the parameters of the top right-hand quadrant. Neither quadrant offers the means to answer questions about the processes and the subjective dispositions to corporate change. The field for such study is in the two quadrants below the horizontal axis. The lower left-side quadrant would contain studies such as Pusey's that identify the impact of restructuring, managerialism and the 'demoralization' of those whose cultures and identities are most affected by codes of economic performativity. Relations between identity and personal development have to be addressed at the level at which Pusey sets his analysis, whether it is through 'humanistic critique' or analysis of another form.

As Foucault (1985, p. 84), mentioned earlier, contends changes to moral codes ask 'new rules of the political game'. It is, in such times, more difficult to define what one is expected to accomplish. 'The formation of oneself (becomes) more problematic'. As such, work done on the lines of 'technologies of self' (Martin, Gutman and Hutton, 1988) and Wexler's (1992, p. 110) notion of institutions, and those in them, being 'desocialized' as an effect of the corporatization of schooling, are examples of how this problem of transition could be understood as a process of subjectivation. As Wexler (1992) indicates in the title of his book, such studies and analyses are a move 'toward a social psychology' but they rest on the development of theory about personal identity which suits the nature of institutional life. This requires not another refinement of structuralism, modernism, Weberian and seemingly forgotten class theories, 'neo' or 'post', but a consideration of prestructuralist problems.

Structuralist-based theory anchors identity, social action, the self, in language, discourse. In prestructuralist theory the emphasis is on consciousness and the assumption is that people know a great deal about the conditions that reproduce society and their position within it. The emphasis here is on action and knowledge, their place and their importance in life careers and related institutional matters. This conscious knowledge is, was and remains, the basis of, if not a universal organizer, then a strong and enduring theme of everyday life — to be somebody, to make it, to get ahead, to be other than we are expected to be. Conscious understanding is directed neither at resisting, or moving out of, nor around structural imperatives. It is tied to the time dimension of the individual life. As Luckmann (1982, p. 255) contends:

> . . . the enchainment of actions in the time dimension of the individual life produces a 'history' of its own: a biography. Here we meet another set of . . . determining factors (that are) self-made. In choosing future courses of action human beings are autonomous, in general principle. But the choices are based on accumulated past experience, an individual stock of knowledge. And the choices are made under the weight of past commitments . . . (but) to try to explain action . . . without allowing for an actor who is a person . . . is downright

absurd . . . A sociological theory of personal identity is therefore urgently needed. Unfortunately, it is still in its infancy . . . (Luckman, 1982, p. 255)

In the analysis of corporatism, the theory of personal identity Luckmann calls for is situated in the lower right-hand quadrant of Figure 9.1. It is also clear that the codes most highlighted in each theory point to a form of identity (one which fits an ideology or a structural change) it assumes, without evidence, that decisions are made on this basis. The focus on structuralist-derived methods means that little or no work of this type exists about corporatism although there is in some analysis about schooling and teaching (Ball and Goodson, 1985; Goodson, 1982; 1990). In the next section, I argue that the direction for a social psychology to explain the subjective transitions to corporatism can be based in part on analysis of 'moral careers' (Goffman, 1961), defined as the social histories of individuals within institutional settings (Harrè, 1979). In each of the positions discussed this far, it is evident that people's places within respect/contempt hierarchies are being re-established within corporate restructuring. Moral careers provide some understanding of individual trajectories through institutions and this is one necessary beginning point for a social psychology.

Toward a Social Psychology

Rom Harrè (1979, Chapter 17) argues that developing a social psychology is a 'political activity'. It depends upon a conception of persons and of the possible forms of social life. It also involves a statement of a moral position underlying it and explicit statements of the political consequences of these views and the political possibilities which adoption of this position would open up. In sketching a position on what a social psychology of corporatism might be, I begin with assumptions from Harrè and Foucault. First, individuals have capacities, personal powers, and with them a right to participate and alter the 'relations of power' within institutions. Power relations should always be able to be entered into and altered to some extent to ensure that 'games' about what is truth and what is not are not always dominated in interactions. The tasks for a social psychology are not so much to liberate one group or individual from the conditions of the fields in which they operate but, to outline the institutional and psychological conditions in which the equilibrium shifts from power over moves within the game to complete domination. Here Bourdieu's analogy to the field and Goffman's range from total and open institutions are useful. Second, the forms of social life in which power is sought result from the formation and construction of hierarchies of respect and contempt. They are relative to the status that people assign to themselves and others, the formation and the continuation of moral orders. For Harrè (1979, pp. 390–4) this leads to a system of moral tension, everyone has the power to deliver an account, they should also have the right to do so. There runs parallel a general political paradox; '(h)ow is it possible to reconcile the interests of individuals and society?' Harrè details two recurring paradoxes that emerge from the general one. To paraphrase Harrè, the first paradox relates to the philosophical question of 'liberty' and the political one of *laissez-faire* government; '(h)ow is it possible to sustain both freedom to construct one's life and character and maintain open economic freedom without one subsuming the other in some form?' The second paradox is tied to philosophical questions of 'equality' and the political concerns of socialism; 'that the activities of all should be managed in the interests of the most exploitable groups within a society'. Both of these political paradoxes run through and are the basis of the tensions in the positions on corporatism and the new managerialism discussed in this chapter. The basic argument has been that as more respect is given to markets and economic performativity, less worth is accorded to those whose positions are based on notions of personal freedom and equality. The disagreements concern the extent to which this accentuation towards the *laissez-faire* should be allowed to continue and the amount and type of management required to do so.

In seeking some type of solution, the differences between Pusey and Hunter (and other similar positions in research and theory) about the place of the bureaucracy within corporatism are crucial. For Hunter, it will be recalled, the Bureau must, because of its historical function, follow whichever of these political paradoxes is seen as in the best interests of the State. His solution is to leave the personal development of those in the private and the public spheres out of the equation. Pusey's contrary position is that the State has created a series of crises. In responding to the economic system, by altering the political-administrative structure of the bureaucracy, it has created a crisis of rationality about performance in the public services and a crisis of motivation and loyalty in the socio-cultural system. Pusey's (1991, pp. 235–6) solution is to take a path in which the State remains the 'true independent variable', not the market and the duty of the State is, to 'culture . . . the processes and internal referents of identity formation and social action'. These solutions are at different ends of the libertarian, social democratic continuum. As Harrè (1979, pp. 394–5) contends, any attempt to suppress one or the other entirely in their political forms will have little effect — as the consequences of allowing liberty clash with the conditions of equality, so the conditions necessary for human liberty clash with the conditions of human equality. Politically, within a social psychology then, the tensions between both of these solutions has to be accepted as a given, both as a political consequence and as a field of possibilities.

One consequence seen in Foucault's analysis of the transitions to Hellenism, and apparent in present studies of corporate bureaucracies, is the recruitment of a cadre of managers to carry out the duties of the State and to ensure that this is done ethically. A second consequence, raised by Harrè (1979, p. 398), of bureaucracies being total institutions, means that managers, as a class, can:

. . . transform themselves so that the moral careers of the function-
aries become dominant over the official work of the institutions, unless
there are other institutions which can conduct a continuous assessment of that total institution and occasionally bring it to heel . . .

This is not a new point but a social psychology which questions corporatism
must be linked to a social psychology of bureaucrats and the relations between
their careers and of those who interact with them. An understanding of these
relations and careers is doubly important in that the central bureaucracy, as
the administrative wing of the State, is one of the few institutions that can
'bring it to heel'.

Corporatism and Moral Careers within Moral Orders

A moral order, to paraphrase Harrè (1983, p. 245), exists among a group of
people when there are rituals for the public marking of respect and contempt;
actions, treated as displays of character and locally typified as an acceptable
and context-appropriate; and, forms of interpretation and talk (potential, and
actual, during and after an event) from which actions can be negotiated, interpreted and cognitively positioned. Some elements of corporatism as a moral
order can be found in the analyses depicted in Figure 9.1 shown earlier.
Corporatism as a moral code in restructuring relations between the State and
the bureaucracy, alters the subjective order through the restructuring to new
employment criteria and devolved work practices. Performativity, is the basis
for measuring, rewarding and punishing the behaviours in institutions. Taking Foucault's differentiation between codes as a guide, most attention is paid
either to codes as new rules of conduct or to how such codes are to be
measured. Little attention is given to moral orders and the moral or ethical
stance which people have to take to these new orders and conditions. The
realm of a social psychology is set in the moral orders in which subjectivity
is established and altered within institutional life and actual lives in progress.
Most analyses of corporatism are not suited to theory and research within this
aspect of the codification of corporate restructuring.

Corporatism has, it is argued, been analysed nearly exclusively within
three quadrants of Figure 9.1. Moral orders, as outlined by Harrè, are appropriate for the study of moral orders within institutional settings. Demonstrating the need, and the place, for a social psychology is in the area depicted in
the fourth quadrant, showing relations between institutions and subjectivation,
has been the purpose of the earlier sections of this chapter. It is here the issue
of the use of one's personal powers to redefine an identity and to centre the
self within corporate restructuring can be more fully understood as a moral
career. Moral careers, following Goffman (1961), cover the social histories of
people according to attitudes, opinions and beliefs others have of them and
their understandings of these attitudes. Moral careers, as institutional life

trajectories, link the psychological and the social to the opinions, beliefs and accounts that are embodied in everyday talk of institutions. Institutional talk, for Harrè (1979, pp. 388–9), offers the possibility for political activity. It brings to the surface the 'private-personal conceiving and a public-social' events within which exist possible ideas about 'alternative social orders' than those operating within a moral order. Seen in this fashion, everyday speech tied to moral careers provides a touchstone between discourse, the intra- and inter-personal dimensions of self and identity and wider ideologies and theories of social change. The extent to which corporate restructures might take hold or become another version of the older order rests on, and includes, a study of the bureaucracy and of the moral careers of managers in relation to the official work they are assigned. Apart from Pusey's study, where the relations between everyday speech and changing moral orders are highlighted but not developed, the voice that is heard is always that of the omniscient theorist.

In dealing with the bureaucracy as an enduring state apparatus, Hunter places institutional and individual tension as outside of the realms of the State and the Bureau. But these tensions need and should be analysed, though not purely as humanistic critique or as the impact of a code of performativity on a system. Understanding how, and through what mechanisms, persons reorient their identities to corporatism raises questions about the life world, Weber's notions of *vestehen*, and Thomas' of the definition of the situation, the powerful demands that confront and demand specific responses to given expectations (Berger, 1963, p. 111). Corporate restructures of bureaucracies constitute a twofold redefinition of bureaucratic situations. Restructures have followed a 'confrontation mode' (Harrè, 1979, p. 400) by the cutting of the workforce, conditions and the introduction of legislation regulation policies to ensure a change to *laissez-faire* economic relationships in the public and private sectors. These changes are for Harrè (1979, p. 402) a 'primary revolution' in that they have changed the practical, operational order. A 'secondary revolution' in contrast, is one in which the conventional signs of respect and contempt in the 'expressive order' are changed. For Harrè, primary revolutions occur without a great effect on the expressive orders.

A central question in the analysis of corporatism is whether or not a primary or a secondary revolution has or is occurring. The tone of most of the recent literature and the ongoing restructuring of public services and the universities from within which critique should originate suggest that the primary revolution is in place and ongoing. The extent of its erosion of the expressive order is evident in the critical and the 'reflexive modernist' writings of Habermas (1975, 1979), Beck, Giddens and Lasch (1994) where moral orders are being separated from established traditions. For Beck (1992) the expressive order is being brought under 'risk' through an interminable and a 'manufactured insecurity'. For younger sociologists such as Wagner (1994) such answers overly simplify the complexity of the issues and alienate them from the possible assistance of lay actors who can offer everyday accounts. Overlaying both the structuralist and modernist explanations and their 'post' versions, social theory has become more and more discursive, its theories are carried in advance by discourse, the stories about more than empirical understandings of the object being sought. The contention in this chapter is that some answers are available in an understanding of how self and identity are being reconstituted in moral orders. Harrè (1979, 1983) has been drawn on to argue that the political underpinnings of the sociological theories about corporate change lack an adequate psychology to understand and suggest how the moral bases are shifting at this level and what directions should be taken. An outline of what directions should be taken toward such a psychology have been generally outlined with an emphasis on moral orders and moral careers. Ultimately, the testing becomes empirical.

Conclusion

The grand theories of structuralism (and functionalism) have set an impossible task, that of conceiving of 'being' and 'becoming' as oppositions. Numerous attempts have been made either to link 'identity to society', to explain structure with and without agency or, to place discourse as a sole mediating mechanism between the two. These approaches support dualisms between the individual and the social and dichotomies between sociology and psychology. Mead, Vygotsky and Goffman have shown that institutional structures and social formations of the self have to be taken together and as relational.

In this vein I have sketched a direction toward a social psychology which highlights the fact that change, at one level within the field of corporate restructure, depends upon the possible schema and worlds that people in institutions must accommodate, can devise and hope for. Politically, it faces the paradoxes of liberty and *laissez-faire* economics and equality within social democracies. Administratively, bureaucratic procedures have to be managed and policed. Within all of this, actors/agents in a wide number of institutions seek and actively strive for places in the hierarchies of respect and contempt that make up moral orders and moral careers. Change; structurally, sociologically, personally and intrapersonally is mutated and never clearly resolved. As many persons as possible, on as many occasions as are possible, have to be involved in what Foucault refers to as games of truth. This depends upon psychological conditions and people with the psychological capacities to be able to intervene in the course of events and reverse the expected balances of power.

The debate about poststructuralism and postmodernism is most often about relations between the State, the bureaucracy and those of academics seeking to establish new positions in theoretical fields which have been disrupted in the corporate restructuring of most national economies and institutions within them. A social psychology, which relates institutional life to actual career paths and positions within moral orders, is needed to take account of the problems of becoming a new person within these changes. Structuralist, modernist and cultural theories, post and neo, have outlined the nature of positioning, by the State, the bureaucracy and social institutions — in Bourdieu's terms, a 'field of struggles'. Within struggle, there is also a 'field of possibilities' and the interconnections between the two fields is the modest dimension of social psychology. Institutional life is conservative, it offers more possibilities to become someone within existing respect/contempt hierarchies than possibilities for escape, and escape can be a category within this hierarchy. Forcing free from positioning is for most a pipe dream — jobs have to be held or sought, bills paid, dependents cared for, given and fought for, reputations have to be upheld. The most obvious possibilities for most people are to become someone of some standing within existing orders.

Here people are forced into positions, they force others into other positions, always with the intent of establishing their position as relative to others. Stylizing of one's life, as Foucault contends, is of singular importance, so too are the provision of technologies to do so morally. This, and the seeking of recognition within moral orders as a dominant institutional and life force, are the beginning of new theory. Neither can follow from a new form of structuralism, nor from newer forms of academic and bureaucratic mutually inclusive, self-perpetuating and self-reinforcing discourses. Such a study begins where structure, history and biography intersect in institutional settings. The paradox is one in which theory aims at liberation, social conditions expect moves to become someone within existing orders.

References

ALTHUSSER, L. (1971) 'Ideology and ideological state apparatuses', *Structure and Society*, Harmondsworth, Penguin.

BALL, S.J. (Ed) (1990) *Foucault and Education, Disciplines and Knowledge*, London and New York, Routledge.

BALL, S.J. (1991) *Politics and Policy Making in Education: Explorations in Policy Sociology*, London, Routledge.

BALL, S.J. and GOODSON, I. (1985) *Teachers' Lives and Careers*, London, New York and Philadelphia, Falmer Press.

BARKER, P. (1993) *Michel Foucault — Subversions of the Subject*, Sydney, Allen and Unwin.

BECK, U. (1992) *Risk Society*, London, Sage.

BECK, U., GIDDENS, A. and LASCH, S. (1994) *Reflexive Modernization*, London, Polity Press.

BERGER, P.L. (1963) *An Invitation to Sociology: A Humanistic Perspective*, Ringwood, Victoria, Penguin Books Australia Ltd.

BERGER, P.L. and LUCKMANN, T. (1971) *The Social Construction of Reality*, Australia, Penguin Books.

BOURDIEU, P. (1977) *Outline of a Theory of Practice*, Cambridge, Cambridge University Press.

BOURDIEU, P. (1987) 'The Biographical Illusion', *Working Papers and Proceedings of the Center for Psychosocial Studies*, no. 14., Chicago, Center for Psychosocial Studies.

BOURDIEU, P. and WACQUANT, L.J.D. (1992) *An Invitation to Reflexive Sociology*, Cambridge, Polity Press.

CODD, J. (1990) 'Educational policy and the crisis of the New Zealand state', in CODD, J. and JONES, A. (Eds) *New Zealand Education Policy Today*, Wellington, Allen and Unwin, pp. 191–205.

CODD, J. (1992) 'Contractualism, Contestability and Choice: Capturing the Language of Educational Reform in New Zealand', Paper presented at the Australian Association for Research in Education, Deakin University, Geelong, November.

CONNELL, R.W. (1983) 'The black box of habit on the wings of history', in CONNELL, R.W. *Which Way Is Up?*, Sydney, Allen and Unwin.

CONNELL, R.W. (1987) *Gender and Power: Society, the Person and Sexual Politics*, Stanford, Stanford University Press.

CONNELL, R.W., ASHENDEN, D., KESSLER, S. and DOWSETT, G. (1982) *Making the Difference*, Sydney, Allen and Unwin.

DAVIS, G., WELLER, P., LEWIS, C. (Eds) (1989) *Corporate Management in Australian Government*, South Melbourne, The Macmillan Company of Australia Pty Ltd.

DEAN, C.J. (1992) *The Self and Its Pleasures, Bataille, Lacan, and The History Of The Decentered Subject*, Ithaca and London, Cornell University Press.

FOUCAULT, M. (1985) *The Use of Pleasure, The History of Sexuality*, Vol. 2 HURLEY, R. (Tr.), Penguin Books.

FOUCAULT, M. (1986) *The Care of the Self — The History of Sexuality*, Vol. 3 HURLEY, R. (Tr.), Penguin Books.

FOUCAULT, M. (1988) 'Technologies of self', Chapter 1 in MARTIN, L.H., GUTMAN, H. and HUTTON, P.H. *Technologies of Self*, London, Tavistock.

FROMM, E. (1955) *The Sane Society*, New York, Holt, Rhinehart and Winston.

FUNNELL, R. (1993) 'Cardigans to corporatism: A state of play analysis of TAFE as an example of micro-economic reform and public sector restructuring', *Australia and New Zealand Journal of Vocational Education and Training*, 1, 1.

GIDDENS, A. (1979) *Central Problems in Social Theory*, London, The Macmillan Press Ltd.

GLEESON, D. (1994) 'Open for business? Knowledge, rhetoric and reality in further education', *Australian and New Zealand Journal of Vocational Education and Training*, 3, 1, pp. 64–87.

GOFFMAN, E. (1959) *The Presentation of Self in Everyday Life*, Harmondsworth, Penguin.

GOFFMAN, E. (1961) *Asylums*, Garden City, Doubleday.

GOODSON, I.F. (1982) 'Life histories and the study of teaching', in HAMERSLEY, M. (Ed) *The Ethnography of Schooling*, Duffield, Yorkshire, Nafferton.

GOODSON, I.F. (Ed) (1990) *Studying Teachers' Lives*, London, Routledge.

GOODSON, I.F. (1991) 'Life history and the study of schooling', *Interchange*, 11, 4.

GOODSON, I.F. and WALKER, R. (1991) *Biography, Identity and Schooling: Episodes in Educational Research*, London and New York, Falmer Press.

HABERMAS, J. (1975) *Legitimation Crisis*, Boston, Beacon Press.

HABERMAS, J. (1979) *Communication and the Evolution of Society*, Boston, Beacon Press.

HARRÈ, R. (1979) *Social Being: A theory for social psychology*, Totowa, NJ, Rowan and Littlefield.

HARRÈ, R. (1983) *Personal Being*, England, Basil Blackwell.

HARRÈ, R. (1993) *Social Being: A Theory for Social Psychology*, 2nd Edition, Totowa, NJ, Rowan and Littlefield.

HARVEY, D. (1989) *The Condition of Postmodernity*, Oxford, Basil Blackwell.

HEARN, S. (1992) 'The revolution in New Zealand Education', *Melbourne Studies in Education*, Carlton, Melbourne University Press.

HUNTER, I. (1992) 'Auditing the critique department: On the humanist understanding of bureaucracy', *Melbourne Studies in Education*, Carlton, Melbourne University Press.

KANTER, R.M. (1985) *The Change Masters, Corporate Entrepreneurs at Work*, London, Unwin Paperbacks.

LIMERICK, D. and CUNNINGTON, B. (1993) *Managing the New Organization: A Blueprint for Networks and Strategic Alliance*, Chatswood, NSW, Business and Professional Publishing.

LINGARD, R., O'BRIEN, P. and KNIGHT, J. (1993) 'Strengthening Australia's schools through corporate federalism?', *Australian Journal of Education*, 37, 3, pp. 231–47.

LINGARD, R., KNIGHT, J. and PORTER, P. (1993) *Schooling Reform in Hard Times*, London, Falmer Press.

LUCKMANN, T. (1981) 'Individual action and social knowledge', in VON CRANACH, M. and HARRÈ, R. (Eds) *The Analysis of Action*, Cambridge, Cambridge University Press.

LYOTARD, J.F. (1984) *The Postmodern Condition: A Report on Knowledge*, Minneapolis, University of Minnesota.

MARGINSON, S. (1993) *Education and Public Policy in Australia*, Cambridge, Cambridge University Press.

McCARTHY, T. (1991) *Ideals and Illusions on Reconstruction and Deconstruction in Contemporary Critical Theory*, Cambridge, MA and London, The MIT Press.

MARTIN, L., GUTMAN, H. and HUTTON, P. (1988) *Technologies of Self*, London, Tavistock.

MILLS, C.W. (1959) *The Sociological Imagination*, New York, University Press.

NIETZSCHE, F. (1967) *Thus Spoke Zarathustra A Book for Everyone and No One*, HOLLINGDALE, R.J. (Tr.), Harmondsworth, Penguin Books.

OFFE, C. (1975) 'The theory of the capitalist state and the problem of policy formulation', in LINDBERG, L.N., ALFORD, R., CROUCH, C. and OFFE, C. *Stress and Contradiction in Modern Capitalism*, New York, Heath and Company.

OSBORNE, D. and GAEBLER, T. (1992) *Reinventing Government*, Ringwood, Australia, Penguin Books.

PARKER, I. (1992) *Discourse Dynamics: Critical Analysis for Social and individual Psychology*, London and New York, Routledge.

PETERS, T. and WATERMAN, R. (1982) *In Search of Excellence: Lessons from America's Best-Run Companies*, New York, Harper and Row.

POSTER, M. (1993) 'The self and its sex: Foucault and the problem of self-constitution', in CAPUTO, J. and YOUNT, M. (Eds) *Foucault and the Critique of Institutions*, University Park, Pennsylvania State University Press.

PUSEY, M. (1991) *Economic Rationalism in Canberra*, Cambridge, New York, Port Chester, Melbourne, Sydney, Cambridge University Press.

SARTRE, J.P. (1967) *Search for Method*, BARNES, H.E. (Tr.), New York, Knopf.

SCHULTZ, A. (1962) *Collected Papers I: The Problem of Social Reality*, The Hague, Martinus Nijhoff.

STEVENSON, J. (1993) 'Competency based training in Australia: An analysis of assumptions', *Australian and New Zealand Journal of Vocational Education and Training*, 1, 1, pp. 87–104.

TERKEL, S. (1972) *Working: People Talk About What They Do All Day and How They Feel About What They Do*, New York, Ballantine Books.

VYGOTSKY, L. (1962) *Thought and Language*, Cambridge, MIT Press.
WAGNER, P. (1994) 'Sociology and contingency: Historicizing epistemology', Paper delivered at the XIIIth World Congress of Sociology, University of Bielefield, July.
WATKINS, P. (1992) 'The Marketing of Education in a Co-ordinated Decentralized Context', Paper presented at the Australian Association for Research in Education Conference, Geelong, November.
WEBER, M. (1968) *Economy and Society*, New York, Bedminster.
WEXLER, P. (1992) *Becoming Somebody: Toward a Social Psychology of School*, London, Falmer Press.
WILENSKI, P. (1987) 'Can government's achieve fairness? Two views of government and society?', in COGHILL, K. (Ed) *The new right's Australian fantasy*, Ringwood, McPhee, Gribble/Penguin, pp. 55–66.
WILLIAMS, R. (1981) *Culture*, Great Britain, Fontana Paperbooks.
WILLIAMS, R. (1983) *Toward 2000*, London, Chatto and Windus, Hoggarth.
WILLIS, P. (1974) *Learning to Labour*, England, Saxon House.
YEATMAN, A. (1987) 'The concept of public management and the Australian state in the 1980s', *Australian Journal of Public Administration*, 46, 4, pp. 339–56.

10 Voicing the 'Other', Speaking for the 'Self', Disrupting the Metanarratives of Educational Theorizing with Poststructural Feminisms

Parlo Singh

Introduction

The task that I have set myself in this chapter is to work through the challenge of deconstructing current poststructural feminist educational theorizing[1] from 'the position of a woman of color'[2]. This concept of taking up positions, and other related concepts such as, speaking for the self, speaking from the margins, and deconstructing the centre, are currently issues of debate within poststructural feminist theorizations in education. It is within this context of debate about the self and the 'other', that theorists using poststructural feminist frameworks, have refused to speak on issues of race[3]. When racial issues are incorporated into poststructural feminist writings they usually take the form of 'triple oppression' (Gilbert and Taylor, 1991), and the 'etc' and 'so forth' of the list of patriarchal oppressions (Luke and Gore, 1992; Luke, 1992). This poststructural feminist silence on issues of race is theoretically justified. The 'sexed self' cannot speak on behalf of 'others', particularly racialized sexed 'others'.[4] There is a 'strong, albeit contested, current within feminism which holds that speaking for others is arrogant, vain, unethical, and politically illegitimate' (Alcoff, 1991, p. 17). While feminists and poststructural theorists 'on the Left' have debated issues centring on the self, the 'other', who has the right to speak for whom (Probyn, 1993), those 'on the Right' have continued to reconstruct racist policies, legislation and practices'.[5] Consequently, it is necessary to re-examine the issues of the self and the 'other', and who speaks for whom, as well as the temporal, spatial, economic and political conditions of speech communities.

I will begin this discussion of the taking up of positions as 'sexed self' and 'racialized self' by analysing the politics of poststructural educational conferencing in Australia. Consider two scenarios, both summarizing discourses produced at a recent conference held at Griffith University — Literacy and Power: Difference, Silence and Textual Practice — where the position of 'woman' and 'racialized man' is taken up to contest the centre and speak on behalf of 'other(s)'.

1   Women use feminist poststructural theories to read, interpret and construct meaning of, participant speaking positions at the conference. The common enemy is 'man', that is 'white, middle class, Eurocentric man'. 'Man' is represented in the confessions of keynote speakers as a 'wife basher' and 'theoretical terrorist'. A woman keynote speaker challenges the male literary canon, and masculine discourses which herald the return to this tradition, with the much applauded statement — 'Well I won't fuck ducks!' Through this statement a position of sexed self is taken up to deconstruct the neuter self of misogynist literary practices.

2   'The day a white middle-class woman stands up and talks not only about gender but problematizes her own racial politics will be a day of celebration.' This statement is authorized from the position of a racialized male self. A white middle-class woman says these words are etched on her brain. Although there are over a hundred participants at the conference, she feels these words are directed at her. She maintains that she is forced in that moment to confront her own racism and later approaches the speaker, apologises and becomes 'quite emotional'.

In both discourses difference is strategically deployed to serve particular political objectives. In the first example, the 'sexed self' or 'woman's voice' is inserted in the discursive politics of traditionally male conferencing. In poststructural feminist terms the masculine voice is challenged and deconstructed. Feminist voices are reconstructed through the organization of feminist pedagogy plenary sessions, feminist networking, feminist interruptions, and feminist interpretations of male speech. The 'sexed self' represents the 'Other' and speaks for the 'Other'. The master's tool, Derrida's deconstruction, becomes *the* politically effective strategy for incorporating the 'sexed self' within the discourses of 'male' conferencing. But the question that remains unanswered is — who is represented by this 'sexed self' and who are the 'others' that she, the 'sexed self', is speaking for?

In the second example, the position of a 'racialized self' is taken up to rebuke 'white women' for not engaging in issues of racism. In this context the 'sexed self' is strategically repositioned first as the centre of oppression, and then, through the deploy of deconstruction, the marginalized voice. The centre now, no longer remains the patriarchal self, masquerading as the neuter self, but the Eurocentric masculine and feminine self. The political effect of this strategy is to deconstruct the power of the centre through the insertion of difference — but what next? Is the centre reconstructed or is it endlessly deferred to 'Others' through the endless suspension of meaning?

It is within this context of the taking up of positions as 'woman' and 'racialized self' that is, the symbolically constructed 'marginalized other' of 'the modernist subject' — patriarchy and/or the grand narratives of modernity (science, reason and individualism), that I want to review and critique poststructural feminist theorizations of education. I believe the central theoretical issues which need to be addressed and reconceptualized are: the self, 'Others', and the strategic deploy of difference and alliance in terms of who has the right to speak for 'Others' and in what contexts (Brah, 1992; Knowles and Mercer, 1992; Perera, 1992; Ram, 1993). I will begin with a brief overview of the sociology of education and the incorporation of the 'woman's voice' within these theoretical texts. I will then move onto a detailed elaboration of concepts taken from four poststructural feminist theories of education. This will be followed by a critique and summary of feminisms, poststructuralisms and education.

Historical Overview, the New Sociology of Education

The objective of poststructural feminist theorizations is to deconstruct binary opposition theorizing which positions woman as the 'Other', and is evident in: the new sociology of education movement; the 'second-wave' new sociology which emphasized the structural determinants in the reproduction of class; and the 'third-wave' new sociology of education known as critical pedagogy (see Luke, 1992; Middleton, 1993). According to Luke (1992) and Moore (1983, 1987), new sociology which began in the early 1970s developed a phenomenological perspective on school knowledge and relations.

> The emphasis was on agency, reality, interaction, and lived experience as co-constitutive of the production of meaning. It was assumed that once educators took into account children's differential subjectivities and background knowledge, schooling could be transformed and students' class-based failure remediated. (Luke, 1992, p. 26)

By contrast, 'second-wave' new sociology emphasized the structural determinants in the reproduction of class and thus of the labour force, social identities and cultures (Luke, 1992). Reproduction theorists emphasized the ideological functions of all state institutions, particularly education, in maintaining the existing class structure of society. Teachers were theorized as agents of the State, working in the bureaucracy of the State, to reproduce particular types of students for the needs of the workforce. Student resistance was theorized as action which could not contest or transform the hegemonic practices of the State. Reproduction became the starting basis of the theory which postulated capitalist structures as invariant.

Critical theorists attempted to move beyond the determinist assumptions of reproduction theory by reintroducing the concept of agency. Luke (1992) proposed that critical theory and critical pedagogy in the 1980s could be seen as constitutive of the 'third-wave' new sociology of education. Critical pedagogy aspired to counteract the pessimism of reproduction theories by centring its project on liberation, empowerment and social justice. Agency was reinstated, but now within the acknowledged constraints or structures of state schooling.

In the Australian context, the 'fourth-wave' new sociology of education attempted to incorporate poststructuralist theories, mainly Foucault and feminist poststructuralist analysis, into an interpretation of schooling. Poststructural feminist theorizations of education are, for the purposes of analysis, categorized as; phenomenological (Davies, 1993; in press), cultural Marxist (Gilbert and Taylor, 1991), psychoanalytic (Walkerdine, 1990)[6] and feminist theories of pedagogy (Luke and Gore, 1992).

Poststructural Feminisms and Education

While there are many theoretical similarities in the poststructural feminist literature on education, there are also points of difference. One of the theoretical similarities in this research includes the use of deconstruction as a strategy to read against the grain of 'patriarchal' texts. Another theoretical strategy deployed by the four poststructural feminist theories is the method of reconstructing texts so that they include the 'woman's voice'. Consequently, all four theorizations, although objecting to the universalizing aspects of 'male' theories, universalize the 'woman's voice'. In this process of universalizing 'women's voices' little attention, apart from the occasional aside, is given to difference within the symbolic category 'woman'. 'Woman' is essentialized not only across cultures, but also space and time, with the sporadic justification that strategic essentializing of 'woman' is necessary as a political strategy (see Luke, 1992). The differences within poststructural feminist theorizations centre on the conception of the self. That is, although all four theorists essentialize 'woman', they arrive at this point through different ontologies.

Drawing on the interpretative or phenomenological sociology of Schutz, Davies (1982, 1989a; 1989b, 1993; in press) theorized about the conceptual frameworks of male and female social identity held by preschool and primary school children. Davies (1982, 1989a) argued that the research method of ethnogeny is based on the philosophical premise that people have the ability to reflect upon, and give meaning, to their experiences. That is, a person is capable of knowing himself or herself through the process of self-reflection. Knowledge is produced as a person comes to know himself or herself through language (i.e., self-reflection). Being and existence is constituted through an interaction with language.

In contrast to the phenomenological position adopted by Davies (1989a), Gilbert and Taylor (1991) and Taylor (1991) appropriated concepts from cultural Marxism for their analysis of the romance genre of popular teenage girls' books. Within this theoretical framework, being and existence are constituted by the capitalist State, which in order to construct a gendered division of labour and specific gendered identities produces patriarchal discourses. Consequently, students' knowledge, in the form of speech and writing, does not produce truth. Rather, students' knowledge is a product of their position within patriarchal discourses. That is, the knowledge or data produced by students (re)produces the power relations of the State. The role of the researcher in this context is to deconstruct the knowledge produced by students to show the workings of patriarchal capitalism (Gilbert and Taylor, 1991).

Rather than focusing solely on the literacy curriculum, Walkerdine (1990) also examined the discourses of postwar schooling, liberal pedagogy and mathematics. By way of contrast to the phenomenological (Davies) and cultural Marxist epistemologies (Gilbert and Taylor) deployed in the two previous categories of poststructural feminist research, Walkerdine (1988; 1989a, 1990) used poststructural readings of the psychoanalytic work of Lacan and Freud to deconstruct the discourses regulating the practices of modern schooling. She argued that when girls enter schooling they have to negotiate difficult and contradictory positions within discourses which expect them to perform as feminine but achieve academically (i.e., rationally) 'as if they were men'. Walkerdine (1990) argued that modern schooling practices simultaneously construct girls as different, that is, the 'Other' of boys, while concurrently silencing difference by constructing discourses of the school child as sanitized, asexual and neuter. Moreover, Walkerdine (1988, 1990) proposed that in the shift from traditional to liberal pedagogy, power relations become invisible and operate through regulating the 'individual'.

By contrast to the feminist poststructuralist project of deconstructing the discourses of liberal humanism and child-centred pedagogy, Luke (1992), Gore (1990, 1993), and Lather (1991) deconstructed the phallogocentrism within the discourses and practices of critical or radical pedagogy. Luke (1992) proposed that educational theorizing, particularly in the form of critical theory, has been historically the project of men and in the interests of the speech community of men. Women, Luke (1992) argued, have traditionally been silenced from this speech community, and therefore, simply granting space for women to critically reflect on their conditions and speak out fails to historize the cultural and social conditions within which girls and women live out their daily lives. Furthermore, Luke and Gore (1992) proposed that speech does not necessarily equate with power. Silence or taking up the position of not speaking can also be a powerful strategy. Furthermore, Lather (1991), Luke (1992) and Gore (1990) argued that critical pedagogy fails to examine the social and historical conditions of speech communities which regulate what girls are allowed to speak about, when, and how their speech may be received by other participants. Moreover, Gore (1990, 1993) argued that critical theorists assume a 'socially reflective' pedagogue with an ability to transfer power, that is, empower oppressed groups. Feminist poststructural theorists however, argued that power is not inherent in one site, that is, the body of the pedagogue, but is exercised through the power–knowledge relation between teacher and student. Consequently, power can not be given to another, but is exercised in and through power–knowledge relations (Gore, 1990; Gore, 1993).

I now turn to a discussion of the two major theoretical concepts advanced by poststructural feminisms in education; discourse and positioning, and power–knowledge relations.

Discourse and Positioning

Within the four categories of poststructural feminist literature in education, Davies and Walkerdine have elaborated the most detailed theorization of discourse and the location of the self within discourse.

Communication and the Self

Davies and Harrè (1990, p. 45) interpreted discourse as an institutionalized use of language and language-like sign systems. They argued that people's understanding and experience of their social identity, the social world and their place in it, is constructed through discourse. Discourses do not identify or describe objects, knowledge and people, they constitute and regulate them and in the practice of doing so conceal their own invention. In addition, particular discourses offer more than one subject position. While a discourse will offer a preferred form of subjectivity, its very organization will imply other subject positions and the possibility of resistance or reversal.

A subject position is defined by Davies and Harrè (1990) through the metaphor of an unfolding narrative. Positioning is the discursive process whereby selves are located in conversations as observably and subjectively coherent participants in jointly produced story lines. In the narrative, persons are constituted in one position or another, or even come to stand in multiple or contradictory positions, or negotiate new positions by 'refusing' the position that the opening rounds of the conversation have made available. According to Davies and Harrè (1990) discursive practices constitute speakers and hearers in certain ways and yet at the same time are a resource through which speakers and hearers can negotiate new positions.

Two forms of positioning namely, interactive and reflexive were identified by Davies and Harrè (1990). In interactive positioning what one person says positions another. Reflexive positioning entails positioning of oneself in discourse. In speaking or acting from a position, people are bringing to the particular situation their history as a subjective being, that is, the history of one who has been in multiple positions and engaged in different forms of discourse. Current understandings of what it means to be a person, Davies (1989b) claimed, require individuals to take up positions in practice as distinctly male or female persons, these terms being meaningful only in relation to each other and understood as essentially oppositional terms.

Davies (1989b, 1993) outlined four processes in the production of subjectivity or sense of oneself. All four processes, Davies (1989b) maintained, arise in relation to a theory of self embodied in pronoun grammar in which persons understand themselves as historically continuous and unitary. The first process involves learning the categories which include some people and exclude others, for example the category of male and female. The second process entails participating in the various discursive practices through which meanings are allocated to categories of masculine and feminine. Positioning of oneself in terms of the categories and story lines is encapsulated in the third process. Positioning implies an imaginative placing of oneself in one category and not in another. The fourth process incorporates the recognition of oneself as having the characteristics that locate one as 'x' or 'not x', that is, the development of personal identity or a sense of oneself as belonging to the world in certain ways and thus seeing the world from one so positioned. Recognition within a category entails an emotional commitment to the category membership and the development of a moral system organized around the belonging.

Proposing a model of agency as a form of discursive practice, Davies (1990) argued:

> ... the person is a person by virtue of the fact that they use the discursive practices of the collectives of which they are a member. Such collectives might include children, boys, students, a particular classroom, one's family etc. Each person can only speak from the positions made available within these collectives through the recognised discursive practices used by each collective. Their desires are formulated in terms that make sense in each of the discourses available to them. (Davies, 1990, p. 343)

Agency, then for Davies (1990), is a matter of location within, or relation to, particular discourses. How that agency is taken up depends upon how the individuals have constructed themselves as a moral being, the degree of commitment to that construction, the alternative discourses available to a person, as well as the subjective history of a person.

Davies and Harrè (1989) theorized that out of the magnitude of conflicting and often contradictory possibilities, persons struggle individually to make themselves a unitary rational being, whose existence is separate from others and yet makes sense to those others. In learning the discursive practices people learn the categories, the relations between categories, and the fine conceptual and interactive detail with which to take up their personhood, and with which to interpret who they are in relation to others. The position of a unitary self however, is more likely to operate at the discourse rather than practice level. According to Davies (1989b), individuals can have multiple contradictory selves or have contradictory social identities situated in different institutionalized narratives. This leads to a certain fragility of self requiring constant maintenance of self. The fact that a consistent and unitary self is never finally achieved makes it possible for new and radically different discourses and positionings to be established and taken on as one's own (Davies and Harrè, 1989).

Discourses of Education and the Constitution of the School-child

Walkerdine (1988) argued that discourse signifies the public process through which meanings are progressively and actively generated in the regulation of practices. Of particular interest to Walkerdine were the discourses of progressive and child-centred education, and mathematics, which she argued regulate classroom life. Walkerdine (1989a, 1990) and Walkerdine and Lucey (1989) were interested in analysing the discourses which regulated the fictional constitution of the child as the object of the pedagogic gaze. Key terms in progressive child-centred pedagogy such as 'the child', the 'facilitating environment', 'active learning', 'stages of cognitive development' were identified by Walkerdine (1989a; 1989b) in order to examine the way in which a regime of truth is constituted in and by the practices. Walkerdine (1989b) argued that

> . . . the discursive practices themselves, in producing the terms of the pedagogy, and therefore the parameters of practice, produce what it means to be a subject, to be subjected, within these practices. (Walkerdine, 1989b, p. 271)

According to Walkerdine (1989b), the discursive practice of the classroom is a complex sign system in which signs are produced and read and have truth effects. The power of progressive pedagogy to construct a truth about schooling is based on its claim to scientific rationality and the fostering of natural, cognitive development. Present practices, Walkerdine (1990, p. 45) argued, assume a universal class-and-gender neutral 'child', who in development, passes from one 'environment' or 'context' to another through utilization and facilitation of cognitive and linguistic capacities. Moreover, the scientific and pedagogical gaze creates a fictional image of 'the child' as an object of adult desire and thereby produces fictional spaces for children to enter.

In examining the discursive spaces constructed for little girls, Walkerdine (1990, p. 118), explored the fictions of a hygienic, sanitized child as compared with a covert, highly sexualized image entering the classroom only at its interstices; the forbidden, denied and suppressed production of children as heterosexual. The fiction is a production and is embodied, built into the very architecture, the seating arrangements, the work cards. The education of girls as children presents something of a dilemma, a dilemma about sexuality suppressed in the pedagogic fantasy itself. Walkerdine (1990) theorized

> . . . what lurks, hidden and subverted, is sexuality — there in the very fictions which are denied in the overt form of the pedagogy. The child whose safety and innocence are worshipped is a far cry

from the sexualised child, object of an overtly sexualised heterosexual gaze. Yet they are not far apart. Such a sexualised child exists as another position, a heterosexual fiction present in the very interstices of the overt pedagogy — its overt and dangerous shadow. (Walkerdine, 1990, p. 121)

On the subject of regulating women, Walkerdine (1990) proposed that sexuality and rationality are integrally intertwined within the discourses of modern schooling institutions. Walkerdine (1990, p. 69) argued that it is important not to see the creation of scientific truth about rationality and women's bodies as a distortion or a simple mistake, but a productive force which has effects. Rationality is located in the sexed body. Moreover, Walkerdine (1990) proposed that the production of male violence is associated with the regulation of sexuality and is evident in schools from infants to secondary. The violence towards girls and female teachers is a fact of the everyday life of the classroom. However, Walkerdine (1990) proposed, while violence is a central feature of the classroom, equally important is female teachers' denial of it. This down-playing, disavowal of boys' violence is endemic to the pedagogic and child-rearing practices on which it is based. The practices actually and positively permit this violence and construct it as the 'natural' way of active boys (Gilbert and Taylor, 1991; Walkerdine, 1989b).

Power–Knowledge Relations

Of the four poststructural feminist theories, Walkerdine's research provides the most detailed account of power relations. Walkerdine (1988) defined power not as an essential property of males or patriarchal structures but as

. . . implicated in the power/knowledge relations invested in the creation and regulation of practices. Here, power is not a single possession of an individual, nor is it located in a unitary, static sense. Rather, power is shifting and fragmentary, . . . Power exists in the apparatuses of regulation . . . (Walkerdine, 1988, pp. 42–3)

Power, for example, is not located in the mother but is exercised in the regulative practices of mothering. Children can and do contest the technologies of mothering practices. Further, Walkerdine (1990) argued power is not only relayed through the construction of silence. Power is productive and consequently regulates or structures desire through the production, circulation and acquisition of discourses. Thus power relations structure the limitations and possibilities of the desire to know.

Walkerdine (1989a) argued that for many women the powerful part of themselves has been so split off as to feel that it belongs to someone else. It is not the case that there is a simple passive wimp femininity, but a power which is both desired, striven after, yet almost too dangerous to acknowledge as belonging to the woman herself. Walkerdine (1989b) concluded that women's success appears to present such a threat to masculine rationality and to the bourgeois and patriarchal power which it underpins, that it is very dangerous for women to admit their own power.

This denial of power, Walkerdine (1988) proposed, can be genealogically traced to the period of the Enlightenment, if not before, when rationality was constructed as a male domain in relation to 'female' knowledge forms which were constructed as irrational. This power–knowledge relation associating masculinity with rationality and scientific truth, and femininity with irrationality continues to regulate the discourses of schooling today. Walkerdine (1990) suggested that

> . . . (for) Rousseau, . . . a 'reasoning woman' was a monster. While Emile's education was a discovery, Sophie's was a lesson in the art of pleasing and being subservient to men . . . What is of particular concern . . . is the transformation of a philosophical doctrine into the object of science in which reason became a capacity invested within the body, and later mind, of the man, from which the female was, by definition, excluded. (Walkerdine, 1990, p. 67)

While individual women may not have fitted this stereotype, Walkerdine (1990) theorized, no woman would be able to stand outside the power of that scientific truth. Women could resist that power, they could dare to be different. But the necessity to struggle and the form that the struggle took was completely bound up with determining that truth. And because the account was located in women's bodies, it immediately placed them as naturally external to a capacity to reason. According to Walkerdine (1988, 1990) in the shift from overt to covert regulation in the classroom, that is the shift from visible to invisible power relations, a capacity for language has been linked to natural reason, and conflict has been individualized, reduced to feelings or a mastery of frustration. The problem, Walkerdine (1990) argued, of reducing powerlessness to a 'feeling' is that it becomes the property of the person. The social construction of authority relations in schooling is disguised in the language of children 'feeling' frustrated and powerless. Powerlessness can hardly be recognized as an effect of regulation in those practices in which power is denied (that is, shifts from overt to covert regulation). Moreover, frustration and powerless 'feelings' can be overcome by the child if he or she is willing to adapt to reality and deal with frustration; in short become a self-regulating, democratic citizen. But, Walkerdine (1990, p. 41) theorized 'as long as "he" experiences frustration, "feels powerless", and so forth, these feelings are pathological'.

From a similar theoretical position, Gilbert (1989a, 1989b) and Gilbert and Taylor (1991) analysed the invisible or naturalized power–knowledge relations invested in discourses of liberal and child-centred literacy classrooms.

They proposed that the social construction of educational discourses as 'natural', 'individualist', 'personalized' and 'child-centred' mitigates against the possibility of equitable practice. Positioned within liberal educational discourse, the teacher does not gain access to ways of identifying and dealing with inequitable relations of power and gender production. Institutionalized inequality becomes naturalized and personalized so that it becomes hegemonic (Gilbert, 1989a).

Power, Desire and Deconstruction

The empowerment of girls, Gilbert and Taylor (1991) and Gilbert (in press) proposed is achieved through the acquisition of strategies of 'reading against the grain' or deconstructing the phallogocentrism within discourses. Gilbert and Taylor (1991) discovered that not all girls read romance novels in the same way. Reading practices were learned because children learned to take up various subject positions which allowed the text to be framed in specific ways. If reading positions, Gilbert and Taylor (1991) argued, are socially constructed, then girls should be taught how to read against the grain of patriarchal texts.

Attempts to change feminine subordination in the classroom must begin with students' experiences. The power of gender ideologies lies in the fact that they work at an emotional level, through the structuring of desires, as well as at a rational level. Deconstructing emotional attachments through analysis of personal lives, however, is problematic. It is personally threatening for many students to place their lives under scrutiny as their very sense of themselves is at stake (Gilbert and Taylor, 1991).

Furthermore, Gilbert (in press) proposed that Kristeva's (1986) three-tier model of women's work provides a guide by which women can challenge and incorporate their voices within the current literacy curriculum. Briefly, the first level of challenge to the patriarchal literacy curriculum is to gain access to the dominant symbolic order. The second phase is to set up oppositional knowledge(s) and construct alternative symbolic order(s) which represent the interests and lived experiences of marginalized groups. The third phase operates on the principle of incorporating alternative meaning systems into the dominant symbolic order. That is, women must create and incorporate alternative ways of reading, writing and speaking in order to express their lived experiences. Moreover, Gilbert (in press) proposed that women must challenge the patriarchal symbolic order which operates on the Cartesian logic of male–female dualisms to create multiple stories and ways of being and living. In this way, both men and women will have available to them, alternative stories by which they can construct their subjectivities and practices.[7]

Power, Desire and Reason's Dream

While Gilbert and Taylor (1991) examined the construction of female desire in romance novels, Walkerdine (1988) analysed the construction of desire within the discourse of primary-school mathematics. She argued that the term 'desire' focuses sharply upon the fantasy of a discourse and practice in which the world becomes what is wanted; regular, ordered, controllable. Emotions have to be suppressed to achieve the fantasy of the mastery of reason.

Walkerdine proposed that 'Reason's dream' is seductive, it offers its subject power over others, oneself and the prediction and control of events. 'Reason's dream' is a fantasy of an omnipotent power over a calculable universe and thereby renders the mathematician an incredibly powerful position. The statements produced by the mathematician are taken to be true. The result of the fantasy is lived as fact. The result of the fantasy is the logical construction of the bourgeois, patriarchal order.

Because the schooling institution defines and delimits normality, it also operates through the regulation of desire. Desire is mastered as control over the 'Other' and of self-control. Control of the 'Other' and narcissistic control of self become one. The pleasure afforded through this mastery is 'somebody else' who is certain, gets right answers, has closure rather than being ceaselessly caught in the web of desire. If desire is controlled, it is not fulfilled or satisfied. Its 'Other', therefore, the loss, the object desired exists in the external reference suppressed in the discourse. The 'Other' of mathematics is uncertainty, irrationality, madness, hysteria. The symbolic is not constituted out of certainty, Walkerdine (1988) argued, but produces certainty out of terror. Control or be controlled. Master the loss. Such a system produces a very powerful body of truth, against a terrifying 'Other' which it must 'know'. That 'Other' constantly threatens those claims and stands outside it.

In the preceding discussion concepts from four poststructuralist feminist theories of education were elaborated. In the following section I will address the limitations of poststructural feminisms. I will focus my critique on poststructural feminisms prioritizing of 'difference' and local contexts of power–knowledge relations, while at the same time, constructing patriarchy as the single source of oppression and essentializing 'woman' and 'women's speaking, reading and writing practices'.

Speech Limitations of the Sexed Self

Before I begin to outline some of the limitations of poststructural feminisms in education, I want to return to the discourses produced in the recent conference held at Griffith University — Literacy and Power: Difference, Silence and Textual Practice — with which I started this chapter. It seems to me, after reviewing the concepts of discourse, positioning, gendered self, power and desire, poststructural feminisms have articulated an elaborate theoretical framework which can be used to analyse local or specific discursive practices (i.e., conversations, teacher–student talk, student learning). Furthermore, poststructural feminisms provide a framework for explaining how taking up a position as a gendered self can be strategically used to disrupt the workings of a traditionally male conference. However, the notion of gender and race subsumed under the single unambiguous signifier of the body, authenticates and authorizes speech (Perera, 1992). The body (racialized and sexed), through the signifiers of chromatism and genitals, is marked as something seemingly promoting difference, but such marking serves simultaneously as an alibi for sameness. The 'unmediated, ahistorical meaning attributed to the . . . body serves in the end to undo difference and to make it recuperable under the agendas of neo-orientalism and humanism' (Perera, 1992, p. 11).

Let me be clear — I am arguing that the racialized subject, like the gendered subject, is positioned in a network of cultural economies which include historical conditions of voicelessness and invisibility in the academy. Consequently, it does matter who is speaking. A speaker's location, that is, social location or social identity 'has an epistemically significant impact on that speaker's claims and can serve either to authorize or deauthorize one's speech' (Alcoff, 1991, p. 7). However, the 'ethnicized critic' is usually present on the privileged stage of the academic conference 'either only as fetishized object or in purely discursified form '(Perera, 1992, p. 19). This does not imply that the 'racialized Other' must be deterministically constructed by the discourses of conferences. Since race and sex are multiple and ambivalent rather than unitary signifiers, 'there are several contradictory ways in which these signifiers can be articulated, received and put into circulation in the construction of social and political meaning' (Perera, 1992, p. 7).

> Location and positionality should not be conceived as one-dimensional or static, but as multiple and with varying degrees of mobility. What it means, then, to speak from or within a group and/or a location is immensely complex. To the extent that location is not a fixed essence, and to the extent that there is an uneasy, under-determined, and contested relationship between location on the one hand and meaning and truth on the other, we cannot reduce evaluation of meaning and truth to a simple identification of the speaker's location. (Alcoff, 1991, p. 17)

Consequently, it is not enough to simply take up positions as racialized or gendered subject and interrupt conferences with personalized confessions. It is necessary to theorize about the social, historical and cultural conditions of the 'rituals of speaking' (Foucault cited in Alcoff, 1991) and representation, that is, the power and control relations which determine who can speak for whom and under what conditions (Alcoff, 1991; Probyn, 1993). 'Rituals of speaking are constitutive of meaning, the meaning of the words spoken as well as the meaning of the event' (Alcoff, 1991, p. 12). This means that the ontology of meaning should be shifted from its location in a text or utterance to a larger space which includes the discursive context. In other words, the meaning of a speech act must be understood as plural and shifting and not essentialized and fixed in the body of the speaker.

I now want to return to the limitations of poststructural feminist theorizing, which similarly focuses on difference, authorized female voice and the local, and consequently neglects the macro-structural reforms taking place in education globally.

The Structure of Pedagogic Discourse

Because poststructural feminist theorizations celebrate difference and thereby focus on the local and the specific, they fail to examine the uniform structures of state-education systems across the world today. Under the conditions of reorganized global capitalism in the latter part of the twentieth century there exists a uniformity in the structure of schooling systems. That is, the pedagogic device by which power and control relations are relayed through schooling systems across national boundaries is similar. The focus on difference and the local fails to account for this global similarity across education systems (Bernstein, 1990).

Theories of cultural reproduction which focus on the surface features of the transmission device such as those of poststructural feminisms in education cannot conceptualize the structural conditions of the pedagogy which constructs positions of marginalization (Bernstein, in press; 1990). Bernstein (1990) proposed that the pedagogic device is the device which structures the power and control relations of knowledge transmission in all state-education systems in socialist, communist and democratically governed societies in the world today. The pedagogic device of education systems is structured by the rules of production, recontextualization and evaluation. These rules are hierarchically organized and are common features of schooling systems in the late twentieth century. Production rules demarcate between 'thinkable' and 'unthinkable' or 'esoteric' and 'mundane' knowledge forms. In this way, state systems regulate the boundaries of legitimate educational knowledge in schools. Recontextualization, Bernstein (in press, 1990) suggested, is the ideological process through which discourses are delocated, relocated and refocused with other specialized discourses, bringing them into new relations with one another and thereby introducing a new temporal, internal ordering. For example, knowledge produced in universities is recontextualized for school use by curriculum writers, authors of textbooks and software producers. During the process of recontextualization the power and control relations internal to the structure of the knowledge are changed. Bernstein (1990) described knowledge transmitted in schools as instructional discourse. Instructional discourse, in turn, is structured by the rules of selection, organization, pacing and evaluation. Moreover, the internal structure of instructional discourse is governed by the regulative discourse of 'macro' (state system) and 'micro' (local) contexts. That is, the social order (division of labour), the social relations (relations within the division of labour) and social identity (self and group) will regulate the process by which knowledge or instructional discourses are selected, organized, paced, as well as the criterion of evaluation (Bernstein, 1990).

Voicing the 'Other', Speaking for the Self. Who get's Left out?

Poststructural feminisms silence on the macro-changes or restructuring taking place in education is symptomatic of what Alcoff (1991, p. 17) calls the 're-treat response'. Alcoff (1991) argued that

> This response is simply to retreat from all practices of speaking for and assert that one can only know one's own narrow individual ex-perience and one's 'own truth' and can never make claims beyond this. This response is motivated in part by the desire to recognize difference, for example, different priorities, without organizing these differences into hierarchies. (Alcoff, 1991, p. 17)

Although this response is sometimes the result of a desire to undertake political work without engaging in discursive imperialism, it significantly undercuts the possibility of political effectivity (Alcoff, 1991). It seems para-doxical that when capitalism is restructuring the State across national bounda-ries in new structures of international education, that social educational theorists attempt to avoid political and theoretical imperialism by speaking only for the 'self'.

I am not implying here that poststructural feminists in education have not recognized the urgency of connecting local and wider political struggles. However, the discussions remain locked into calls for developing 'connec-tions', 'affinities' and 'networks'. The research does not explore the interre-lationship between the various forms of social differentiation empirically and historically. The research does not question the similarities and differences between members of the social category — the 'Other'. Furthermore, post-structural feminisms assume that the oppressions of 'others' are derived from a single determining instance such as; patriarchy, capitalism or the modernist project.

Although poststructural feminisms recognize that the category 'woman' is a social construct, their analysis does not examine how 'woman' is con-strued in specific instances by agencies in the public domain with which women come into contact (Knowles and Mercer, 1992). Rather, poststructural feminisms in education tend to theorize 'woman' as a victim of omnipresent, overarching discourses of patriarchy and modernism. This means that the category 'woman' which has become the significant category of 'difference' within poststructural feminisms and educational theory is essentialized. Women are not inevitably oppressed by men or capitalism. Oppression is not inevi-table for all women and 'Other(s)'. Rather, power relations which may op-press some women, in some circumstances, at particular times are negotiated, struggled over and can be challenged. Theoretical focus on the local context must differentiate between the 'demarcation of a category as an object of social discourse, as an analytical category, and as a subject of political mobilisation without making assumptions about their permanence or stability across time and space' (Brah, 1992, p. 138).

My central question now is: How do poststructural feminists in education strategically deploy 'difference' in order to make a political difference? Poststructural feminists theorizing in education clearly have talked about the way in which 'woman' as a symbolic category is constructed in a differential power relation to 'man'. In this context, 'man' and the masculine represent rationality, scientific truth and knowledge, 'woman' as the 'Other' of 'man', the second in the binary couplet is always represented in the negative or deficit. But is there difference outside of this binary?

It seems to me that the only difference made significant in the writings of poststructuralist feminisms is the biological difference of woman to man. Moreover, poststructural feminists claim that by deconstructing the grand narratives of academic patriarchy they are serving the interests of all 'Others' in all contexts. Although — they do attempt to denounce this universalizing tendency — by adding on the 'so forth', the 'etc', and the structural hierarchies of double and triple oppression in constituting the people(s) that have been, and continue to be, oppressed by the 'western phallocentric order' (see for example, Davies, in press; Gilbert, in press; Gilbert and Taylor, 1991; Luke and Gore, 1992). For example, Luke and Gore (1992) proposed that

> The politics of difference rationalized by the western phallocentric order subjugates not only women in general as well as women marked by particular differences, but men outside the normative (white heterosexual) representation of 'inside'. The vision of the normative subject has authorized not only sexist discourses and practices, but extends its rule across multiple dimensions of difference: from race, ethnicity, sexuality to religion, nationality, ability and so forth. *The exclusions and subjugations women experience under patriarchal and sexist discourses are in many ways not that dissimilar from the personal and structural discrimination many women of color or gay men experience within that same regime* (my emphasis). (Luke and Gore, 1992, p. 196)

The implicit starting point of poststructural feminism(s) is that educational theorizing, although masquerading as universal, rational, scientific and objective is essentially masculinist. This implies that women have no speaking positions within the academy unless they take up masculinist positions. The project of poststructural feminisms is to deconstruct the masculinist project of educational theorizing and insert the 'woman's voice'. Epistemological and ontological priority is given to the power relations of patriarchy. In other words, patriarchy as opposed to racism, classism, capitalism, for example, is given ontological priority as the source and site of oppression. Modernity and its associated patriarchal symbolic order become 'synonymous with terroristic claims of reason, science and totality' (Giroux, 1992, p. 43).

I have three problems with this analysis. In the first instance, the project of modernity and the Enlightenment are constructed as totalizing, patriarchal and misogynist discourses. This is erroneous and misleading. Political modernism constructed a project that rested on a distinction between political liberalism and economic liberalism. While economic liberalism promoted the instrumental rationality of capitalist market economics, political liberalism has been associated with the principles and rights embodied in the democratic revolution that has progressed in the West over the last three centuries. The ideals of the political project of modernism were founded in the capacity of individuals to act upon conditions which cause human suffering, to define the principles of equality, liberty and justice, and to create social conditions in which human beings will develop the capacities to transform ideologies and material forms which legitimate and are embedded in relations of domination (Giroux, 1992).

This does not imply that discrepancies did not exist between the glowing principles of the Age of Europe, the Enlightenment, and the actual practices. Nor does it imply that the discourses of rationality, science, progress and civilization were not used to define, through the power of conquest, the position of 'Others' (women, Blacks, indigenous people). However, it is the very contradictions and the ambivalence of the modernist project which have created the spaces, the interstices from which 'Other(s)' can speak. By taking up these speaking positions in the ruptures or fissures of modernist discourses, subjects 'Other' than those of the European male subject, have been able to reconstruct and thereby change the discourses of the Enlightenment.

My second point of concern is the desire by poststructural feminists to use the Master's tools of deconstruction and logocentrism. This desire for explanation in terms of binary, centre/margin categories, that is logocentrism, is a strategy of colonization (Spivak, 1987). Poststructural feminisms by placing 'woman' symbolically as the significant oppressed 'Other' within modernist discourses, colonises all 'Others' who have been, and continue to be, marginalized. In addition, the focus by poststructural feminists on speaking for the 'self', and granting epistemic privilege to the ontological space of the margin, is of concern because it does not move the marginalized from this discursive and material space. Marginality and sites identified as 'places of pain' are 'now celebrated as the permanent dwelling place from which to produce stirring critiques of the Eurocentric (masculinist) subject' (Ram, 1993, p. 6). While celebrating difference and heterogeneity, the deconstructive linguistics of poststructuralism homogenizes the 'Other', and thereby silences issues of economic underdevelopment, colonialism and racism. Because they rely solely on logocentrism as a set of explanations and deconstruction as a tool of critique and resistance the texts of poststructural writers are assimilationist and represent the cultural and feminine 'Other' as mute (Ram, 1993).

The postmodern is described in such all-inclusive terms, as in Liz Grosz's version, that it ends up being a tool of an assimilationist and universalising drive all the harder to name as such because of the continual celebratory rhetoric of difference, diversity, heterogeneity and localisms. (Ram, 1993, p. 11)

The only way to avoid mutism is to deconstruct phallogocentric discourses, using the Master's tools, from the position of the margin. Does this imply that those marginalized 'Others' who do not engage in the deconstructive strategies of poststructural European and feminist theorizing remain 'voiceless'? It seems problematic that while poststructural feminisms celebrate difference and diversity, strategies of resistance although localized, are homogeneous.

My third point of concern is the epistemic privilege granted to the feminist (read as white, middle-class academic) voice of critique or deconstruction within feminist poststructural theories of education. The politics of poststructural feminist theorizing in the academy have been captured well by Luke (in press) and Luke and Gore (1992) who argued that a universal feminist position is necessary to destabilize the literary canon and the patriarchal centre of academic discourse. Luke (in press) claimed that

Feminist discourse *is* ultimately the most visible and powerful part of the postmodernist move to local sites and valorization of voices from the margins. (Luke, in press, p. 17)

However, this universal feminist position is in sharp contrast to that of anti-colonial theorists such as Bhabha (1986, 1990), Young (1992), and West (1993) who proposed that the disruptures in the universalizing discourses of modernity have been produced by Afro-American and Third-World activists and writers, for example, prior to the much exalted social movements of 1968, historically venerated as the key turning point of power–knowledge relations in the writings of Foucault. While deconstruction has been a strategy used by black activists through cultural products such as the blues and jazz, it gained political legitimacy on the Left when a male, European subject began to write on this issue. Derrida did not invent deconstruction. It had been invented by oppressed and marginalized groups long before the events in France of 1968.

Rather than looking to the centre of the western academy for explanations about the changing social, cultural and historical circumstances in the late twentieth century, anti-colonial theorists have analysed the decolonization of the 'Third World', that is, the rise of nations which were once the colonies of Europe.

With the first defeat of a western nation by a non-western nation — in Japan's victory over Russia (1905); revolutions in Persia (1905), Turkey (1908), Mexico (1911–12), China (1912); and much later the independence of India (1947), China (1948); and the triumph of Ghana (1957) — the actuality of a decolonized globe loomed large. Born of violent struggle, consciousness-raising, and the reconstruction of identities, decolonization simultaneously brings with it new perspectives on that long festering understanding of the Age of Europe (of which colonial domination represents the *costs* of 'progress', 'order', and 'culture'), as well as requiring new readings of the economic boom in the United States (wherein the Black, Brown, Yellow, Red, White, female, gay, lesbian, and elderly working class live the same *costs* as cheap labour at home as well as in U.S. — dominated Latin American and Pacific rim markets). (West, 1993, p. 207)

The process of decolonization has changed irreversibly the practices of colonization (Hall, 1992; West, 1993). Since the Second World War during which, for the most part, the decolonization of the European empires has taken place, there has been an accompanying attempt to decolonize European thought and the forms of its history. This project, Young (1992) argued was initiated in 1961 by Fanon's The *Wretched of the Earth*. I am not implying that new forms of colonial practices (i.e., neo-colonialism and postcolonialism) do not exist. What I am saying is that the political, economic and cultural relationship of Empire and colony, centre and periphery has changed. There is no going back.

Decolonization and the accompanying resurgence of Asian-Pacific economies, languages and cultures has ushered in a New World Order (West, 1993). Japan has emerged as an economic leader. And south-east Asian countries, recently represented as 'undeveloped', 'too traditional' or 'Third World' are now the fastest growing economies in the world (Alexander and Rizvi, 1993; Hall, 1992). In addition, mass worldwide immigration has dislocated and relocated people from the former colonies of Europe. As immigrant people, the former colonized now constitute part of the black diaspora.

The diaspora experience as I intend it here is defined, not by essence or purity, but by the recognition of a necessary heterogeneity and diversity; by a conception of 'identity' which lives with and through, not despite, difference, by *hybridity*. Diaspora identities are those which are constantly producing and reproducing themselves anew, through transformation and difference. (Hall, 1990, p. 235)

Through the process of anti-colonial struggles, the English-speaking world has been forced to listen to the point of view of 'others', of those selves who have been colonized, and continue to be oppressed. Speaking and writing in English, from the geographic heart of English cultural production (i.e., London, New York, Brisbane), the point of view of the colonized is increasingly seen as a part of English-speaking culture (Brennan, 1990). It is a situation in which, as the Indo-English writer Salman Rushdie (1982, p. 8) points out, English 'no longer an English language grows from many roots; and those whom it once colonized are carving out large territories within the language for themselves'.

Conclusion

In this chapter I have argued that poststructural feminisms have disrupted the metanarratives of educational theorizing through the insertion of the 'woman's voice'. I have outlined my concerns about the logocentric and deconstructive strategies of this poststructural project. The disruption of the 'masculinist voice' has relied on the use of the Master's tool of deconstruction and logocentric explanation which has celebrated the position of the 'marginalized'. Concepts such as discourse and positioning, and power–knowledge relations have focused on the 'I' of the sexed self as the 'Other' of the Eurocentric masculine self and in the process revered the position or location of the margins. Further, I have proposed that the focus on the local and the claim of speaking for the 'sexed self' while developing 'connections' with 'Other' struggles has not forged alliances. The focus remains on the individual, the sexed individual of humanism. I have suggested that modernity and the discourses of the Enlightenment are not the omnipresent and misogynist discourses portrayed in the texts of poststructural feminisms. Rather, the discourses of the Enlightenment have created the democratic spaces from which 'Others' can speak and change practices. Moreover, I have urged the importance of poststructural feminisms to engage with theorizations which explore the political-economic dimensions of educational restructuring.

Most importantly I have argued that the differences of 'Others' within the category 'Other' are *significant differences* and should not be classified as the *same differences* of 'white middle-class women' in the academy. By granting epistemological and ontological priority to the similar differences of 'Others', women in the academy reveal their reticence to implicate men as allies. This reticence may symbolize a reluctance by white middle-class feminists in the academy to identify and engage with racism, for feminist theory is still puzzling over the relationship between race, class and gender as forms of social division. It is not sufficient for poststructural feminisms to merely tag on other forms of oppression with the words 'etc', 'so forth', and 'triple oppression' in order to engage with the 'linguistic acrobatics' (Luke, 1992) of academic theorizing and political activities. Epistemological privilege must be granted to the 'etc' and the 'so forth' of oppressions, for as they are currently written into poststructural feminist texts they are merely the negative binary 'Other' of the 'woman' constituted as the negative patriarchal 'Other'.[8]

Notes

1 In this chapter postmodern feminist sociology and postmodern feminism have not been conceptualized as distinctly different from poststructural feminisms in

educational theorizing. This in no way implies a unified conception of poststructuralism or postmodernism. Rather, the similarities of the postmodern cultural, social and literary critiques to poststructuralism as outlined by Flax (1987) are used in this study. Flax argued that the postmodern philosophy attempts to disrupt the beliefs prevalent in (American) culture derived from the Enlightenment, such as:

- The existence of a stable, coherent self.
- Reason and its 'science' — philosophy — can provide an objective, reliable, and universal foundation of knowledge.
- Knowledge acquired from the right use of reason is truth and represents something real, unchanging and universal about the human mind and the structure of the natural world.
- Reason has transcendental and universal qualities.
- There are complex interconnections between reason, autonomy and freedom.
- By grounding claims to authority in reason, the conflicts between truth, knowledge and power can be overcome. Truth can serve power without distortion. Knowledge can be both neutral and also socially beneficial.
- Science is the discipline of reason and also the paradigm for all true knowledge. Science is neutral in its methods and contents but socially beneficial in its results.
- Language is in some sense transparent. Language is merely the medium in and through which the representation of the 'real' occurs.

A similar position on postmodern literary, cultural and social critiques can be found in the work of Luke and Luke (1990), Murphy (1989) and Yeatman (1992).

2 In the second section of the chapter I will theorize on the issue of taking up positions as a 'woman of color' and 'man of color', that is 'racialised sexed selves' (Probyn, 1993). I am not clear about what Carmen Luke is attempting to signify by the use of this phrase. I assume, however, that Carmen Luke is suggesting that 'women of color' insert their voice in the texts of poststructural feminisms through the discursive strategies of deconstruction. However, I am not clear why Luke needs to demarcate between the symbolic category women and 'women of color'. My immediate question is why has she chosen the racialized body as the signifier of difference, rather than, say for example, the social, cultural and historical experience of colonization (i.e., Aboriginal women) or immigration (i.e., non-English speaking women). While the bodies of 'women of color' may be visibly marked in similar ways, that is chromatism (Spivak, 1988), their personal and social selves are markedly different. The taking up of a position as 'woman of color' theoretically essentializes and universalizes 'woman' on the basis of skin colouring which seems to be contrary to the project of poststructural feminisms.

3 Notable exceptions are:
Luke, C. (1992) 'Women in the academy: Gendered discourse and cultural power', Paper prepared for the Victoria University of Technology Conference: 'A Gendered Culture: Educational Management in the '90s'.
Luke, C. (1992, under review). 'The politicised "I" and depoliticised "We". The politics of theory in postmodern feminisms', *Social Semiotics*.
Carmen Luke engages with Afro-American and Third World feminist literature in

an attempt to deconstruct her own position as a white, female, middle-class and North American teacher in her interactions with male and female Islander, Aboriginal and Kanaka students.

4   Elspeth Probyn (1993) in her book *Sexing the Self*, introduces the concept of the sexed self. Probyn argued that the self as a neutered self, concealing the masculine self, and speaking as the organic intellectual of the working class has been the dominant theoretical conception of the self in cultural sociology prior to feminist theorizing. The concept of the sexed self attempts to synthesize the ontology of being female and the epistemology of speaking of the self (me) and the Other (she).

5   (a) Note particularly here the recent press coverage of the Australian High Court's Native Title Ruling (MABO), former Prime Minister John Gorton's comments regarding Australia's Indigenous people, the response of the Liberal Opposition to the Labor Government's attempts at reconciliation with Indigenous people, and the attempt to 'suspend' the 1975 Commonwealth Racial Discrimination Act in order to appease the interests of the mining and pastoral industries in relation to the High Court's Native Title Ruling particularly in the states of Queensland and Western Australia. In addition, Aboriginal groups claim that Daniel Yock's death in police custody in Brisbane, Australia recently is yet another example of state racial violence against indigenous people. The protest by Aboriginal groups was supported by a wide sector of the Australian community in all major Australian cities and many rural Queensland towns.
(b) The discourse between the Australian Prime Minister, Mr Keating and the Malaysian Prime Minister, Mr Mahathir, can be read as a politics of the self and the 'other', the centre and the margin in the play of economic politics. Mr Mahathir deconstructed the power/knowledge relations within Mr Keating's discourse which represented Australia as a postindustrial First World and Malaysia as a traditional Third World country through threats of economic sanctions against Australia. These threats represent, not a personal offence taken by a culturally traditional Malaysian Prime Minister, but the voice of a 'Third World country' demanding a place as a rapidly growing 'Second World modernist nation' in the 'New World Order'.

6   Although Valerie Walkerdine is a Britain-based researcher, her work has been used extensively in the Australian context to theorize the dynamics of gender interaction, as well as to analyse mathematical and literacy texts.

7   Pam Gilbert (in press) theorizes about the stages of a poststructural feminist project using Kristeva's work. After deconstructing masculinist assumptions in the literary canon from the position of the 'other', the objective is to mainstream feminist reading and writing practices. Similarly, Davies (1993) writes about moving beyond the binaries of male and female dualism and mainstreaming feminist strategies for reading and writing.

8   I am grateful to Basil Bernstein, Richard Smith and John Knight for their enthusiasm and encouragement for this project which was part of my doctoral dissertation. I thank Leanora Spry for the many discussions on the concept of the sexed, racialized self.

References

Alcoff, L. (1991) 'The problem of speaking for others', *Cultural Critique*, 20, pp. 5–33.

ALEXANDER, D. and RIZVI, F. (1993) 'Education, markets and the contradictions of Asia-Australia relations', *The Australian Universities' Review*, 36, 2, pp. 16–20.

BENHABIB, S. (1990) 'Epistemologies of postmodernism: A rejoinder to Jean-Francois Lyotard', in NICHOLSON, L.J. (Ed) *Feminism/Postmodernism*, London, Routledge.

BERNSTEIN, B. (1990) *The Structuring of Pedagogic Discourse: Class, Codes and Control*, (Volume 4), London, Routledge.

BERNSTEIN, B. (in press) 'Code theory and research', in BERNSTEIN, B. (Ed) *Class, Codes and Control*, (Volume 5), London, Routledge, Barcelona, El Roure.

BHABHA, H.K. (1986) 'Of mimicry and man: The ambivalence of colonial discourse', in DONALD, J. and HALL, S. (Eds) *Politics and Ideology*, Milton Keynes, The Open University Press.

BHABHA, H.K. (1990) 'DissemiNation: Time, narrative, and the margins of the modern nation', in BHABHA, H.K. (Ed) *Nation and Narration*, London, Routledge.

BRAH, A. (1992) 'Difference, diversity and differentiation', in DONALD, J. and RATTANSI, A. (Eds) *'Race', Culture and Difference*, London, The Open University Press.

BRENNAN, T. (1990) 'The national longing for form', in BHABHA, H.K. (Ed) *Nation and Narration*, London, Routledge.

DAVIES, B. (1982) *Life in the Classroom and Playground: The Accounts of Primary School Children*, London, Routledge and Kegan Paul.

DAVIES, B. (1989a) *Frogs and Snails and Feminist Tales*, Sydney, Allen and Unwin.

DAVIES, B. (1989b) 'The discursive production of the male/female dualism in school settings', *Oxford Review of Education*, 15, 3, pp. 229–41.

DAVIES, B. (1990) 'Agency as a form of discursive practice: A classroom scene observed', *British Journal of Sociology of Education*, 11, 3, pp. 341–61.

DAVIES, B. (1993) *Shards of Glass*, Sydney, Allen and Unwin.

DAVIES, B. (in press) *Poststructural Theory — Classroom Practice*, Geelong, Deakin University Press.

DAVIES, B. and HARRÈ, R. (1989) 'Explaining the Oxbridge figures', *Oxford Review of Education*, 15, 3, pp. 221–5.

DAVIES, B. and HARRÈ, R. (1990) 'Positioning: The discursive production of selves', *Journal of Theory of Social Behaviour*, 20, 1, 43–63.

FLAX, J. (1987) 'Postmodernism and gender relations in feminist theory: Signs', *Journal of Women in Culture and Society*, 12, 4, pp. 621–43.

FLAX, J. (1990) 'Postmodernism and gender relations in feminist theory', in NICHOLSON, L.J. (Ed) *Feminism/Postmodernism*, London, Routledge.

GILBERT, P. (1989a) 'Personally (and passively) yours: Girls, literacy and education', *Oxford Review of Education*, 15, 3, pp. 257–65.

GILBERT, P. (1989b) *Writing, Schooling and Deconstruction: From Voice to Text in the Classroom*, London, Routledge.

GILBERT, P. (in press) 'Discourses on gender and literacy: Changing the stories', in FREEBODY, P., MUSPRATT, S. and LUKE, A. (Eds) *Constructing Critical Literacies: Teaching and Learning Textual Practices*, New York, Falmer Press.

GILBERT, P. and TAYLOR, S. (1991) *Fashioning the Feminine: Girls, Popular Culture and Schooling*, Sydney, Allen and Unwin.

GIROUX, H. (1992) *Border Crossings: Cultural Workers and the Politics of Education*, London, Routledge.

GORE, J. (1990) 'What we can do for you! What *can* "We" Do for "You"?: Struggling over empowerment in critical and feminist pedagogy', *Educational Foundations*, 4, 3, pp. 5–26.

GORE, J. (1993) *The Struggle for Pedagogies: Critical and Feminist Discourses as Regimes of Truth*, London, Routledge.

HALL, S. (1992) 'New ethnicities', in DONALD, J. and RATTANSI, A. (Eds) *Race, Culture and Difference*, London, Sage.

KNOWLES, C. and MERCER, S. (1992) 'Feminism and antiracism: an exploration of the political possibilities', in DONALD, J. and RATTANSI, A. (Eds) *'Race', Culture and Difference*, London, The Open University Press.

LATHER, P. (1991) *Getting Smart: Feminist Research and Pedagogy With/in the Postmodern*, London, Routledge.

LUKE, C. (1992) 'Feminists politics in radical pedagogy', in LUKE, C. and GORE, J. (Eds) *Feminisms and Critical Pedagogy*, London, Routledge.

LUKE, C. (in press) 'The politicised "I" and the depoliticised "We": The politics of theory in postmodern feminisms', *Social Semiotics*.

LUKE, C. and GORE, J. (1992) 'Women in the academy: Strategy, struggle, survival', in LUKE, C. and GORE, J. (Eds) *Feminisms and Critical Pedagogy*, London, Routledge.

LUKE, A. and LUKE, C. (1990) 'School knowledge as simulation: Curriculum in postmodern conditions', *Discourse*, 19, 2, pp. 75–91.

KRISTEVA, J. (1986) 'Women's time', in MOI, T. (Ed) *The Kristeva Reader*, Oxford, Blackwell.

MIDDLETON, S. (1993) *Educating Feminists: Life Histories and Pedagogies*, New York, Falmer Press.

MOORE, R. (1993) 'Education and Production. A Generative Model', Unpublished doctoral dissertation, Institute of Education, University of London, London.

MOORE, R. (1987) 'Education and the ideology of production', *British Journal of Sociology of Education*, 8, 2, 227–41.

MURPHY, J.W. (1989) 'Making sense of postmodern sociology', *The British Journal of Sociology*, 39, 4, pp. 600–14.

PERERA, S. (1992) 'Making difference: Language, corporeality and the protocols of conferencing', Paper delivered at 'Dealing with Difference' Conference, University of Melbourne, November 21.

PROBYN, E. (1993) *Sexing the Self: Gendered Positions in Cultural Studies*, London, Routledge.

RAM, K. (1993) 'Too "traditional" once again: Some poststructuralists on the aspirations of the immigrant/third world female subject', *Australian Feminist Studies*, 17, pp. 5–28.

SPIVAK, G.C. (1987) *In Other Worlds: Essays in Cultural Politics*, New York, Methuen.

SPIVAK, G.C. (1988) 'Can the subaltern speak?', in NELSON, C. and GROSSBERG, L. (Eds) *Marxism and the Interpretation of Culture*, Chicago, University of Illinois Press.

TAYLOR, S. (1991) 'Feminist classroom practice and cultural politics: Some further thoughts about "Girl Number Twenty" and Ideology', *Discourse*, 11, 2, pp. 22–47.

WALLACE, M. (1993) 'Negative images: Towards a black feminist criticism', in DURING, S. (Ed) *The Cultural Studies Reader*, London, Routledge.

WALKERDINE, V. (1988) *The Mastery of Reason: Cognitive Development and the Production of Rationality*, London, Routledge.

WALKERDINE, V. (1989a) *Counting Girls Out*, London, Virago.

WALKERDINE, V. (1989b) 'Femininity as performance', *Oxford Review of Education*, 15, 3, pp. 267–79.

Parlo Singh

WALKERDINE, V. (1990) *Schoolgirl Fictions*, London, Verso.

WALKERDINE, V. and LUCEY, H. (1989) *Democracy in the Kitchen? Regulating Mothers and Socialising Daughters*, London, Virago.

WEXLER, P. (1987) *Social Analysis of Education*, London, Routledge.

WEST, C. (1993) 'The new cultural politics of difference', in DURING, S. (Ed) *The Cultural Studies Reader*, London, Routledge.

YEATMAN, A. (1992) 'Postmodern epistemological politics and social science', Unpublished manuscript, New Zealand, Massey University.

YOUNG, R. (1992) 'Colonialism and humanism', in DONALD, J. and RATTANSI, A. (Eds) *'Race', Culture and Difference*, London, The Open University Press.

Part 4

Politics

11 Educational Intellectuals and Corporate Politics[1]

James G. Ladwig

> If I am incomplete, don't fill the gaps
> Save me from the people
> who would save me from myself
> *Gang of Four* (the rock group)

Toward the continuing agenda of re-articulating and understanding the nature of intellectual work, in this chapter I attempt to link some current Australian and US educational critique with what are probably some fairly obscure notions about intellectuals and their work. The current criticisms I address are those which have been constructed against 'corporatism' in education. The reason for choosing to focus on these debates lie in what I take to be an unseen conception of corporatism, a conception which reveals more potential than risk. The alternative notions of intellectual work I present pivot around a construct named 'the nomadic intellectual'.

To facilitate the intended dual functions of this essay, I organize the discussion below in two main sections. First, I attempt to present a critical analysis of some of the current critique of educational corporatism. I then turn toward the task of presenting this alternative image of intellectual work, an image I take to be both more accurate and more modest than the image I find guiding much of the current critique of corporatism. I close with a brief overview of the alternative corporatist agenda I just mentioned, an agenda not yet widely discussed in educational research.

Here my intent is simply to present this other conception of corporatism as one alternative, as one offering that might nurture future collective debates about the role of corporatism in the work of educational intellectuals. I should note that much of the historical and social outline lying behind the image I am presenting of nomadic intellectuals in education has already been articulated by Popkewitz (1991). Drawing connections between Foucauldian inflected socio-historical analyses of intellectuals in US educational history, Bourdieu's critique of ethereal universalism, feminist analyses of the tensions between poststructuralism and a broader feminist politics, Popkewitz incisively cuts away much of the taken-for-granted common sense of 'populist' English-speaking educational intellectuals who seem blindly committed to an appropriated and simplistic form of Gramscian intellectual nostalgia. In the attempt to construct an alternative I seek not to fill any gaps, but simply to document the way in which anti-statist educational thought might find spaces of freedom within the gaps that already exist.

What of the Critique of Corporatism?

To begin this offering, I shall argue that contemporary academic criticisms of so-called corporate politics in education seem to be premised on the strength of a dangerously beguiling discourse, a discourse that can be seen as a discourse of pure intellectualism. Within this discourse, I argue, many authors of academically better-known criticisms of corporatism in Australian education interweave predictable slogans of radical critique with an analytical posture that is neither empirically accurate nor pragmatically productive. While the specific criticisms raised against corporate competitiveness and new forms of Australian federalism are undoubtedly sound, I find currently repetitive appeals to nostalgically simplified political stances neither particularly enlightening nor politically useful.

On the surface of it, like most 'new' theories in education, these specific theoretical developments in educational policy are, for many students of educational theory, rather mundane and quite predictable. There is, however, one aspect of the current reliance on 'corporatist' explanations within Australian and US-based educational theory which is quite interesting. That is, it is really very interesting to ask why these 'new' explanations seem somehow unique or even needed. As a general rule of thumb, I think, explanations of supposedly 'new' social formations which gain wide currency in the academy become much more interesting when we ask how these explanations became plausible in the first place.

Whence the 'corporatist' critique? Current restructuring movements in education undeniably have become a global phenomenon. The so-called corporatist reorganization identified, for example, in the US by Wexler (1993), and in Australia by Lingard (1991) and Yeatman (1993), is traceable along the planet's colonial bureaucratic flows and the pathways of post-WWII economic organizational networks such as the OECD. In countries typically identified as industrialized or even postindustrial, such as the US and Australia, the common-sense language accompanying many educational restructuring manoeuvres is equally undeniably economically based. Thus it is that educational scholars in many parts of the world currently face a major task in trying to construct adequate explanations and understandings of the current post-Fordist rearticulation of educational policy and the associated bureaucratic reorganization.

On the one hand, in countries where federal governments have been unabashedly neo-conservative throughout the 1980s, such as the US and

England (as obvious examples), the economic agenda of concurrent educational reform has carried some rather obvious intents. On the other hand, in countries where federal governments have been relatively more progressive (as compared to their formal opposition, in name at least), an economic agenda of educational reform, similar to that of other nations, has apparently been a little more difficult to understand. After all, traditionally progressive political parties have historically been associated with educational agendas that are less obviously driven by economic concern.

So it is that the association between the current Australian federal government, controlled by the Australian Labour Party (the ALP), and evidently economically driven educational policy has led 'critical' educational scholars to proffer explanations of this ostensible contradiction under the banners of 'neo-corporatism', 'corporate politics', and (when specifically targeting the current federal government), 'corporate federalism' (e.g., Bartlett, Knight and Lingard, 1991; Bartlett, Lingard and Knight, 1992; Lingard, Knight and Porter, 1993).

In the case of the Australian rise of corporatist explanations in education, the turn to 'corporatist' explanations relies on one of the most long-standing interests of social and sociological theory. In crude terms, social theorists are often confronted with the need to explain how seemingly whole populations of human beings allow or even encourage governments to take up policies that are, from the perspective of one or another particular social theoretical framework, clearly not in the interest of that wider population. In neo-Marxist terms, this dilemma is the source of state theories of 'legitimation' and one of the central tasks addressed in analyses of ideology.

In fact, in this case, the analytical ties with neo-Marxist sociological literature are quite direct. With direct citations of Offe's (1975, 1984, 1985) explanations of state legitimation and the relative disorganization of capital, Schmitter's (1974) ordinant essay on neo-corporatism, and Panitch's (1986a) socialist analysis of governmental impasse in social democratic states, the intellectual genesis of current corporatist explanations within Australian educational literature is rather evident. This turn to the European-based neo-Marxist social theory is certainly understandable, given the Australian academic intellectual heritage. The concern about issues of legitimation is also understandable given the rather stark mid- to late- 1980s turn to the Right of the Australian Federal Government under the ALP.

To be fair, it is certainly true that European-oriented intellectuals were publishing additional material on neo-corporatism well into the 1980s (e.g., Schmitter, 1985; Grant, 1985; Panitch, 1986b). However, it should at least be recognized as a curiosity that in response to late 1980s circumstances Australian and United States commentators felt it appropriate to appropriate theoretical lenses originally developed in political conditions from nearly twenty years earlier, on the opposite side of the planet. Appropriating far-flung theoretical constructions is not necessarily a problem; but in this case, I believe this appropriation of criticisms of corporatism has led to some disconcerting limitations within current radical educational theory.

For the moment I would like to focus specifically on the interrelation between two such limitations. These two limitations can be named with rather direct criticisms. First, I argue that with both a lack of conceptual clarity and a flawed structure of argument, current critiques offer up a dubious under-standing of economic interest in public policy debates. Second, as mentioned earlier, I simply pose the reminder that the intellectuals who pen these criti-cisms are themselves well incorporated into the socioeconomic systems which are being criticized. These two points, I think, become much more interesting and important when the interconnections between them become clear.

A dubious economic critique from pure intellectuals with some rather subtle play on some not-so-subtle dichotomous values (pitting the non-eco-nomic against the economic, or the public against the private, etc), conven-tional criticisms of corporatism fail to emphasize the profound extent to which social reality has been incorporated within institutional systems, at both the level of the social and at the level of desire. Perhaps more importantly, these criticisms also seem to reveal that incorporation occurred right under the historical noses of these analysts. To speak autobiographically for a moment, as one born in the US in the wake of JFK's assassination, the intertwining of social and economic institutions has been a fact for my entire life. And so it goes that much of the current criticism seems more historically quaint than informative when attacks on corporatist agendas are defended by obvious statements of nostalgia. Consider, for example, Wexler's (1993) observation that:

> There is no longer any pretence of an organized public institutional mediation between education and economic production. From 'the school to work transition', to the redefinition of educational knowl-edge and, finally, the subject of schooling, the student, education is to be reorganised to both mirror restructured workplaces as organi-zations and to match them by a smoother flow and transfer of the product, from the student to worker. (Wexler, 1993, p. 2)

Beyond personal observations, the long-standing tradition of educational cri-tique which opposes an economic vision of education demonstrates the tenu-ousness of an historical memory which suggests education once was not economically rationalized in very direct ways. From at least the early twen-tieth century educational efficiency movement in the US, from commonly cited educational statesmen such as Dewey and his so-called 'progressive' colleagues, from radical authorities of the 1950s and 1960s such as C. Wright Mills and Jules Henry, from the nineteenth century feminist rationalizations of more humane educational practices, from the well-known debates between Washington and DuBois, it is clear that if ever there was a dominant common sense of education in industrialized countries, it has been that education is fundamentally taken to be primarily a concern of national economies. Without denying the important impact more sociocultural images of schooling have had in the reasonings of influential social circles, it is very difficult to see current and very basic economic rationality as either something new or historically different. To base a critique on a differing image of education is to elevate alternative images of education well above the rather marginal status they have historically held.

Similar nostalgic observations accompany much of the Australian literature, but is particularly evident in Yeatman's (1990, 1993) concern over Australia's ostensible loss of a publicly minded corps of public servants. For example, in her analysis of corporate managerialism, Yeatman (1993) begins from the premise that a new managerial culture has developed in the welfare state. On the surface of it, this point seems quite sound. However, when turning to a presentation of the supposedly virtuous past managerial culture, Yeatman seems to use an overly clean memory to claim that in the past,

> . . . it was a good thing to recruit public servants from people committed to and motivated in terms of public service . . . (and) . . . while it was important to keep your senior and middle public servants remunerated at average senior and middle professional salaries levels, these were not people motivated by interests of private gain. (Yeatman, 1993 pp. 3–4)

As with nostalgic images of macro-level public educational rationale, I find this image of past public servant life in Australia more than a little deceptive. Assigning motivational interests in private gain to the other of corporate managerialism seems to me both a bit too self-righteous and probably empirically wrong (after all, did those past important remunerations really carry no motivational influence?).

With these two points of nostalgic fudging I think it is possible to see the image of economics presented in current criticisms of educational corporatism at both the macro- and micro- level (in this case at the level of the nation and at the level of the person). I have already pointed out that I take these points to be of dubious empirical accuracy. Parts of this inaccuracy I would attribute to an underdeveloped conception of economic interests, in which economics and motivations toward personal gain are somehow not social or cultural.

On the macro-level, this view of economic interests denies the basic fact that the principles of capitalist economics and corporatism are fundamentally cultural. As Marxist analyses have so strongly demonstrated, basic beliefs in property ownership and the legal systems which defend such ownership and control are at the heart of so-called materialist analyses. As collectively shared unconscious beliefs and norms, propositions about ownership are certainly more cultural and social than material. Consequently, setting up economic political interests as somehow opposed to so-called social interests seems, to me, conceptually blurry.

On the micro-level, the view of interest in personal gain as somehow opposed to interests in public service denies the intense complexities of the connections between personal gain and so-called public service. As a general point, I would suggest educational analyses of corporatism (and perhaps even all social critique) might be better served if one worked from the premise that both personal and social interests serve as motivational forces in almost all sociopolitical systems. As one of the long litany of analytically constructed dichotomies (along with 'us and them' and, of course, 'good and bad'), the split between public and private interests is often only as clear as the analyst makes it. After all, many corporatist supporters would argue that their policy formations are in the public interests (whether or not 'we' like those interests).

Most importantly for this essay, though, I think it is possible to see that the image of economics and economic rationality presented in these critical essays holds the status of the 'other' — as something outside of, or different from, the sociocultural or existential interests of the authors. Some of the empirical and conceptual inaccuracy discussed above I would attribute to the narrative structuring of arguments in which the 'good' and the 'bad' are pretty clearly defined. Aside from the exogenous empirical problems of these analyses, this narrative structuring endogenously positions the authors of these narratives in an equally unlikely posture.

To explain the posture constructed by these criticisms of corporatism, I think it is clear from the analysis above that the critique of corporatism gains saliency by investing in what I call a discourse of pure intellectuals whereby the authors of these 'analyses' set themselves outside the very corporatism shunned by critique. While risking the seemingly inevitable epistemological break with the object of one's analysis may be necessary for any social analysis, failure to recognize this break as the construction of the analysis can lead to a failure to recognize the structures which make such critique possible in the first place. Not only do such analyses rely on simple, normative, forms of intellectual puritanism, the depictions of social reality presented by these critiques are, at best, partial. Of course, constructing partial depictions of reality is not necessarily a problem; but, in this case, the empirical blind spot created by current criticisms of Australian corporatism can be associated with significantly limited political strategies.

That is, it seems to me that while pure intellectuals have been busily constructing partial depictions of corporatism, they have also failed to recognize the potential offered by the systems into which they themselves are already incorporated toward advancing struggles to which official allegiance has been pledged. In addition to the limits individuals may place on their own explicitly political activities, the moral final word seems already to have been pronounced over corporatism as a form of social organization. It is important, and interesting, to keep in mind that the analyses of corporatism conducted in the 1970s western European Marxist tradition (i.e., the very sources cited by current critics of educational corporatisms) were addressing the overall agenda of analysing the 'transition costs' of moving from capitalism to socialism. In these neo-Marxist analyses, it was an open debate as to whether or not corporatism was (or was not) a point along that transition.

Here the international appropriation of meanings seems to have allowed for muddled conceptual applications. Whereas US-based literature is typically built from within a capitalist state where the notion of a social wage has virtually no meaning (and hence US critics of corporatism work from a fairly stark and clear notion of a 'capitalist pig'), the social welfare states of northern Europe seem to work with a more fluid meaning of corporatism. Neither meaning could be imported into the Australian context in a simple fashion, and yet clarification of this appropriation and what is meant by 'corporatism' in the Australian context has been largely left to assumption and presumption. In the current Australian context, things get all the more complicated, of course, when an attempt is made to actually analyse the relations between corporatist organizations and social movements other than those based on economic class (e.g., consider many of the other essays included in Lingard, Knight and Porter, 1993).

This international ebb and flow of theoretical constructs, however, also serves as a reminder that the current social systems identifiable as nations are (and have always been) part of global systems of exchange, control and desire. With the relatively high levels of information technology currently available on an amazingly large portion of the planet, with the ongoing expansion of market-driven capitalist forms of organizational structures, with what is commonly misrecognized as 'the Americanization' of popular culture, and with the development of an international 'security' force supplied by a very extensive military-industrial complex, the global conditions in which most academic workers make a living and construct knowledge are exceedingly more complex and interconnected than we might be led to assume within the discourse of pure intellectuals.

To better understand the nature of intellectual work and, perhaps more importantly, the nature of the social institutions that make such work possible, I turn below to articulating what I take to be an emerging alternative to conventional postures of puritan intellectual work. Before beginning that explication, however, I should emphasize that I do not take this emerging alternative to be the result of some ever more crafty theoretical construction. On the contrary, I take the alternative theoretical views of intellectual work to be a matter of socially recognizable, historical, fact.

In response to an essay in which Steven Seidman was advocating the virtues of postmodernism (Seidman, 1991), Charles Lemert (1991) offered the following reminder:

> Postmodernism, if it means anything at all, means to say that since the midcentury the world has broken into its political and cultural parts. The very idea of the world revolving on a true axis has proven finite. The axial principles of the twentieth-century world — European culture, British administration, American capitalism, Soviet

James G. Ladwig

politics — have come apart as a matter of fact, not of theory. The multiple identities and local politics of which Seidman speaks are not just another way; they are what is left. (Lemert, 1991, p. 167)

To the extent Lemert's reminder helps curtail excessive theoretical pretence, I would simply accept his point. To the extent that I hope to reframe understandings of corporate politics in education, the conceptual outline offered below might be best seen as an attempt to construct different and less pure patterns amongst the rubble left behind the world's shattered colonial empires, overextended modernist economic orders, and inflationary post-modern hypertextual cultural appropriations. For the sake of constructing a signifier, I refer to this emergent alternative as an understanding of the nomadic intellectual.

Nomadic Intellectuals and Education

Every thought is already a tribe, the opposite of the state. (Deleuze and Guattari, 1987, p. 377)

The specific phrase, 'nomadic intellectual', I have taken relatively directly from *A Thousand Plateau*, the second volume of *Capitalism and Schizophrenia* (Deleuze and Guattari, 1987). In *A Thousand Plateau*, Deleuze and Guattari set out an exceedingly complicated and complex traversal of history, geology, literature, biology, philosophy, politics and psychoanalysis (*inter alia*). While there may be a secondary industry attempting to explain what Deleuze and Guattari are up to, I prefer to read this work in the same manner I read most philosophy — but particularly Spinoza (a connection made by Deleuze and Guattari). That is, I take much of what is valuable in this work to be that which can be gained when viewing the work as a set of thought experiments, or as the authors would have it, as a constellation of plateau interconnected in the manner of a potato (as rhyzomatic nodes, that is).

As a general point, I think it is important to keep one's reading of the overall project of Deleuze and Guattari's *Capitalism and Schizophrenia* in the foreground. Roughly speaking, if we keep in mind the position of this work in the wake of the events of May 1968 (French epochal time), this work and the ideas presented by Deleuze and Guattari can be seen as an attempt to address a very long-standing and continuing dilemma of revolutionary politics. That is, as a general rule, it seems common that when a radical shift occurs in structures of power, a new power structure eventually emerges to take the place of the old structure — sometimes in even more solidified fashion. (Forgetting the obvious examples for the time being, consider the poststructural feminist critique of neo-Marxist educational theorizing as a case in point). Having observed this, Deleuze and Guattari present a series of concepts, ideas, categories, propositions and conclusions which would be very

216

difficult to congeal in any fixed structure. Underscoring the importance of this general point, it may help to note that in the introduction to *Anti-Oedipus* Foucault referred to the book as an 'introduction to non-fascist life' (Deleuze and Guattari, 1983, p. xiii).

While it might violate the intent of this work to worry about somehow marring its incoherence by simply pulling out one of its often used images for my own use, I think the notion of a nomadic intellectual carries a related set of distinctions, concepts and categories which make it comprehensible. Consequently, before attempting to explain the connections I see between education and nomadic intellectuals, I first turn to a brief extrapolation of this borrowed image.

Most importantly, I think, from among a related set of distinctions I foreground the fact that Deleuze and Guattari construct an image of the 'nomadic' as interlinked with 'the war-machine' which is itself in opposition to (or rather in obliteration of) things of the State. Hence, readers are presented with a series of oppositions: 'nomadic philosophy' as opposed to 'state philosophy'; 'nomadic science' as opposed to 'royal science'; 'nomadic war machine' as opposed to the 'state apparatus', etc.

Having just framed these two sets of images as 'opposing', I should point out that I do not mean they are 'opposites'. Rather, having introduced the metaphor of 'machine' in *Anti-Oedipus* (Deleuze and Guattari, 1983) as a system of interruptions, an intertwining of production, consumption, reproduction and desire, Deleuze and Guattari refer to the 'war machine' as irreducible to the State, lying outside the State altogether. In their words:

> In every respect, the war machine is of another species, another nature, another origin than the State apparatus. (Deleuze and Guattari, 1987, p. 352)

The nature of this other origin Deleuze and Guattari first explain by way of a contrast between Chess and Go (the Chinese board-game). Many other depictions follow. Nevertheless, the war machine is nomadic and exterior to the State apparatus.

Deleuze and Guattari presented the general notion of 'machines' in their initial work toward *Capitalism and Schizophrenia* (volume one, *Anti-Oedipus*), as a way of linking what an Althusserian analysis might have conceived of as the structural conditions of society with what can fairly be called a libidinal economy (as did Lyotard). In this way, Deleuze and Guattari presented a very interesting analytical connection between a political economy and psychosocial life. Unlike Althusserian interpretations, however, it would be very difficult to not recognize the so-called agency of individuals within this schizoanalytical focus on desire and 'desiring machines'. Linking the work of some intellectuals into an analysis of 'the war-machine' allows both an interesting (and perhaps uncompromising) angle for re-examining intellectual work and a repositioning of the function of their own analyses.

James G. Ladwig

Within the larger concern for reframing 'structural' matters in territorial terms, the notion of nomadic subjects (in at least two senses of that term) takes on a very compelling point. An important counterintuitive notion of the relationship between nomads and space needs to be underscored here. Where common sense understandings of nomadic life may misrecognize nomads as non-territorial, in this view, nomadic life has an alternate relationship with territory — a relationship Deleuze and Guattari refer to as 'deterritorialized'. In this view, unlike migrants who move from one point to another only to resettle or reterritorialize again, nomads live by an inverted set of principles where every point is 'reached only in order to be left behind; every point is a relay and exists only as relay' (Deleuze and Guattari, 1987, p. 380).

This deterritorialized relation carries significant consequences. Rather than working as 'sedentary roads . . . which parcel out closed space to people', a nomadic trajectory 'distributes people (or animals) in an open space' (p. 380). This character of nomadic life, as described by Deleuze and Guattari, is strongly related, in my view, to radically differing understandings of ownership or control, and alternative understandings of humans' relation to the earth and each other, as might be found in some of the so-called indigenous cultures colonial empires once pejoratively named nomadic as a means of shunning, ignoring and discarding nomadic life.

One final analytical dimension of nomadic life relates to current issues of identity and representation. Where past notions of class members might be seen as 'internally' focused on ostensibly 'organic' relations, nomadic understandings take representation and identity to be clearly concerned about issues which were once considered 'external'. Analyses of the body, the corporeal, used to be external to issues of consciousness and ideas (according to Descartes at least). Questions of personal desire were external to matters of the State (according to many Marxists and, of course, Gramsci himself). And the whole idea of worrying about representation over 'the real' used to seem a bit external. Hence, given current political debates, and the postmodern focus on performity, the notion of accepting externality as a basic analytical category also seems wise.

Connecting this general image of nomadic life with the work of intellectuals is, I think, fairly straight-forward. In making the point that nomadic science has its own division of labour (lest we think it has no divisions), Deleuze and Guattari draw out a poignant analysis of the relationship between things nomadic and things statist. There, Deleuze and Guattari say:

The state does not give power (*pouvoir*) to the intellectuals or conceptual innovators; on the contrary, it makes them a strictly dependent organ with an autonomy which is only imagined yet is sufficient to divest those whose job it becomes to simply reproduce or implement of all of their power (*puissance*). This does not shield the State from more trouble, this time with the body of intellectuals it itself engendered, but which asserts new nomadic and political claims. In any case, if the State always finds it necessary to repress the nomad or minor sciences, if it opposes vague essences and the operative geometry of the trait, it does so not because the content of these sciences is inexact or imperfect, or because of their magic or initiatory character, but because they imply a division of labor opposed to the norms of the State. (Deleuze and Guattari, 1987, p. 368)

Leaving aside the question of what division of labour is implied by nomadic work, it probably should be of some concern, (to academics who might consider themselves at least vaguely Left), that Deleuze and Guattari present a rather persistent argument which basically suggests that academic intellectuals are, to a very large degree, intertwined in the mechanisms of the State (as they define it, of course).

Given the (perhaps inscribed) agenda of Deleuze and Guattari, that is, given the task of creating non-statist thought, this view of intellectuals as symbiotically intertwined with the centrist movements of the State's interior raises a long-standing problematic. Textual self-questioning of the role of the revolutionary intellectual is something of a literary genre in its own right, and the basic tension is not new; but Deleuze and Guattari's intertwining of political and libidinal economies places that old tension in a very new light (at least very new for those who took the feminist personal/political merely as a sign that men could do some child care).

By the Deleuze and Guattari categorization, most academic intellectuals are far from nomadic. Given most academic paychecks are literally backed by state monies, this is hardly an empirical insight. But, if there is reason to accept past claims about the intimate connection between the social structures and the structure of thought; at a time when most academics I call colleagues are disgusted at the not-so-recent turns of public desires, before any definitive form comes to public argument, perhaps it is also a time to curb any desire to call for revolutionary action long enough to see whence that desire comes. And in Australia, more specifically, given the recent not-so-subtle centrist moves of the 'new' industrial order of academics (Australian academics' unions have recently amalgamated into one large national union), perhaps it is also time to consider the role of a nomad in more depth — to look for potential realizations, possible insights, and potential avenues of action.

What is a nomadic educational intellectual? I think there are some everyday realities of academic work in education (among vaguely politically left thinkers), which point to the way in which some intellectual work already is nomadic. First, I think it is important to realize that recognizing the global nature of schooling and school systems not only provided insights for our 'forefathers', but the growing global common schooling experience has also opened a whole line of documentary research. That is, there is a growing body of literature in the sociology of education which examines the global expansion of industrialized forms of schooling and which is working with a general notion of schooling as a world culture in itself (Benavot, *et al.*, 1991;

Boli and Ramirez, 1986; Boli, Ramirez and Meyer, 1985; Meyer, 1980; Meyer, Ramirez and Soysal, 1992). The lines of this international traversal are fairly predictable. Without even considering the influence of UNESCO and the World Bank, after all, the sun has yet to set on the British Empire (to see this image, simply map out the national origins of research in bilingual or ESL education).

On a more subjective/personal side of life, consider the way in which many small educational research conferences develop (such as the one leading to this volume). While there may well be a strong tendency toward a monocultural identity amongst/between the members of such groups, the analytical lines which tie these groups together are not exactly nation specific — they are, I would suggest, understandable as a counterpart of the world schooling culture Meyer, Ramirez, Boli and co. are studying. It is probably worth nothing, as well, that there is another growing body of literature in the sociology of education which may even more directly connect such events with a global expansion of professionalism among educational reformers (e.g., Popkewitz, 1991). It is one dynamic of this global expansion which allows us to 'speak' with one another at the speed of light on Email, at the expense of the US Department of Defence. As a matter of daily life, not wanting to wait for communication from the other side of the planet certainly marks an important link in the growing desiring machine of educational research and the intellectual work of education, for me at least. Here it is important to recognize that the historical connections between the current internet information superhighway and the post-WWII 'allied' intelligence networks are notably more direct than most observers would care to mention.

Further, even if there has been a fall of the new sociology of education (Wexler, 1987), the social networks set up by the new sociology (as just one example) have certainly not passed away. Even if Bernstein has pronounced the field unfulfilled, I know I can travel to much of the industrialized world and find at least someone who knows what I talk about. In fact, I have done so, on three continents other than North America.

Along many other planes lie the flows and channels of possible nomadic intellectual travels in the educational world. In such a world, is it really possible to think of the home-grown organic intellectual as a safe reality? Is such a creature really going to produce thought which can come from outside statist thought anyway?

Conclusion

To connect this discussion of nomadic intellectual life back into this essay's opening concerns about criticisms of corporatism in education, I present one notion of corporatism, attached to a very practical agenda, left aside in the puritan rejection of incorporation. That is, I would ask my educational colleagues to consider the relationship between this image of nomadic intellectuals and a proposal put forward by Bourdieu for a corporatism of specific intellectuals (Bourdieu, 1989). As I think will become apparent, Bourdieu's understanding of corporatism is substantially more favourable than those presented in past educational criticisms. In part, I take this to be due to a recognition of the possibilities that lie in organizational politics and a continuing insistence to produce theories that are reflexively strategic.

In an analysis of the current role of intellectuals, Bourdieu builds on the insights of Foucault's well-known call for specific intellectuals in light of a widely perceived threat to the autonomy of academic intellectual life. In response to these current threats (threats which are associated with the 'corporatism' named by US and Australian educational critics), Bourdieu suggests a wide collective of specific intellectuals might offer some defence of the social institutions which allow for the existence of intellectual work.

Contrary to Habermas's notion of an ideal speech situation, Bourdieu (1989) suggests:

> . . . There is no such thing as a transhistorical universal of communication, but there are socially instituted forms of communication favoring the production of the universal — forms whose logic is already registered in the social logic of public and regulated communication represented paradigmatically by generalising the kind of exchange that takes place within the scientific microcosm. Here competition, or a *bellum omnia contra omnes* is organized in such a manner that no one can succeed over anyone else, except by means of better arguments, reasonings and demonstrations, thereby advancing reason and truth. (Bourdieu, 1989, p. 104)

Thus, those institutions which allow for existence of intellectual work are, for Bourdieu, to be defended. As Edward Said (1993) points out, as part of the 'war-machine' these institutions are not necessarily statist in function but can be potential relays for nomadic thought (p. 402).

The connection between Bourdieu's notion of a corporatism of intellectuals and nomadic intellectual work seems clear to me as Bourdieu describes the organizational model and function of his corporatism. When read in light of my earlier discussion and in light of some of the contributions to this volume (in particular see Allan Luke's strategic contribution to this volume), I think Bourdieu's (1989) own description might best be recounted at length. As he puts it:

> What must be invented today are forms of organisation which permit the creation of a voice for a large collective of intellectuals, combining the talents of the ensemble of specific intellectuals . . . This means, first of all, the invention of a model of organisation which, by exploiting every aspect of modern means of communication, such as micro-computers, allows all competent intellectuals to give their symbolic support to well-constructed public interventions. The dilemma of

centralism and spontaneity would be resolved by the establishment of a true international network which could take the form, according to the formula of Nicholas of Cusa, of 'a circle in which the center is everywhere and nowhere'. Each member would be able to propose an intervention that all others would be free to accept or reject. This type of network, with its own organs of expression, could be mobilised against all attacks on the autonomy of the intellectual world, and especially against all forms of cultural imperialism. It could contribute to the establishment of a groundwork for a true cultural internationalism, which would seek to abolish protectionisms and particularisms, thus creating access to universality for the most specific conquests of each national tradition. (Bourdieu, 1989, pp. 108–9)

Where Bourdieu sees the potential of such a network as something of the future, I see it as something of the present. In the remnant channels of postcolonial realities, such networks have already developed in the world of educational research; and they are likely to continue functioning.

Undoubtedly, during much of the so-called corporatist educational era, governmental authorities on both sides of the Pacific have applied decision-making procedures which effectively limited public debate. Equally undoubtedly, the interests of corporations set up and protected by colonial and capitalist regimes have been well served by some of the educational corporatisms. But these regimes are never entirely stable and there are other opportunities available at this historical juncture (whether or not oppositional writers care to make these public). To the extent alternative conceptions of intellectual work may help recognize these possible opportunities, I take the image of nomadic intellectuals to be a worthy thought. And, more specifically, to the extent such nomadic life can employ its own conceptions of corporatism, I take the historical role of educational corporatism to remain an open book.

To conclude, three years ago (at the time of this writing), when an Indian colleague and then fellow graduate student, discovered I (a native born US citizen) had decided to take up a position at a university on the opposite side of the planet, he said, in a very friendly manner, 'welcome to the Empire'. That conversation took place in Madison, Wisconsin. If there was a moment when I began to consciously and concretely recognize the lines of flight, the paths of freedom, which appear and disappear around the globe, it was then. To say intellectual work is nomadic is simply to recognize the anti-statist possibilities that already exist in the intermezzo regions which connect the locales of our work. And, to say an international corporatism may aid the continuing attempt to maintain gaps in our institutional structures is simply to name what already exists.

Note

1 This chapter has benefited from the thought of many people, notably Thomas Griffiths, Gavin Hazel, Jennifer Gore, and Allan Luke.

References

BARTLETT, V.L., KNIGHT, J. and LINGARD, R. (1991) 'Corporate federalism and the restructuring of teacher education in Australia', *Journal of Educational Policy*, 6, 1, pp. 91–5.

BARTLETT, V.L., LINGARD, B. and KNIGHT, J. (1992) 'Restructuring teacher education in Australia', *British Journal of Sociology of Education*, 13, 1, pp. 19–36.

BENAVOT, A., CHA, Y.-K., KAMIENS, D., MEYER, J.W. and WONG, S.-Y. (1991) 'Knowledge for the masses: World models and national curricula, 1920–1986', *American Sociological Review*, 56, pp. 85–100.

BOLI, J. and RAMIREZ, F. (1986) 'World culture and the institutional development of mass education', in RICHARDSON, J.G. (Ed) *Handbook of Theory and Research for the Sociology of Education*, New York, Greenwood Press, pp. 65–90.

BOLI, J., RAMIREZ, F. and MEYER, J.W. (1985) 'Explaining the origins and expansion of mass education', *Comparative Education Review*, 29, pp. 145–70.

BOURDIEU, P. (1989) 'The corporatism of the universal: The role of intellectuals in the modern world', *Telos*, 81, pp. 99–110.

DELEUZE, G. and GUATTARI, F. (1983) *Anti-Oedipus: Capitalism and Schizophrenia*, HURLEY, R., SEEM, M. and LANE, H.R. (Trs) Minneapolis, University of Minneapolis Press.

DELEUZE, G. and GUATTARI, F. (1987) *A Thousand Plateaux: Capitalism and Schizophrenia*, MASSUMI, B. (Tr) Minneapolis, University of Minneapolis Press.

GRANT, W. (Ed) (1985) *The Political Economy of Corporatism,* New York, St. Martin's Press.

LEMERT, C. (1991) 'The end of ideology, really', *Sociological Theory*, 9, 2, pp. 164–72.

LINGARD, B. (1991) 'Policy-making for Australian schooling: The new corporate federalism', *Journal of Educational Policy*, 6, 1, pp. 85–90.

LINGARD, B. (1993) 'Corporate federalism: The emerging approach to policy-making for Australian schools', in LINGARD, B., KNIGHT, J. and PORTER, P. (Eds) *Schooling Reform in Hard Times*, London, Falmer Press, pp. 24–35.

LINGARD, B., KNIGHT, J. and PORTER, P. (1993) *Schooling Reform in Hard Times*, London, Falmer Press.

MEYER, J.W. (1980) 'The world polity and the authority of the nation-state', *Studies in the Modern World System*, BERGESEN, A. (Ed), New York, Academic Press, pp. 109–37.

MEYER, J.W., RAMIREZ, F. and SOYSAL, Y.N. (1992) 'World expansion of mass education', *Sociology of Education*, 65, pp. 128–49.

OFFE, C. (1975) 'The theory of the capitalist state and the problem of policy formation', in LINDBERG, L.N., ALFORD, R., CROUCH, C. and OFFE, C. (Eds) *Stress and Contradiction in Modern Capitalism*, Massachusetts, Lexington Books.

OFFE, C. (1984) *Contradictions of the Welfare State*, London, Hutchinson.

OFFE, C. (1985) *Disorganised Capitalism*, Cambridge, Polity Press.

PANITCH, L. (1986a) 'The impasse of social democratic politics', in MILLIBAND, R. and SAVILLE, J. (Eds) *Socialist Register 1985/86*, London, Merlin Press.

PANITCH, L. (1986b) *Working-class Politics in Crisis*, London, Verso.

POPKEWITZ, T. (1991) *A Political Sociology of Educational Reform*, New York, Teachers College Press.

SAID, E. (1993) *Culture and Imperialism*, London, Vintage.

SCHMITTER, P. (1974) 'Still the century of corporatism?', *Review of Politics*, 36, pp. 85–131.

SCHMITTER, P. (1985) 'Neo-corporatism and the state', in GRANT, W. (Ed) *The Political Economy of Corporatism*, New York, St. Martin's Press, pp. 32–62.

SEIDMAN, S. (1991) 'The end of sociological theory: The postmodern hope', *Sociological Theory*, 9, 2, pp. 131–46.

WEXLER, P. (1987) *Social Analysis of Education*, New York, Routledge.

WEXLER, P. (1993) 'Educational corporatism and its counterposes', Unpublished manuscript, University of Rochester.

YEATMAN, A. (1990) *Bureaucrats, Technocrats, Femocrats: Essays on the Contemporary Australian State*, Sydney, Allen and Unwin.

YEATMAN, A. (1993) 'Corporate managerialism and the shift from the welfare to the competition state', *Discourse*, 13, 2, pp. 3–9.

12 Academic Work Intensification: Beyond Postmodernism

Richard Smith and Judyth Sachs

Introduction

This chapter explores the connections between economic rationalism, managerialism and the intensification of academic work. The position we adopt is that in the current economic, social and political conditions, the nature and purpose of universities has changed and what was once represented as the core of university life, 'collegial work', is historically out-flanked. We document at a general level the conditions that have precipitated this situation and the impact of changed conditions on the working lives of academic staff. We are particularly interested in the tendency to attribute work intensification solely to economic rationalism and managerialism and consequential attempts to reconstruct organizationally the tenets of a previous academic culture. We argue that these directions are mistakenly identified as new and appropriate directions for academics and universities in the 1990s.

Economic Rationalism and Managerialism

There is little doubt that the Australian higher-education sector since the late 1980s has been progressively attuned to the 'national (economic) interest' in research funding policy, in the establishment of the Committee for the Advancement of University Teaching (CAUT) in 1992 and in the current drive to establish 'quality' profiles and indicators. These global trends (Offe, 1984; Handy, 1990; Wexler, 1987; Wasser, 1990) put a premium on productivity, efficient uses of resources and value-for-money so that the role of management via a 'managerial ideology' has dominated universities in recent years (Pollitt, 1990; Pusey, 1993). Peters (1992) has commented:

> What we can say, without doubt, is that we have witnessed a fundamental change in the political ideology in higher education, a change that will set the parameters within which higher education is to be conceived and practised for a considerable period to come. Underlying

the change is the call for a greater productivity and for improved efficiency and effectiveness. (Peters, 1992, p. 127)

Following Schuller (1990), the new elements which have impinged on university governance and academic practice in the 1980–90s can be summarized as:

- reduction in public funding to institutions leading to first contraction, then expansion at reduced cost per EFTSU. This development has placed heavy emphasis on alternative funding sources, accountability and market responsiveness as both academics and institutions seek to cope with these new conditions;
- diversification and expansion of higher education to account for the collapse of the youth labour market, the demand for higher degrees and the search for 'market niches' in areas such as new spheres of knowledge, continuing education and sub-degree programmes; and
- central government attempts to tie higher education to the 'national interest' via so-called 'wealth production' needs so that financial pressures have been applied to higher education to become more 'business-like'.

These trends indicate an increased growth of, and role for, the State in higher education. As Smart (1991) and Lingard (1991) have shown, the Australian State has moved in a flexible way to achieve its educational goals. Under the National Unified System established in 1988–9, the federal government controls agreed profiles, the funding model and the competitive bidding process while leaving management and internal distribution of resources to the institutions. In turn, the management and internal distribution of resources are highly sensitive to specific funding mechanisms such as the research and training agendas of the federal government and to accountability arrangements (Marginson, 1993, pp. 125–6). Underlying the public-sector accountability arrangements is a belief in the use of market forces to induce greater efficiency (Peters, 1992, p. 127).

Such mechanisms are embedded in the demand pressures on higher education. Between 1983 and 1991, higher-education enrolments increased by 29 per cent with a projected increase of a further 13 per cent by 2001. Even so, the estimated unmet demand for higher education in 1992 was 34,000–49,700 (Trinca, cited in Marginson, 1993, p. 89). During the 1983–1991 period, the percentage of national wealth dedicated to education fell from 5.7 per cent to 4.2 per cent with a projected decline to 3.5 per cent in 2001 (Bates, 1992). Simultaneously, salaries for teachers and academics have declined as a percentage of average weekly earnings. Pusey's (1991, 1993) analysis shows how the new agendas ultimately affect cultural values, social conventions as well as central elements of national identity.

Pusey's point is quite central. In the 1990s, developments in the education sector, exemplified by the universities, are less about the relevance and quality of a new pedagogy and more about regulation and the realization of symbolic control in the transition to a communications age (Bernstein, 1990, p. 88). In short, the present novel experiments in industrial organization, political and social life are the early signs of a new regime of capital accumulation and its attendant system of political and social regulation (Bernstein, 1990; Harvey, 1989; Wexler, 1987).

It would be surprising if such measures, coupled with micro-economic reform, did not affect work practices across the higher-education sector. While there has been relatively little attention paid to the intensification of work in higher education (see Harman and Wood, 1990; California/Princeton Fulfilment Services, 1994), the trends in school teaching provide a reference point.

Work Environment: The Erosion of Community

In the school system, educational 'reforms' such as the decentralized, collegial 'self-managing' school have meant that teachers spend extraordinary hours doing administrative and other non-teaching-related tasks (Seddon, 1992; Preston, 1992). Similarly, in the universities, academic work is intensified by the internal redistribution of resources generated by institutional attempts to fulfil profile requirements with diminished staff and increasing centralized surveillance. The pressure to maintain and increase student enrolments while fulfilling industrial award expectations to 'perform' better for continuation and promotion procedures, creates difficulties for individual academics (Porter, Lingard and Knight, 1993). In particular, the urgency to undertake higher degrees and research has fallen especially on former CAE staff who were primarily recruited and promoted on the basis of teaching (Harman and Wood, 1990; Williams, 1992, p. 287).

While change has been a constant feature of higher education (Taylor, 1987), a discernible effect of the intensification of academic work is a perceived decline of what is referred to as 'collegial' activity, thought by many to be the core of academic culture and practices. There are several emergent tendencies generated by the new environment of higher education which reinforce a change in academic culture away from the complex of values centred on collegiality.

A prime element, as in the rest of the economy, is the increasing division between a core of permanent staff and a periphery of marginal workers in the academic labour force. The former have security while the latter are employed on a part-time basis with little or no discernible occupational career path. In addition, permanent staff, compared to part-timers, are relatively well-paid.

Part-time work as a category is broad in its application, ranging from weekly hours to contract work which falls only just short of 'permanent'. What is clear however is that part-time work is not a staging point for tenure. The point is that the university 'community' is increasingly a small elite of 'conversationalists' flanked by substantial numbers of predominantly women temporary teachers, contract researchers and others whose deadlines are short (Schuller, 1990, p. 5). The idea of a university 'community' of equals is suspect in this scenario.

A further outcome of the intensification of academic work is the skewing of the reward structure. People doing the same work — teaching and research — are rewarded differently. In addition, with the increasing use of differential pay packages in universities and different conditions of employment which allow for consultancies and other remunerative rewards, commitment to ideals of a community are further weakened. The apparent career path of marginal workers in this scenario, despite the recent academic industrial award, is arduous if for no other reason that most peripheral workers are employed to teach. As we argue later, this is a fatal focus for aspiring academics, even under the new-found interest in teaching at the national and institutional levels.

Similarly, consultancy and contract work diminishes the idea of an academic 'community'. Such work raises issues of control and autonomy. It affects the types of problems that scholars pursue in two ways. It draws them away from serious problems that have few immediate pay-offs and from those problems that afflict people who cannot afford to pay consultants. As Guttman (1987, pp. 198–9) argues, consultancy and contract work provide freedom for academics to pursue their interests but in doing so, is less likely to sustain the collective autonomous scholarship which forms a defence against political control of ideas. In this way, consultancies and contracts weaken university ideals about scepticism towards the conventional wisdom of society (Annan, 1970, p. 467) by lessening the possibility of universities acting as socially sanctioned sites of dissent.

Moreover, in large cities, as cost constraints on plant and utilities increase, different forms of industrial structures are emerging. Already in some places it is proposed that university staff be present on site for lesser periods (Schuller, 1990). In such cases, staff contracted on an internal consultancy basis for a specific amount of teaching and research will have less time for the interchange that supposedly holds the university 'community' together. This is one of the implications of the attempt to make fuller use of university human and physical capital of which the intensification of academic work is a symptom.

Furthermore, external consultancies affect the internal fiscal operations of universities as elements seek resources to sustain or expand the capacity to generate income. Such competitive pressures detract from the sense of community and common purpose. Schuller's (1990, p. 7) conclusion is that consultancies and contract work signal a significant shift in the prevailing conceptions of what university academic work is, particularly as the shift from knowledge as a process to knowledge as a product for audit purposes accelerates (Scott, 1984).

The punishing work environment of the evolving university system, relatively poor remuneration in comparison with other occupations and lack of clearly tenured opportunities, are bound to have their effects on university staff recruitment. It might be predicted that universities will face what Kerr (1983) has observed of school teaching:

> . . . We can reasonably expect only the numb and the dull to linger in teaching careers. That some exceptionally able teachers appear and remain in the classroom reflects the heroic commitment and extra-ordinary sacrifice of those rare individuals and not the wisdom of our institutional arrangements and expressed values. (Kerr, 1983, p. 530)

Some Empirical Evidence

Before proceeding and by way of testing the discussion so far, we draw on a university-wide survey study of university life conducted by Bond, Simons, Pitts, Horrigan and Dempster (1993). This study collected information about work conditions, teaching and research across a major urban institution which has in recent years grappled with the difficulties of amalgamating several previously non-university elements. The examples are intended to exemplify the changing nature of academic relations resulting in the erosion of an 'academic community' and the progressive alienation of academic staff.

Teaching

Teaching is a major aspect of work for 92 per cent (N = 375) of the target university's academics. Its significance is underlined by the importance placed on a desire for further training in teaching reported in the survey. Bond *et al.* (1993, p. 25) make the point that academics are especially sensitive to the changing nature of higher education and the characteristics of cohorts of students new to the universities.

The contemporary conditions of higher education are underlined by the teaching 'issues' identified by academics in the survey. While heavy teaching loads and insufficient support for teaching were nominated by 14 per cent of the sample (N = 409), 71 per cent were junior staff. Reported comments indicate that new academics are bearing the costs of reduced funding and pressure to maintain or increase student numbers. Work conditions are characterized by '(I)ncreasing teaching loads primarily as a consequence of cuts in part-time teaching resources . . .', large classes and high contact hours. There is concern also about the effects of heavy teaching loads on future prospects, thus:

> Too much teaching . . . in relation to what is considered to be important for promotions . . . ; [and] There is never an opportunity for

uninterrupted research time of a sustained nature. (Bond *et al.*, 1993, pp. 31, 37)

While pressures to 'teach' more are felt by staff, it is also perceived that teaching is undervalued and unrecognized (Bond *et al.*, 1993, p. 31), exemplified by: 'There is not enough support for teaching activities. The administrative support hinders, not enhances, academic endeavours'; and 'More acknowledgment of the needs associated with course development especially with regard to time'.

Research

Research is regarded as a major aspect of academic work by 74 per cent of the sample (N = 302), with expressed needs for assistance evident in the more junior members of staff, especially in the newly amalgamated faculties (Bond *et al.*, 1993, p. 37). The authors of the report comment that: '. . . staff perceived the need to perform well in the research area . . . However, the realities of a large workload in one or more areas tended to intervene' (Bond *et al.*, 1993, p. 47). As one respondent put it:

. . . the most useful thing would be availability of time to complete my higher degree. Junior staff appear to find themselves doing so much teaching that this aspect of their development, which is absolutely crucial to career prospects, can get neglected. I am absolutely no exception to this general syndrome. (op. cit.)

Another observes:

. . . In my view we are on the verge of a crisis. On the one hand, (the Deputy Vice Chancellor — Research) encourages us to do research, as he should. On the other, he mentions that the resources available to teach our students are steadily declining. (op. cit.)

Administration

42 per cent of the sample identified some form of administration as a major aspect of their work. The academics in this survey perceive that they are doing too much of it and in contrast, that administration overwhelms teaching and research. Thus, 'The University always seems to act as if its administrative activities, requests, demands etc should take precedence over scholarly activities, and this can be very frustrating and stressful'. More bluntly, '"Top-down" management policies which create anger, misunderstanding, and paranoia among staff who feel no ownership of changes' (Bond *et al.*, 1993, p. 76).

Echoing Middlehurst and Elton (1992), Bond *et al.* (1993, p. 76) remark that '(t)here is a perception that the University is driven by its administrative processes rather than its other functions, and in particular those of teaching and research.'

Most of the features that have engaged the energies of educators in recent years can be interpreted as reactions to the emergence of this new socioeconomic reorganization. 'Postmodernism' then is a *state of things*, not a structured and coherent ideology (Olalquiaga, 1992, p. xi, our emphasis). It is perhaps not surprising that Bond *et al.* (1993, p. 79) report academics are frustrated by, and angry about, both their own professional progress and managerial pressures on their work. They are particularly concerned about what they perceive to be unclear and changing criteria for appointments, tenure and promotion, job security and equity.

Threat and Interpretation

It is evident that academics in the survey are worried about the clash between what they perceive to be 'traditional' generic university values and those of an emergent university culture. The particular expressions within the specific institution can be taken as symptomatic of the whole sector. Remarks about retreat from scholarship and the impact of economic rationalism on scholarly activity in the form of diminished resources, and fears that the 'university' will lose its status, indicate that academics feel themselves under threat.

Our view is that the threat/crisis complex is more complex than the listing of contemporary woes revealed by the Bond *et al.* (1993) and comparable surveys. In a wider context, Olalquiaga (1992) argues that the postmodern age brings about the loss of coherent, integral social and cultural wholes and creates fragmentation and segmentation. We interpret the academic experience of lost personal responsibility and individual impotence as the social-psychological dimensions of contingency, randomness, and a disbelief in the meaning or logic of history (Holton, 1990, p. 5; Pusey, 1991, 1993).

Because crisis and threat have been normalized as the most symptomatic root metaphors of the late twentieth century and the particulars of daily life in the university (Holton, 1990) confirm the perception of threat, people feel afraid to begin the future. For many academics, the university of the 1990s provides little or no sense of what it is to be true to self. The management languages that are available in the institution (by definition 'rationalist' or 'managerialist') set limits to what counts as legitimate memory. As Gergen (1991, p. 150) proposes, if one holds to the notion of an authentic self, acting in any other way is a form of forgery or deceit. In responding to the new and different demands of universities in the 1990s, academics argue that present practices and trends are unacceptable *because* they endanger privileged historical and professional achievements (Hirschman, 1991). In particular, the search for the past and the desire for self-realization can become a withdrawal into narcissism and a search for a 'regressive utopia of a safe and transparent environment which enables individuals to be themselves by becoming identical to others' (Melucci, 1989, pp. 209–10).

Our concern is that under conditions in which 'real self' and personal memory are anchored in metaphors of 'the university' and collegial management and there is little confirmation of identity or patterns of authentic action, academics tend to blame 'economic rationalism' and 'managerialism' uncritically for their predicament. In what Zurbrugg (1993, pp. 7–12) refers to as the apocalyptic fallacy or B-Effect, university governance and management theories and practices in the present are discredited and identified with the end of universities. Zurbrugg (1993, pp. 5–6) argues that by mistaking 'morsels of postmodernism's mischievous bark for the entirety of its bite', attempts to defend such theories are 'absurdly reductive'. This often leads to proposals for models of university governance which pay scant attention to the structural relationships between universities, the State and civil society or the ideological constructions of academic practices. In contrast to a catastrophic sense of crisis, the C-Effect considers the possibilities of restarting by rejecting the limitations of the past and worrying about the limitations of the present and the future (Zurbrugg, 1993, pp. 8–10).

Image of Academic Management

An important ingredient of the perceived threat is the recurrent contrast between an implicit image of a generalized 'university' and the perceived effects of economic rationalist policies and managerialist forms of administration on it. On the one hand, while definitions of the 'university' are diverse (Jaspers, 1960; Schuller, 1990; Bates, 1992), the implicit B-Effect model resembles 'a series of communities held together by a common name, a common governing board, and related purposes' (Kerr, 1983, p. 1). Birnbaum (1988) for example, argues that distributed rational decision-making and 'spontaneous corrective action' between academics working harmoniously within a common culture, is the most appropriate for higher education and indeed business and industry. The rhetoric however is stretched by the reality of university life in the postwar period.

First, academic units such as departments and faculties and individual academics within them, are largely concerned with competition. Academic life is, and has always been, inseparable from matters of resources and their distribution in the search for reputational work. At the individual staff-member level, there is competition for resources, grants and positions. Specialization and changes in the nature of knowledge put strains on individual academics to look outside academic units and the institution for intellectual partnerships. Academic units jostle for shares of centrally allocated funds for research and teaching. Under contemporary funding arrangements, they not only seek sufficient students to fill profile requirements, but also the best of them.

Second, what is relatively focused now in universities is the traditional concern for reputational work. The press for reputational work that benefits the institution is explicitly required. Universities recognize that there is an emergent ranking of institutions on a centrality/marginality continuum. The ranking is tied to prestige which in turn affects the guaranteed continuity and saleability of professional services within a market orientation determined by the State and civil society. These circumstances directly challenge the notions of interdependent academic exchange within a collective, scholarly culture. In the emergent university structure, relations are better understood as individualized, bilateral, competitive and monetarized (Schuller, 1990, p. 9). Such relations challenge the right of university professionals — who standardize the production of professional producers — to defend the universalistic guarantees of professional competence in ways that legitimate their own claims of autonomy and monopoly (Larson, 1977, p. 34). Moreover, as Larson (1977, p. 227) and Rice (1986) argue, they challenge the ideological construction of a 'career', which is as resilient as that in medicine, tied to an essential dimension of the self.

Third, academic careers are traditionally dependent on the idea that teaching is a 'job' while research is an academic's 'work'. Teaching has always been a necessary but not a sufficient criterion for individual prestige (Fox, 1992, p. 302). It is paradoxical that academics who argue against the institutional press for research performance and the possession of higher degrees invoke images of the past. While 'collegiality' and 'community' may seem to be appropriate ramparts against the acquisitive, economic rationalist society and the managerialist institution, professions are always defined by their elites, by the 'central power structure of the society' (Larson, 1977; pp. 226–7; Bourdieu, 1986). It is a convenient myth to explain academic workload, work conditions and the demands for advanced qualifications and 'research', solely by the deprivations of managerialist administrative practices and economic rationalist policies. The seemingly new performance-based agenda is fundamentally that which has always characterized the high-status liberal university.

Platt (1988, p. 525) points out that if people only do the kind of work for which their age, experience and ability fits them, then it does not matter what the institutional context is like. Platt's proposition appears to be supported by Hattie's (1990, p. 265) study of performance indicators in Australian university education departments and faculties that shows the strong statistical relationships between publications in refereed journals and percentage of PhD students and percentage of staff with PhDs in an academic department.

Hattie's findings suggest that people interested in, and prepared for, research will undertake it regardless of age, size of department, number of staff or research monies (see also Platt, 1988, p. 519). In a national study of academic work of social science staff in the United States, Fox (1992, pp. 299–300) reports that with teaching load constant, faculty who publish more have a higher interest in research than teaching and the effect increases with the degree granting level of the department.

Fourth, while it is possible to conceive of collegially organized academic units, they always operated within a framework of established systems, rules and procedures (Kotter, 1988), including those set by 'collegial' decision-making. While it is has always been difficult to separate academic and administrative activity, the latter serves the purposes of either academic leadership *or* management.

Fifth, 'collegiality' has always entailed a need for increased numbers of administrative staff, thus detracting from academic resource allocation, or demands on academics to do administrative work. Academics, intent on reputational academic work, have long recognized the advantages of avoiding administrative work. Fox's (1992, p. 302) national study of social scientists in the United States, confirms the view that ideas, the laboratory, the library and external funding are more important for active researchers than people, teaching, faculty meetings and internal budgets.

Sixth, Middlehurst and Elton (1992, p. 255) point out that external shock, unacceptable levels of intra-institutional performance and the need for radical or urgent change create special conditions. In these circumstances, collegial management practices may not be the interests of either academics or the institution and in turn, students. 'External shocks' were faced by Australian universities in the 1980s and continue to be faced by them in the 1990s. They take the form of priority setting against system and institutional financial stringency and the linking of levels of institution and individual performance to quality audits.

Where institutions or subsystems within them perceive themselves to be in survival mode, 'strong institutional management' to initiate and maintain rapid procedural and structural changes seem to be required, no matter what the institution (Middlehurst and Elton, 1992, p. 257). In the new universities, there is a sharp edge to 'survival mode' as individuals and institutions attempt to reach base levels in qualifications and performance. Middlehurst and Elton (1992, p. 257) hypothesize that under 'survival' conditions, academics will become 'progressively alienated', that academic goals will suffer and that academic standards will drop. The data contained in the Bond *et al.* (1993) study lend weight to the first of these hypotheses.

Seventh, there is compelling evidence that the long-term condition of the university sector is a conflict of interests between academic loyalties, institutional and governmental goals (see Bendix, 1956, p. 136 for the continuity of this concern). Such organizational structural problems, exemplified in Bond *et al.* (1993), are endemic to large institutions in which expert professionals are embedded, whatever the macroeconomic conditions of the day.

The idea of the university as a 'community' of autonomous individuals governed by collegial values centred on teaching them, is certainly an historical myth (Smith, 1989, p. 217). Even if this were not the case, changes in the nature of academic employment and the material circumstances of universities render the image 'increasingly inaccurate' both as an account of current practice and implausible as a view of the future (Schuller, 1990, p. 4).

The predisposition to treat catastrophic 'experience' as an explanatory rather than a descriptive idea, ignores or misrecognizes the transformation of the university sector and its relations with civil society. It does not specify the link between the university system and the occupational practices of academics. Consequently, the potential to reconstruct the knowledge base and social practices of the traditional university are dissipated in the present period of disorganization and uncertainty. It is imperative that theory, practice and analysis appropriate for dealing with a new political situation is confronted.

Bauman (1992, p. 102) argues that under postmodern conditions the relationships between academic work concerned with the reproduction and renewal of culture, social integration and the role of the State have changed. His view is that in a society that is not culturally unified or uniform, the need for authoritative solutions to questions of truth, moral judgment and aesthetic taste are relativized and eroded. The growing irrelevance of legitimation has coincided with the growing freedom of intellectual debate and in turn, with the indifference of political power to intellectual debate. Accordingly, he identifies a shift in the mechanisms of social integration from those concerned with legitimation to new forms of institutionalized knowledge-based expertise and market dependency. At the same time, academics suffer a 'status crisis' as what was previously their rightful control over the consumption of education and information, passes to the control of agents of the market such as gallery owners, TV managers, bureaucrats and publishers (Bauman, 1992, p. 95).

Bauman's analysis is quite central to this chapter. We interpret the conditions reported by Bond *et al.* (1993) and the trends discussed so far as the de-institutionalization of education for an emergent internationalized society. As Wexler (1987) argues, there are several possibilities for the reconfiguration of the university–society relation in these conditions. Universities may be incorporated entirely so that knowledge production is synonymous with technology; or they may retreat into a socially insignificant concern with internal analysis. In both cases, universities will lose their autonomy.

The third element of Wexler's prognosis is that by engaging with popular concerns and demands in a critical way, with all of the attendant dangers of incorporation, they may forge a new knowledge and operational base that enhances their social contribution. The third possibility then seems mandatory for faculties and departments concerned with professional preparation and development. The development of new technologies has accelerated the expropriation of culture in a market-centred form and its expansion so that the market has now widened the circle of cultural consumers. Paradoxically, '(T)he market will thereby achieve what the intellectual educators struggled to attain in vain: it will turn the consumption of information into a pleasurable, entertaining pastime' (Bauman, 1992, p. 101). The new demands of developments such as these deauthorize conventional courses and methods of delivery. In turn, 'client'-centred demands affect the way in which a university is governed and managed because the possibility exists that universities or parts of them will become redundant (see Whitty, 1993).

Concluding Remarks: Post-postmodern Management

Our view is that the new element in academia through the 1990s is the uncertainty in university governance and academic work that is an effect of the unstable postmodern environment (Piore and Sabel, 1984). Failure to cope with postmodernity in general and to the need for growth in a period of stable or reducing student numbers, volatility in student recruitment patterns, increased competition amongst universities, changing student profiles and demands universities has and continues to deauthorize universities. Deauthorization is exacerbated by the emergence of DIY electronic technologies and higher-education providers outside the university sector.

These characteristics of postmodern sociopolitical life, what we referred to earlier as external shock, create an imperative to turn fluctuations in the environment to advantage by creating patterns of work that fit the specific needs of the organization (Streek, 1987, p. 288). In addition, in keeping with Wexler's cautious but optimistic prognosis, there are opportunities to create new forms of knowledge that link university and everyday concerns. In these circumstances, flexibility in organization and teaching orientation is an intelligent option for academics to support and pursue.

In the face of uncertainty, universities seek to increase the general capacity to adapt in several ways that go beyond mere cost-cutting. Part-time, temporary and casual subcontract staffing of programmes meet demand fluctuations. Academic redeployment and training schemes and pressure to acquire new qualifications are aimed at new tasks. The organization of work is subject to the unrelenting need for continuous fast adjustments ('shifting the goal posts') as external conditions change. These conditions generate a constellation of difficulties for academics and administrators alike as the Bond *et al.* (1993) data show. In turn, workplace governance based on a managerial line of command 'is less economically rational than ever' (Streek, 1987, p. 298) and the collegial model of management is peculiarly non-adaptive. These models are incapable of adaptation to changed sociopolitical conditions because they are embedded in assumptions about a previous historical age.

In respect to teaching and research, flexible delivery modes offer opportunities to investigate and expand some relatively radical options. Most university management rules and regulations are tied to taken-for-granted presuppositions about the connections between time, content and organization (e.g., a semester is x weeks in duration; year-long courses). Flexible delivery modes require the space to transcend such restraints and in this sense they challenge elements of university governance such as enrolment and examination procedures, library hours, staff teaching loads and so on. But the key to understanding the potential of flexible delivery modes is that they tend to change the *relationships* between the teacher and the student; the student and the subject matter; and the teacher and the subject matter. These elements are close to the 'relay' of university work and as they change, with or without the endorsement of academics on the supply side of the equation, the nature of the university operation will change (Bernstein, 1990).

Paradoxically, the B-Effect position perceives pressures like the intensification of work as the *outcome* of a virulent form of managerialism driven by evil or unwitting managers rather than as an effect of postmodernism. It fails to apprehend the institutional need to engage with the rest of society in a *post-*postmodern style rather than in a Taylorist, industrial-age method of improving productivity alone. In characterizing contemporary university initiatives as a hightech-driven version of Fordism, academics tend to miss the already apparent and future significance of the shift from mass markets to customized products which are judged primarily from the demand side. This points to a new focus on innovations in the *rules by which the game is played* rather than marginal adjustments to existing activities.

The economic fate of the employer depends on the cooperation and identification of academic staff with institutional aspirations. It also depends on the collective pursuit of efficiency in 'quality' regimes (Streek, 1987, pp. 294–5) which imply a new form of academic-status rights centred around images of the 'professional' and employment protection. In this sense, status-oriented flexibility-management strategies are not necessarily neo-liberal solutions which deny the status of the individual academic. Moreover, it is not clear why redesigned jobs, more flexible organization of work and multifunctional team-work, together with market-control devices such as quality-performance measures to make work more accountable to management and students, should be interpreted as deskilling rather than reskilling, as job enlargement and work intensification rather than job recomposition (Davidson, 1990).

Exploration of alternative patterns postmodern work are required *of academics* if they are to deal with post-postmodern conditions rather than being repressed by them. Such an exploration is central to the survival of universities and their purposes and as Wexler (1987) suggests, represents the future, a strategy of farewelling the served-markets to which academics have become accustomed. The future is not easily achieved in models of university governance made clumsy and bureaucratic by changed historical circumstances and bolstered by the B-Effect position. Yet, as Bauman (1992, p. 112) remarks of sociology, the alternative is irrelevance.

References

ALEXANDER, J.C. and SZTOMPKA, P. (Eds) (1990) *Rethinking Progress: Movements, Forces and Ideas at the End of the 20th Century*, London, Unwin Hyman.

ANNAN, N. (1970) 'The university and the intellect', *Times Literary Supplement*, 3557, pp. 465–8.

BALL, S. (1992) *Policy and Policy-making in Education*, London, Routledge.

BATES, R. (1992) *The Emerging Culture of Educational Administration and What We Can*

Do About It, Darwin, National Conference of the Australian Council for Educational Administration.

BAUMAN, Z. (1992) *Intimations of Postmodernity*, London, Routledge.

BENDIX, R. (1956) *Work and Authority in Industry*, New York, Harper and Row.

BERNSTEIN, B. (1990) 'Social class and pedagogic practice', in *The Structuring of Pedagogic Discourse: Class, Codes and Control*, Volume 4, London, Routledge, pp. 63–93.

BIRNBAUM, R. (1988) *How Colleges Work: The Cybernetics of Academic Organisation and Leadership*, San Francisco, Jossey-Bass.

BOND, C., SIMONS, R., PITTS, E., HORRIGAN, L. and DEMPSTER, N. (1993) *Staff Development at Griffith University*, Griffith Institute for Higher Education, Griffith University (mimeo).

BOURDIEU, P. (1986) 'The production of belief: Contribution to an economy of symbolic goods', in COLLINS, R., CURRAN, J., GARNHAM, N., SCANNELL, P., SCHLESINGER, P. and SPARKES, C. (Eds) *Media Culture and Society*, London, Sage, pp. 131–63.

CALIFORNIA/PRINCETON FULFILLMENT SERVICES (1994) *The Academic Profession: An International Perspective*, New Jersey.

COHEN, M.D. and MARCH, J.G. (1986) *Leadership and Ambiguity: The American College President*, 2nd ed., New York, McGraw Hill.

DAVIDSON, J.O'C. (1990) 'The road to functional flexibility: White collar work and employment relations in a privatised public utility', *Sociological Review*, 38, 4, pp. 689–711.

FOLLERT, A. (1988) 'Dismantling flexibility', *Capital and Class*, 34 (spring), pp. 42–75.

FOX, M.F. (1992) 'Research, teaching and publication productivity: Mutuality versus competition in academia', *Sociology of Education*, 65, 4, pp. 293–305.

GERGEN, K. (1991) *Dilemmas of Identity in Contemporary Life*, New York, Basic Books.

GUTTMAN, A. (1987) *Democratic Education*, Princeton, NJ, Princeton University Press.

HANDY, C. (1990) *The Age of Unreason*, London, Arrow.

HARMAN, G. and WOOD, F. (1990) 'Academics and their work under Dawkins: A study of five NSW universities', *Australian Educational Researcher*, 17, 2, pp. 53–74.

HARVEY, D. (1989) *The Condition of Postmodernity*, London, Basil Blackwell.

HATTIE, J. (1990) 'Performance indicators in education', *Australian Journal of Education*, 34, 3, pp. 249–76.

HIRSCHMAN, A.O. (1991) *The Rhetoric of Reaction: Perversity, Futility, Jeopardy*, Cambridge, Mass., The Belknap Press of Harvard University Press.

HOLTON, R. (1990) 'Problems of crisis and normalcy in the contemporary world', in ALEXANDER, J.C. and SZTOMPKA, P. (Eds) (1990) *Rethinking Progress: Movements, Forces and Ideas at the End of the 20th Century*, London, Unwin Hyman, pp. 39–52.

JASPERS, K. (1960) *The Idea of a University*, London, Peter Owen.

KATZ, H. and SABEL, C. (1985) 'Industrial relations and industrial adjustment in the car industry', *Industrial Relations*, 24.

KERR, D.H. (1983) 'Teaching competence and teacher education in the United States', *Teachers College Record*, 84, pp. 525–52.

KOTTER, J. (1988) *The Leadership Factor*, New York, Free Press.

KOTTER, J. (1990) 'What leaders do', *Harvard Business Review*, May/June, pp. 103–11.

LaBIER, D. (1989) *Modern Madness: The Hidden Link Between Work and Emotional Conflict*, New York, Simon and Schuster.

LARSON, M.S. (1977) *The Rise of Professionalism: A Sociological Analysis*, Berkeley, University of California Press.

LAZARSFELD, P.F. and MENZEL, H. (1972) 'On the relation between individual and collective properties', in LAZARSFELD, P.F. *et al.* (Eds) *Continuities in the Language of Social Research*, New York, Free Press, pp. 225–36.

LINGARD, R. (1991) 'Policy making for Australian schooling: The new corporate federalism', *Journal of Education Policy*, 6, 1, pp. 85–90.

LONG, J.S. and McGINNIS, R. (1981) 'Organisational context and scientific productivity', *American Sociological Review*, 46, pp. 422–42.

MARGINSON, S. (1993) *Education and Public Policy in Australia*, Melbourne, Cambridge University Press.

MELUCCI, A. (1989) *Social Movements and Individual Needs in Contemporary Society*, London, Hutchinson.

MIDDLEHURST, R. and ELTON, L. (1992) 'Leadership and management in higher education', *Studies in Higher Education*, 17, 3, pp. 251–64.

OFFE, C. (1984) *Contradictions of the Welfare State*, London, Hutchinson.

OLALQUIAGA, C. (1992) *Megalopolis: Contemporary Cultural Sensibilities*, Minneapolis, University of Minnesota Press.

OZGA, J. (1990) 'Policy research and policy theory', *Journal of Education Policy*, 5, 4, pp. 359–63.

PETERS, M. (1992) 'Performance and accountability in Post-Industrial Society: The crises of British Universities', *Studies in Higher Education*, 17, 2, pp. 123–39.

PIGNON, D. and QUERZOLA, J. (1976) 'Dictatorship and democracy in production', in GORZ, A. (Ed) *The Division of Labour: The Labour Process and Class Struggle in Modern Capitalism*, Hassocks, The Harvester Press.

PIORE, M.J. (1986) 'Perspectives on labour market flexibility', *Industrial Relations*, 25, 2.

PIORE, M.J. and SABEL, C.F. (1984) *The Second Industrial Divide: possibilities for prosperity*, New York, Basic Books.

PLATT, J. (1988) 'Research policy in British higher education and its sociological assumptions', *Sociology*, 22, 4, pp. 513–29.

POLLERT, A. (1987) *'The Flexible Firm': A model in Search of Reality or a Policy in Search of Practice?*, Warwick Papers in Industrial Relations 19, Industrial Relations Research Unit, University of Warwick.

POLLITT, C. (1990) *Managerialism and the Public Services: The Anglo-American Experience*, Oxford, Basil Blackwell.

PORTER, P., LINGARD, R. and KNIGHT, J. (1993) Changing administration and administering change: an analysis of the state of Australian education, University of Queensland, Unpublished Manuscript.

PRESTON, B. (1992) 'Teacher professionalism: Implications for teacher educators, teachers and democratic schooling', Geelong, Joint Australian Association for Research in Education/New Zealand Association for Research in Education Annual Conference.

PUSEY, M. (1991) *Economic Rationalism in Canberra*, Melbourne, Cambridge University Press.

PUSEY, M. (1993) 'Reclaiming the middle ground', *Quadrant*, XXXVII, 7–8, pp. 57–65.

RICE, E. (1986) 'The academic profession in transition', *Teaching Sociology*, 14, pp. 12–23.

ROSENZWEIG, R.M. (1994) 'The permeable university: Academic life in an age of special interests', *Interchange*, 25, 1, pp. 11–17.

SCOTT, P. (1984) *The Crisis of the University*, London, Croom Helm.

SCHULLER, T. (1990) 'The exploding community? The university idea and the smashing of the atom', *Oxford Review of Education*, 16, 1, pp. 3–14.

SEDDON, T. (1992) 'Teachers' work: How it is changing and who's changing it?', *Education Australia*, 16, pp. 9–12.

SMART, D. (1991) 'Higher education policy in Australia: Corporate or coercive federalism?', *Journal of Education Policy*, 6, 1, pp. 97–100.

SMITH, P. (1989) *Killing the Spirit*, New York, Viking.

STREEK, W. (1987) 'The uncertainties of management in the management of uncertainty: Employers, labour relations and industrial adjustment in the 1980's', *Work, Employment and Society*, 1, 3, pp. 281–308.

TAYLOR, W. (1987) *Universities Under Scrutiny*, Paris, Organisation for Economic Cooperation and Development.

WASSER, H. (1990) 'Changes in the European university: From traditional to entrepreneurial', *Higher Education Quarterly*, 44, pp. 110–23.

WEXLER, P. (1987) *Social Analysis of Education: after the New Sociology*, New York, Routledge and Kegan Paul.

WHITTY, G. (1993) 'New Schools for New Times? Education Reform in a Global Context', Paper presented to an international conference on 'Educational Reform: Changing Relationships between the State, Civil Society and the Educational Community', Madison, University of Wisconsin, June.

WEICK, K. (1979) *The Social Psychology of Organizing*, Reading, Addison Wesley.

WILLIAMS, B. (1992) 'The rise and fall of binary systems in two countries and the consequences for universities', *Studies in Higher Education*, 17, 3, pp. 281–94.

ZURBRUGG, N. (1993) *The Parameters of Postmodernism*, London, Routledge.

ZEITLIN, J. (1985) 'Markets, Technology and Collective Services: A Strategy for Local Government Intervention in the London Clothing Industry', in GLC *Strategy For the London Clothing Industry: A Debate*, Economy Policy Group Document No. 39, May.

13   Epilogue: From the Inside Out

Philip Wexler

The Verandah

Although I was the keynote speaker at Richard Smith's invited conference, my talk was not at all a keynote for the conference. It was an insider's meeting, not because it was Australian, but because it was a generic, high-level, in-house conversation among theoretically oriented, politically interested educationists arguing between critical theory and poststructuralism (and/or postmodernism). These are media I have worked in, but what I was attempting to do, at least in my paper, was to move outside both of those languages, to reinterpret and uncover traditions that would enable social understanding for what I hope are anticipatory fragments of an emergent civilization, or at least its as yet uncollected sparks.

So, in Morgan's and McWilliam's engaging spatial, academic house metaphor, I was on the margin of the conversation, sitting outside the house, on the 'verandah'. That wasn't accidental, since what I had been trying to do was to offer a non-positivist rereading of Durkheim and Weber, emphasizing the centrality of religion for them, and their interest in the possibilities of religious ways out of the 'cold', 'iron cage' of their social times (Smith remarked that I was offering the group an 'introductory sociology lecture'). At the same time, I was trying to bring up — as a theoretical resource — relatively neglected social theoretic offshoots of romanticism as diverse as Buber, Brown, Reich and Fromm in order to theorize beyond the pale of instrumentalism, either in its monopolistic, triumphant modern phase or in an ironic, parodic and more pluralized, flexible postmodernism. In other words, to theorize on the grounds of 'the irrational', in its various guises that I subsumed as 'energy'. Like a well-trained sociologist, I was trying to persuade — by authorities as untrendy as Sorokin and recent empirical research on contemporary expressions of spirit — that such revisited discourses, in a New Age wrapper, were occasioned by shifts in generative social conditions, and that like all such social and theoretical shifts, they would finally be represented in educational theory and practice: beyond critical theory and poststructuralism.

Philip Wexler

From the Inside

Not that there weren't good arguments on the inside. 'Politically incorrect socialist feminists' (by her own account) like Jane Kenway tried (as we did in *Critical Theory Now*) to read through and cull critique from poststructuralism, to rescue feminist poststructuralism from academic insularity and to reappropriate it for the academic, educational, and wider political responsibilities of oppositional intellectuals. Fitzclarence, Green and Bigum lined up with critical theory, calling for 'a new critical sociology of education' that would restore social class to the centre of social analysis, from which it had putatively already been displaced by a more plural understanding of difference. But even 'difference' is not different enough, for a poststructuralist feminism critical of masculinist essentialisms deserves to be deconstructed, according to Singh, for its 'universalizing the woman's voice', forgetting race, and the global macrostructure of European hegemony and the ascendant anti-colonialism in social practice and in theory. Knight is critical from the vantage point of a foundational essentialism of hope for a 'new humanism', beyond cyborgs and corporatism (Relatedly, Luke did refer to my paper in the conversation, unhappy with my resuscitation of old European essentialist humanists, like Martin Buber). Funnell too is interested in the 'pre-modern', reading Foucault through the binocular of Goffman's moral orders and the contemporary transformations of the everyday social psychology of life in the economically rationalized world of public-sector employees. Deeper into the foundation, Young looks for the 'hidden humanism' of poststructuralist philosophy, to preserve the liberal hope of dialogical critique and the possibility, if not of undistorted communication, then at least of 'authentic self-representation'.

On the other side of the house (although very much inside the meliorist political language that assumes academic workers at the cusp of social evolution), Luke argues for a social, cultural, personal 'hybridity' that invites and enables 'provisional political coalitions' that would 'write the subject differently', to foster a broader and more effective individual and social development through curriculum interventions that should not be judgmentally barred by the uptight standards of old-time critique that Ladwig sees as 'puritan' intellectualism. Instead, 'nomadic intellectuals', operating in 'a true international network' can 'recognize the potential' of the current corporatism to maintain 'gaps' in institutional structures. Along the same lines as Luke's dirtier, more 'muddied' provisional politics of hybridity, Gore takes Foucault into the classroom, in a systematic empirical study of the institutionalization of power in pedagogy, understood as specific and 'more complex' discursive social practices. Smith and Sachs follow the reflexive interest in academic work, and, like Luke and Ladwig, express the desire for a less snooty, unitary dismissal of postmodern social trends by critique. They see in the transformation of universities, in 'an unstable postmodern environment' not only possibilities, but 'an imperative to turn fluctuations in the environment to advantage'; revealing again the meliorist — or what Smith would call 'pastoral' — interest even in a more hard-headed poststructuralist postmodern perspective, by 'engaging with popular concerns and demands in a critical way', under the postmodern condition of the 'de-institutionalization of education'.

Out

I have been digging my way out of critical theory and poststructuralism, and probably sociology as well. Archaeology is really a good term, but it doesn't fully capture the image of originals that have been painted over during the epochs now scraped through the layers, reaching a more primal, original representation; not to restore the original, but to bring it to life, in a different historically concrete time.

Current social conditions, within which a strong dynamic polarity between commodification and resacralization operates (Wexler, in press), work to delegitimate sociology and other modern discourses as uncertain wedges between a fully profaned instrumentalism and a tenuous questing toward sacred experience and religious language. New Age social movements may be merely both new fodder for commercialized lifestyle engineered products or illusory compensations for the full success of the 'mechanized petrification' of a rationalized European culture that Weber dreaded. Still, they open a gate to a very different cosmology of everyday life, of an interpretive organization of experience and being on the other side of what the conference colleagues call, in their language, 'economic rationalism'.

The gate they open is toward the core civilizational cultures, particularly in their gnostic forms (Merkur, 1993), that offer religious hermeneutics, or as Foucault had it, 'ethics'. What this means is an alternative to the secularized social cosmology of modern Enlightenment sociology and its antithetical, but joined binaries in postmodernity — both in everyday life as well as in theorized sublimations. It is an historically conditioned, culturally inchoate, simultaneously individualized and commodified opening to new/ancient practices and discourses. It is 'dangerous' and approached from a 'narrow ridge', fraught with all the destructive capacity of mystical escapes from the world, narcissistic onanism behind the pretense of various unions with the world, or reimmersion in natural ecology, and of course, worst, of organized social irrationalism — a too close reminder of what no one at this or most such conferences, speaks: the Holocaust.

This socially generated cultural unpeeling of modern secular social explanatory cosmologies to religious aspiration, experience and language only repeats Durkheim's explicit claim and Weber's scholarly practice that religion is the paradigmatic social phenomenon. Recall Durkheim's *Année Sociologique* declaration that I quoted in the conference paper:

> . . . it is these phenomena which are the germ from which all others
> — or at least almost all others — are derived. Religion contains in

itself the very beginning, even if in an indistinct state, all the elements which in dissociating themselves from it, articulating themselves and combining with one another in a thousand ways, have given rise to the various manifestations of collective life. (Durkheim, 1960)

This sociological truth, the New Age opening to resacralization, and the historical recency of the Holocaust, together, press me toward a particular religious hermeneutic, the language from the archetypal margin, the difference within the difference that Singh identifies for 'women of color', the revivification of the redemptive calling of the Jews, the primal pariahs. This is not an historically entirely novel path, as Lowy (1992) shows so well in his analysis of the intersection of libertarian utopianism and Jewish messianism between the world wars. Handelman (1991) also traces this route, in the works of Walter Benjamin, Franz Rosenzweig, and Emmanuel Levinas.

This epilogue is only a clue to one path that lies beyond critical theory and poststructuralism. It is a path toward Fromm's (1976) 'city of being', and Levinas' (1993) infinity that is an alternative to the totalizing languages and philosophies of his renowned European teachers, who complied with the Holocaust. Before, beyond and outside west-European culture lies the ethos of the East in the core religions and their dissenting aspect, which the turmoil of the present epoch unwittingly churns to the surface.

It is a renewal of this premodern core, in a postmodern historical context, that goes to pre-humanism's original, creative redemptive revelation and its possibilities for a lived, interhuman being that we seek: as a way of life, and as a language of social understanding. A truly 'new', transformative education is the practice of that social form.

It is not the qualifying complexity and more sober realism of poststructuralism's revision of critical theory that I see as the historically revolutionary possibility. Rather, it is the collectively creative ingathering of the fragmentary, holy sparks from their current exile and dispersion. What that entails at every level — from the body that is not docile but enlivened, through a renormed recultured structure or discipline of being, to the possibility of an institutional collective life that is vital and creative — is what we shall now begin to address.

References

DURKHEIM, E. (1960) 'Preface to L'Anée Sociologique, vols 1 and 2', in WOLFF, K. (Ed) *Essays on Sociology and Philosophy*, New York, Harper and Row.

FROMM, E. (1976) *To Have Or to Be?*, New York, Harper and Row.

HANDELMAN, S.A. (1991) *Fragments of Redemption: Jewish Thought and Literary Theory in Benjamin, Scholem and Levinas*, Bloomington, Indiana University Press.

LEVINAS, E. (1993) *Nine Talmudic Readings*, Bloomington and Indianapolis, Indiana University Press.

Lowy, M. (1992) *Redemption and Hope*, Stanford, Stanford University Press.

Merkur, D. (1993) *Gnosis: An Esoteric Tradition of Mystical Visions and Unions*, Albany, NY, SUNY Press.

Wexler, P. (in press) 'Alienation, New Age Sociology and the Jewish Way', in Geyer, F. (Ed) *Alienation, Ethnicity and Postmodernism*.

Index

One Hundred Names

By the same author

PS, I Love You
Where Rainbows End
If You Could See Me Now
A Place Called Here
Thanks for the Memories
The Gift
The Book of Tomorrow
The Time of My Life

Short stories
Girl in the Mirror